D0403334

Managing Core Public Services

MANAGING
CORE
PUBLIC
SERVICES

DAVID McKEVITT

BLACKWELL
Publishers

JF 1351
M365

Copyright © David McKevitt, 1998

The right of David McKevitt to be identified as author of this work has been asserted in accordance with the Copyright, Designs and Patents Act 1988.

First published 1998

2 4 6 8 10 9 7 5 3 1

Blackwell Publishers Ltd
108 Cowley Road
Oxford OX4 1J
UK

Blackwell Publishers Inc.
350 Main Street
Malden, Massachusetts 02148
USA

All rights reserved. Except for the quotation of short passages for the purposes of criticism and review, no part of this publication may be reproduced, stored in a retrieval system, or transmitted, in any form or by any means, electronic, mechanical, photocopying, recording or otherwise, without the prior permission of the publisher.

Except in the United States of America, this book is sold subject to the condition that it shall not, by way of trade or otherwise, be lent, resold, hired out, or otherwise circulated without the publisher's prior consent in any form of binding or cover other than that in which it is published and without a similar condition including this condition being imposed on the subsequent purchaser.

British Library Cataloguing in Publication Data

A CIP catalogue record for this book is available from the British Library.

Library of Congress Cataloging-in-Publication Data

McKevitt, David.
    Managing core public services / David McKevitt.
        p.   cm.
    Includes index.
    ISBN 0–631–19311–1. — ISBN 0–631–19312–X
    1. Public administration.   2. Administrative agencies—Management.
3. Civil service—Personnel management.   4. Government productivity.
5. Organizational effectiveness.   I. Title.
JF1351.M365   1999
351—dc21   98–20901
                                                                        CIP

Commissioning Editor: Catriona King
Desk Editor: Linda Auld
Production Controller: Rhonda Pearce
Text Designer: Rhonda Pearce

Typeset in Galliard 10/12pt
by Graphicraft Limited, Hong Kong
Printed in Great Britain by TJ International, Padstow, Cornwall

This book is printed on acid-free paper

CONTENTS

CONTENTS

CONTENTS

ACKNOWLEDGEMENTS

Writing a text which spans a number of years and many countries inevitably means that the writer gathers obligations and debts to many people. This study would have been impossible without the generous co-operation of civil servants and managers in England, New Zealand, Germany, Sweden and Ireland who must remain anonymous, if only to protect their honesty! I gratefully record here my debt to them – they have made possible a practitioner perspective on reform in core public services. The study began while I was on study leave from the Open University Business School, the Open University, and I thank the Dean, David Asch and Professor Andrew Thomson for the opportunity to travel to Germany, Sweden and New Zealand. My colleagues at the Open University, Dr Geoff Mallory, Dr Alan Lawton, Dr Geoff Jones have always supported me and they made many helpful comments on the draft chapters. In the UK, I have also received help and advice from Mike Dempsey, Dr John Connaughton, Professor Ron Glatter, Dominic Newbould and Gillian Marshall.

The text began as a joint effort with Professor L. Wrigley, my doctoral supervisor, colleague and former External Assessor on the public management MBA course at the Open Business School. Professor Wrigley's contribution is evident in chapter 2, which forms part of the core conceptual part of the study. This chapter draws heavily on our joint paper 'Professional ethics, government agenda and differential information', Open University Business School. I acknowledge here Professor Wrigley's contribution to the text and express my thanks for his significant input into the study. I am also grateful to Blackwell Publishers for granting permission to use the five case studies in the appendix from *Cases in Public Sector Management* by McKevitt and Lawton.

I would like to record my special thanks to the following persons in New Zealand: Chris Lovelace, Don Huhn, Noeline Alcorn, Rosalyn Noonan, Ken Rae, Coleen Pilgrim, Neil McDonald, Graeme Marshall. My visit to New Zealand was facilitated and supported by Ruth Mansell to whom I owe a special debt of thanks. In Germany, I was helped by Frau Hotz-Demmer, Hessisches Kultusministerium and Dr Clive Hopes, German Institute for International Educational Research, Frankfurt; Dr Hopes helped me in my field work with school

ACKNOWLEDGEMENTS

principals in Germany. In Sweden, Professor Borgenhammar, Torbjorn Bredin, Ingemar Eckerlund, Per Lodding, and Monica Hallberg all gave me their time and co-operation and I thank them for their help.

This study was completed at the Department of Management and Marketing, College of Business, University of Limerick. I would like to thank the Dean of the College, Professor Noel Whelan for his continued support and help in my bad times and for his ongoing interest in public management research. My head of department, Mr Jim Dalton has always supported this work and my colleague Jim Donoghue has commented on the draft chapters. My doctoral and post-graduate students Larry Loughnane, Michelle Millar and Justin Keogan have ably assisted me and put up with my occasional esoteric requests. Ms Bernie O'Connell has, as always, proved to be of inestimable help.

I dedicate the book to Una and Martha who have sometimes been asked to make sacrifices beyond reason in its production. My debt to them is immense and beyond repayment.

The author and publishers gratefully acknowledge the following for permission to reproduce copyright material:

The National Health Committee, National Advisory Committee on Health and Disability, Ministry of Health, Wellington, New Zealand.

Her Majesty's Stationery Office, Norwich.

The OECD, Paris, France.

The Core Services Committee, Wellington, New Zealand.

The publishers apologize for any errors or omissions in the above list and would be grateful to be notified of any corrections that should be incorporated in the next edition or reprint of this book.

Dr David McKevitt
University of Limerick
July 1997

LIST OF TABLES

LIST OF TABLES

LIST OF FIGURES

GLOSSARY OF TERMS

Citizen–client	Members of the general public recognized as both citizens and clients, with their concomitant expectations, rights, etc.
Core skill (or competence, capability)	Key activities and the ability to perform them at professional level.
Institutional memory	The history, or individuals' collective perceptions, of an organization; belief in the nature of an institution; how things used to be done in an organization.
Merit goods	Public 'good', such as health and education, where all benefit.
Next Steps agency	A new form of UK government agency set up in the 1980s to perform executive functions.
Occupational community	A profession, or community of people grouped according to their occupation.
Pareto optimality	Fairness.
Rationing	In, for example, housing allocation, distribution according to a system that limits entitlement.

LIST OF ACRONYMS AND ABBREVIATIONS

CBA Child Benefit Agency
CCT Compulsory competitive tendering
CSA Child Support Agency
DRG Diagnostic Related Groupings
ERO Education Review Office (NZ) – similar to UK's Ofsted (Office for standards in education)
HEWS Health, education and welfare services
NZEI New Zealand Education Institute
OECD Organization for Economic Co-operation and Development
LMS Local Management of Schools
PI Performance Indicator
PSBR Public Sector Borrowing Requirement
PSO Public Service Organization
RAWP Resource allocation formula used in healthcare
SIPGs Single Interest Pressure Groups
SLPO Street Level Public Organizations
TQM Total Quality Management
STEP Social, technical, economic and political
WHO World Health Organization

CHAPTER

1

Introduction

The aim of this study is to explore how core public services can be managed best. Core public services may be defined as those services which are important for the protection and promotion of citizen well-being, but are in areas where the market is incapable of reaching or even approaching a socially optimal state: health, education, welfare and security provide the most obvious and best known examples. (These core services will be abbreviated to 'HEWS' for convenience.) For the provision of services in those areas the relevant public organizations include hospitals, schools, welfare offices, police and fire stations. The study examines, therefore, how these organizations can be managed, including the design of structures to support excellence in service delivery, where such excellence makes for social optimality. The text discusses the responsibilities of core public service managers to manage effectively and efficiently three *functions* – servicing clients, developing service capacity and raising finance – and three *processes* – control, organization and human relations.

These management functions and processes have their counterparts in private enterprises. However, I do not intend to adapt and apply to public organizations the concepts and categories developed originally for private enterprise. This book is concerned to develop and promote a conceptual structure for public management itself. Precisely for the reasons why health, education, welfare and security are in the public domain, we see that the management of core public organizations is different in kind from the management of private enterprise and merits its own special attention. Therefore, chapters 2 and 5 will explore some key characteristics of core public services and the requirements for strategic control that arise from this study. These chapters form the central conceptual part of the text: the remainder of the text is concerned with exploring recent public service reforms in a number of countries and the examination of best practices in core public management.

The text is directed at public service managers who are concerned to improve their management practice and to understand how the characteristics of core public services impact on and shape that practice. The research for this study included field work in England, Germany, New Zealand and Sweden and whenever possible the text uses the direct reports and experiences of managers as they deal with the conflicting pressures on their organizations. This direct experience, together with the case studies in the appendix, brings a practical emphasis to many of the chapters. The comparative focus of the study also helps to show that there are common management problems across countries, and that the study of best practices can help UK managers and others to see their operational concerns in the context of other countries' experience. In exploring the management of core public enterprises, this study continuously deploys three particular concepts:

- the concept of differential information between providers and clients in service delivery;
- the concept of core public organizations providing socially important, interdependent, non-marketable services for social optimality; and
- the concept of professionalism as a relation of trust and agency between providers and clients.

In most, if not all, previous texts on public management, these concepts have been treated as independent of each other. For this study, by contrast, the three are taken to be interrelated and, in consequence, are taken to call together for the development of a different kind of management than that appropriate for private enterprise, or even for public organizations in the non-core areas.

In seeking its objective, this study is less an attempt at theoretical formulation and more an effort to re-interpret existing studies of best practices in management functions and processes in the area of core public services in modern social democracies, particularly in the United Kingdom, Sweden, New Zealand and Ireland, and in other modern or modernizing regions of the world. When examining best practices across a number of countries one particular feature emerges: changes in public management practice, to be successful, must rely on the co-operation of service professionals including managers. It is striking how many proposed changes ignore this feature and this accounts for shortcomings in many of the reform proposals.

The idea for the study arose from reaction to the decades since the Second World War on the relative scale and scope of public and private enterprises. Debates occurred in the press, in periodicals and in learned journals, and constituted the form and substance of conflict between rival political parties and rival social ideologies. However, the course of the debate swung greatly over time. The debate passed through two major swings. First, the 1945–75 swing, which saw a world-wide shift of revolutionary scale in expectations of what government can do, causing a major trend towards public enterprise, and towards enlargement of the role of government as social provider. Secondly, from 1975 to date there has been a great change in sentiment: a decline of faith in government action and, indeed, in collective effort as a whole, as well as a containment in the role of public enterprise. Thatcherism and Reaganism did not initiate this great change towards private enterprise. Thatcherism and

Table 1.1 Government spending, percentage of GDP

	1870	1913	1920	1937	1960	1980	1990	1996
Austria	–	–	14.7	15.2	35.7	48.1	48.6	51.7
Belgium	–	–	–	21.8	30.3	58.6	54.8	54.3
Canada	–	–	13.3	18.6	28.6	38.8	46.0	44.7
France	12.6	17.0	27.6	29.0	34.6	46.1	49.8	54.5
Germany	10.0	14.8	25.0	42.4	32.4	47.9	45.1	49.0
Italy	11.9	11.1	22.5	24.5	30.1	41.9	53.2	52.9
Japan	8.8	8.3	14.8	25.4	17.5	32.0	31.7	36.2
Netherlands	9.1	9.0	13.5	19.0	33.7	55.2	54.0	49.9
Norway	3.7	8.3	13.7	–	29.9	37.5	53.8	45.5
Spain	–	8.3	9.3	18.4	18.8	32.2	42.0	43.3
Sweden	5.7	6.3	8.1	10.4	31.0	60.1	59.1	64.7
Switzerland	–	2.7	4.6	6.1	17.2	32.8	33.5	37.6
United Kingdom	9.4	12.7	26.2	30.0	32.2	43.0	39.9	41.9
United Sates	3.9	1.8	7.0	8.6	27.0	31.8	33.3	33.3
Average	**8.3**	**9.1**	**15.4**	**18.3***	**28.5**	**43.3**	**46.1**	**47.1**
Australia	–	–	–	–	21.2	31.6	34.7	36.6
Ireland	–	–	–	–	28.0	48.9	41.2	37.6
New Zealand	–	–	–	–	26.9	38.1	41.3	47.1
Average	**–**	**–**	**–**	**–**	**25.4**	**39.5**	**39.1**	**40.4**
Total average	**8.3**	**9.1**	**15.4**	**20.7**	**27.9**	**42.6**	**44.8**	**45.9**

* Average without Germany, Japan and Spain undergoing war or war preparations at this time.
Source: Adapted from OECD Main Economic Indicators, 1955–97

Reaganism – and also the whole set of management ideas associated with the concept of competitive advantage – were the outcome.

In the first phase, 1945–75, governments everywhere were proactive in their domestic environment in seeking for ways to exploit public enterprise to reach a socially optimal state. Nationalization of the means of production, was the political slogan favoured by the electorate. Not only were the traditional areas such as health and education, but wholly new areas, such as banking, electrical supply and steel making, were gathered into the public domain. Public enterprise grew as did government expenditure as a proportion of national income (GDP), as can be seen in table 1.1. The economic arguments used to justify this increase in the public domain rarely became more specific than market failure, that is, the incapability of the market to promote the well-being of the people. When political opinion turned against public enterprise in the 1970s, the argument was that markets had improved in their effectiveness and efficiency. At the same time, 'market failure' continued to be the explanation for government to be responsible for the traditional public services – services such as health and education which always were, and which remained, in the public domain.

Everywhere from the mid-1970s, from Washington to London, to Moscow and to Beijing, there has emerged a tremendous faith in the power of markets to promote the well-being of the people, and, certainly, their material prosperity. The consequences have been democratic. A whole social order in one country after another, based on the writings of socialists such as Karl Marx, has been overturned.

Moreover, because socialist countries performed badly in economic terms relative to non-socialist economies, not only has the role of private enterprise been enhanced, but the role of public enterprise also has been sharply contained. This containment can be seen in the trend in the data in table 1.1.

Since the 1980s the tide has continued to flow against public enterprise. There has been a massive loss of faith in the capability of governments, of public enterprise to get things done, particularly to get things done through people. Public enterprise has become widely seen as totally ineffective and inefficient; but this view is in respect of such areas as banking and steel production where the original reason for nationalization was power for government to control the commanding heights of the economy, not the failure of the market to promote social optimality. As the data in table 1.1 show, public enterprise remained on a major scale in the traditional areas: health, education and welfare.

It remains, however, that there has been no serious exploration of the specific reasons why certain services (such as health and education) have tended to develop and to remain in the public domain. Indeed, the whole notion of core public services has not hitherto been recognized. It had to be developed – from the original writings of Coase (1937), Oakshott (1991) and Wrigley (1970 and 1988) for this study. The traditional explanation for public enterprise was 'market failure'. This is plausible but incomplete. Certainly, the government, at least in the provision of important social services, is usually explicitly or implicitly held out as the institution which substitutes for the market failure (Baumol, 1952). This position has long been assumed in most discussions of the functions of government (Arrow, 1975). The idea that society will seek to achieve optimality by government (or other social) action if it cannot achieve it in the market is amongst the oldest roots of western civilization; and modern governments have been very sensitive to pressures for public enterprise to make up for the failure of markets in important areas.

But, if core public management is to develop on well-grounded ideas, then there has to be a precise articulation of why exactly the market system is unable to reach – or even approach – an optimal state in respect of goods and services in certain areas. In other words, we need to locate and understand why the market has failed and why, precisely, it continues to fail in that particular location.

More simply put, the question is why are certain socially important services, such as health and education, non-marketable? This important question deserves an answer if public sector management is to develop as a field of study. Privatization versus public ownership did not confront that question. Yet an answer is needed if the management of core public services is to be placed on a proper basis.

▰▰▰ **Non-marketability** ▰▰▰

For the purpose of exploring why certain socially important services are non-marketable, we have to make certain assumptions. Let us assume that society will always organize itself through one arrangement or another to seek an optimal state. Let us also assume that society will have reached an optimal state when it is precisely in the following condition:

> There is no other allocation of resources to services which will make all participants in the society better off. *(Arrow, 1985, p. 397)*

This particular state is known as 'Pareto optimality'. A definition is just a definition, and implies a neutral stance on matters of value. Whether a Pareto optimal state is what society should seek is a value judgement – a judgement which, particularly, involves a view on the fairness of the original distribution of income.

Nevertheless, it seems reasonable to assume that a change in resource allocation which will make all members of a society better off is a change that should ordinarily be made. In the event, for this study, the term 'social optimality' refers to Pareto optimality, as defined above.

Given a universally acceptable distribution of income, and assuming certain conditions are satisfied, then the competitive market will promote a socially optimal state. Amongst the conditions to be satisfied is the marketability of all goods and services relevant to costs and utilities in the society. Here is where reality intrudes. In practice not all goods and services are marketable.

Such non-marketability may be due to the intrinsic characteristics of a product preventing a suitable and just price from being agreed and enforced; for example, it may concern health care for a contagious disease, or it may be due to social values which prohibit a sale of a product because of social repugnance at the consequences, such as the sale of human organs. But the factors making a service non-marketable that are of direct relevance to this study are twofold: first, differential information in favour of the producer as to the consequences for a client of the acquisition of a product or service; secondly, social interdependence in the act of service consumption. Here, in these two service characteristics, lie the features that distingush core public service management from commercial/industrial sector management.

▰▰▰ **Differential Information** ▰▰▰

Differential information in favour of the provider as to the quality of the product or service is a characteristic of HEWS. Since these areas are so complex, the provider has to be specially trained, and the information possessed by the provider (as to the consequences for the client of acquiring the service) is necessarily very much greater than that of the client. In such circumstances, a price relationship is not practicable and, therefore, the product is 'non-marketable'.

The most obvious areas where such conditions of differential information hold sway are health care and the law. Let us focus here on health care. The complexity of the human body and the complexity of modern techniques to cure the sick require the doctor to undergo highly specialized training before being qualified to practice. Once qualified, the doctor possesses far more information than the client on the consequences for the client of particular forms of treatment. Therefore, the client has to rely on the doctor to determine the appropriate type and quality of health care. Thus the doctor is not merely a provider of medicine, but is also, necessarily, an agent of the client. This duality of roles has important consequences: doctors are duty bound in their professional work by society not to seek to maximize their own profit, but to seek to maximize the welfare of the client. These duties also apply in greater or lesser degree in education, welfare and security, including the law. The very basis for a market does not exist when there is such duality of roles in one individual professional.

It is necessary to emphasize that the existence of differential information that is relevant here is a difference of information as to the *consequences for the client* of the acquisition of the service. It is not a difference of information as to method of production. In both private and public enterprise, there is likely to be an inequality of information between the producer and client as to production methods.

It is also important to note that the information disparity as to the consequences of acquiring a service has to be significant to render the product non-marketable and therefore the market system itself incapable of approaching a socially optimal state. In those areas where the client can have as good or nearly as good an understanding of the utility of the product as the producer, then the product is likely to be marketable and suitable for the relevant resources to be allocated by the market system. But where there is differential information of a major kind, and where universal availability of a service is important for social cohesion, then society has in practice organized itself, in one country after another, to supersede the market and to compel the government to take responsibility for delivery of that service.

Interdependence

Core public services are also characterized by the quality of interdependence. What does that quality mean on the ground? This is not an easy question, but an attempt must be made at an answer.

Clearly, if acquisition or non-acquisition of the service by one member of society affects in significant measure the welfare of the other members of that society then there is interdependence. In other words, interdependence implies a relationship between people. Interdependence as a variable in the human condition does present a dilemma, which was expressed by the Rabbi Kalel thus: 'If I am not for myself, who then is for me? But if I am only for myself, who am I?' Obviously, the claims of interdependence are countered by the claims of individualism. In the UK, the issues are politically thrashed out in the traditional polarization between Labour and Conservative policies.

For this study, the relevant interdependence is of two kinds. First, there is the individual's concern for their own welfare arising from the actions of others, such as the elimination in all others of contagious disease. Secondly, there is individual concern for the general welfare of all others, such as the elimination in society as a whole of absolute poverty. The difference between the two kinds of interdependence is vast in theory, but less so in practice, because in relation to each kind there is strong pressure for collective action through public enterprise to provide the necessary services.

The problem is that, because of interdependence, the services have to be provided free (or heavily subsidized) if society is to approach an optimal state in resource allocation. But although the goods are free to the client, they have to be paid for by society as a whole. The problem then becomes one of rationing.

This is particularly so for some services. In the case of HEWS, the trend in recent decades has been for public demand to increase disproportionately to the resources that society as a whole has been willing to make available through taxation. Hence, each core public service organization has to develop a rationing system to allocate supply to individual clients. The term 'rationing' here means allocation by a system other than price, for example, queuing – allocation on a points basis as in housing.

Hospitals, schools, welfare offices, all have to develop a system of rationing to ensure 'fairness' – or optimality – in distribution. The need to ration the service at an operational level is another major factor that clearly differentiates the management of core public services from the management of business firms in the market system, where supply and demand are equated by movements in price.

Management has to cope with the problems resulting from rationing, particularly the problem articulated through the political system as pressures to make special arrangements for some particularly vulnerable or needy person or class of person.

Stewart has argued that a central concern of public service managers has to be the political dimension inherent in their work. In his words:

> The Manager needs to be aware of political aims and priorities, possible areas
> of conflict, and sources of political difficulty. Awareness requires understand-
> ing of the political process and its workings, not merely the formality of struc-
> ture but the reality of practice. *(1989, p. 171)*

Nowhere is the political dimension more significant than in areas and conditions where rationing of a core public service has to be severe because of demand or supply conditions.

Thus, it is not only differential information, but also social interdependence that push the responsibility for HEWS into the public domain. They also call for a particular social status for the public service managers involved, namely, the status of profession.

▬▬▬ **Professionalism** ▬▬▬

In areas of socially important activity where the condition of differential information and/or of interdependence exists such as health or education, it is apparent from reports over time and from observations in a number of countries that society expects the behaviour of service providers to be quite different from that of business managers in general. In a technical sense, these expectations may be assumed to relate to the fact that the service on offer by the provider belongs to that category of economic goods where *the product and the activity of production are identical* therefore the client is not only excluded from information about the nature of the product, but is also unable to test the value of the product before consuming it.

Necessarily in these circumstances, there has to be a major element of trust in the relationship between provider and client. More than that, because of interdependence, society places ethical restrictions on the provider, such as a nurse or a teacher. The provider's working behaviour is expected to be governed by a concern for the real welfare of the client, and consequently for the real welfare and optimality of society as a whole.

Here, indeed, is the real distinction between the professions (doctors, teachers, police officers and lawyers) and business, where self-interest is the accepted and expected norm. Because of social expectations as to behaviour, the activities of core public organizations are restricted, which affects the way management can operate. They must operate for the real benefit of clients and of society. Another restriction is that the various organizations are expected to stay within their area of specialization, and not diversify their activities in search of custom and profit maximization, as is normal for private businesses.

In the 1980s and 1990s, the claims of such professionals to do a professional job have had to compete with the claims of clients for better service delivery – for better medicine, better education, better welfare and better security.

Supporting that claim by clients are experiences of improvements in the market system, for example, better cars, better houses, better TV. These expectations among clients – and, therefore, of their political leaders – have emphasized the need for better management of the public services.

The nature of management in the core public services has, therefore, changed greatly in the past few years. From being mere custodians of institutions in a steady state, they have had to aim to be dynamic professional administrators offering excellence in service delivery to clients, who themselves are articulate in their needs and demands. These managers are also under the eye of politicians who, in turn, are articulate in promoting ideals of public service, not necessarily with the provision of ideal levels of resources. All this makes the management of core public organizations the most challenging of all the administrative tasks society has to offer.

HEWS

For ease of exposition, the general area – embracing health, education, welfare and security – is here defined as the *core public services*. The proportion of gross national product expended since the Second World War varies greatly between countries and over time. In broadest measure the proportion in the western world was about 20 per cent in 1950, about 30 per cent in 1960, and has remained about 40 per cent since then – but 40 per cent of an increasing size of GDP.

Although concern for the effectiveness and efficiency of the management functions and processes of the core public service was first placed on the public agenda only in the 1970s it seems likely to remain there for the foreseeable future as a challenge to management because of the sheer magnitude of the sums involved. HEWS is a big area. HEWS may or may not be popular or seize the public imagination. Clearly it is important.

The Structure of this Study

Chapter 2 Managing in the core public services

This chapter structures the environment in a rigorous manner using a model we have developed which has its roots in the writings of Richard Caves and Michael Porter. For our purposes the environment is categorized into three major areas:

1 central government, with its politics and pressures;
2 professional associations with their concern for standards and income;
3 citizen–clients with their changing expectations, demographic and family characteristics.

This is the core conceptual part of the book; the models presented here are used to structure the data presented throughout the text. The models are derived from field work and general management models so as to locate the study and management of core public services as a distinct area from general business management.

Chapter 3 Service delivery – meeting citizen needs

This chapter focuses on the relationship between the SLPO (street level public organization) and the citizen–client. The rationing of public services is examined in the context of having appellate structures for citizen redress. The relevance of using consumer models of service delivery in core public services is appraised.

Special emphasis will be given to the problem of substituting priority or rationing by professionals according to the need for the price mechanism according to income.

Chapter 4 Managing resources for social gain

This chapter is concerned with capacity planning in core public services. On a comparative basis, the question of investing in new capacity will be addressed including the input from political forces, professional associations and the community. Particular attention will be given to public investment capacity decisions in New Zealand and Sweden.

Chapter 5 Strategic control of core public services

This is the second major conceptual chapter in the text, and examines the legislative frameworks that provide for the control of public service delivery systems. It focuses in particular on the model of control adopted by New Zealand, which is seen as the most radical restructuring of public service control in modern economies. It looks at the processes of strategic control (objective setting, measurement of objectives against the investment decision described in chapter 4). Another central study in this chapter is the examination of strategic control in the health services of Ireland, the UK, Sweden and New Zealand.

Chapter 6 Organizational structures for effective service delivery

This chapter looks at the relationship between street level public organizations (SLPOs) and their environment. It examines how organizational structures can be designed to cope with different environments, organic and mechanistic. The chapter's focus is again comparative and examines changes in education management in the UK, Germany and New Zealand.

Chapter 7 Managing professionals

This chapter examines the performance measurement frameworks that have been developed for the management of professionals within the public services. It draws on extensive fieldwork in a number of countries and it examines how inappropriate operational control can damage satisfactory relationships between professionals and managers. It looks at the measurement of results promulgated as the basis of reform in different countries and their impact on the delivery of services to the citizen–client.

Chapter 8 Review of reform programmes

What do the public service reforms mean for the relationship between government, professional associations and the citizen–client? What are the education and training requirements for public service managers in a changing environment? Lessons are drawn from our comparative studies and the implications for the success of UK reforms are examined.

Appendix

In addition to the many examples given of public service reform, the text also contains five case studies of UK examples, which describe major change in public service organizations. These examples, which are referred to in the relevant chapters, include change in a Next Steps Agency, local government, the police, community care and in professional public sector accounting. The case studies, which include self-assessment questions, help further our understanding of changes in core public management. The case studies can be treated as stand-alone examples or used to illustrate particular features of change when combined with the models and frameworks presented in the chapters.

CHAPTER

2

Managing in the Core Public Services

This chapter, which is the core conceptual part of the text, provides the public service manager with models for understanding the environment within which public organizations deliver services. It can be argued that, without such a structured understanding as presented in these models, managing social inter-dependence will not be effective. Throughout the text, examples are provided of activities of government where inappropriate controls and management models were applied to the core public services. Appropriate management requires understanding of the organization in its environment; that is a central objective of this chapter. In developing the conceptual framework of this study a major impetus was the need to describe the management of core public services so as to capture the realities and challenges of managers. The writings in this area, hitherto, have tended to describe public management either as a distinctive process (the differentialist perspective represented by writers such as Stewart) or management as a generic activity broadly similar in the public and private sector (this perspective is represented in the writings of Rainey). The conceptual framework developed in this chapter draws on the concepts and categories of general management combined with the data and experience of practising managers.

The chapter examines:

- differential information as between the provider and client of core public services;
- a model of the SLPO in its environment;
- the concepts of professionals and social obligation as they relate to rationing of public services.

The important themes of this chapter, set out in the models, are taken up in much greater detail throughout the remainder of the book.

The proposition is that in modern (OECD) countries, in socially important areas (such as HEWS), where there exists differential information in favour of the producer, progress is necessarily the responsibility of government, and the service delivery activities of SLPOs in these areas is properly structured not by the market, but – contingent on good relations between central government and professional associations – by the influence of central government through general legislation, resource allocation, organizational design and performance measurement, and by the influence of professional associations through ethical codes (or 'rules of the game'), as portrayed in figure 2.1. Each of these modes of influence and 'rules of the game' will be examined in later chapters; the important point to note here is the different sets of forces which impact on service delivery to the client. How can these sets of influence be balanced? I consider this question later in the chapter.

It might be noted that this proposition has its practical roots in my research on public sector management in Britain, Germany, Ireland, New Zealand and Sweden, and its theoretical roots in the writings of Herbert Simon, Michael Oakshott, and Kenneth Arrow (see References). The field research began with an extended on-site study of the workings of a regional hospital in Cork, Ireland. Field research continued with a study of the workings of schools in England. Next, I examined central government in its reform activities in New Zealand (in conjunction with corresponding reforms in schools and hospitals), and observed with close attention in that country the nature of the relationship between central government and the schools and hospitals, that is the SLPOs. Next, health-care delivery activities in Sweden were examined. Finally, I studied the effects and the actual management of the schools, and the effect of legislation on community and school participation in Germany and the UK. The basic research model was comparative, with special attention to differences as well as similarities between countries.

In developing the proposition outlined in figure 2.1, my thinking was influenced by field work and discussions with public service professional associations in Sweden and New Zealand. Their aim was to develop partnerships with clients and central government so as to orient change in a manner mutually suitable to themselves and the politicians directing the reform programmes. Legislation in countries such as Germany emphasized partnership and consensus in public management whilst in the United Kingdom the legislative emphasis was much more concerned with specifying detailed operational controls and performance measures. Particularly notable were the differences in the process of public sector management between countries. (The nature of legislation as an instrument of strategic control is examined in detail in chapter 5.)

My thinking was also influenced by the intellectual movement, labelled as the 'New Public Management', which began to sweep through the western world from the late 1980s. The central theme of this movement is the notion of removing organizational differences between the public and the private sector so to reduce public sector inefficiency by the method of a sharp focus on getting results through 'hands-on' management. According to Christopher Hood (1995), this movement is felt most strongly in Australia, New Zealand, Canada, the United Kingdom and Sweden – countries which, as it happens, were also the focus of my field research.

Figure 2.1 Relationship between government agenda, differential information and professional ethics

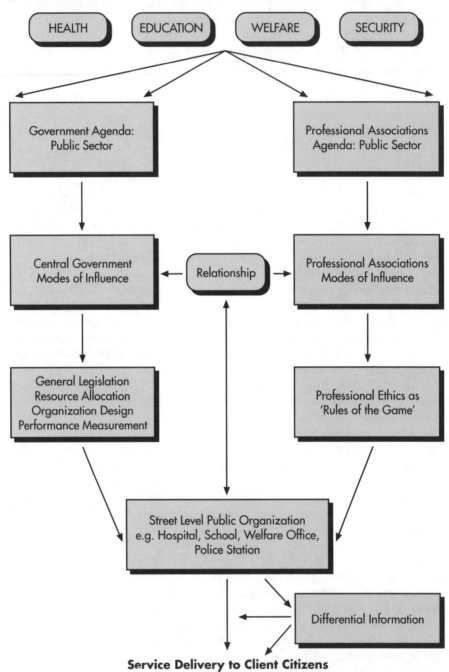

Source: Wrigley and McKevitt 1995

Concept of Progress

To develop the criteria of progress, I make three assumptions. First, I assume that society is the historic personality known as the nation-state, working through innumerable arrangements, traditions and customs, where all the participants are nurtured 'from their mother's milk' with a sense of community and interdependence, and with a shared culture, including a common language and set of social skills.

Secondly, I also assume that society over the long term will always seek to organize itself to achieve an optimal state and, correspondingly, to escape from a sub-optimal state. And thirdly, I further assume that society will have reached an optimal state when it is exactly and precisely in the following condition:

> There is no other movement of activities or resources which will make all the participants of society better off. *(Adapted from the writings of Arrow, 1975, p. 397)*

Correspondingly, we may assume society is in a sub-optimal state if there exists a feasible movement of activities and resources which would make all participating members better off.

In the literature, these states are known respectively as Pareto optimality and Pareto sub-optimality. Accordingly, I define progress as that change of activities and resources that move society from a Pareto sub-optimal state toward a Pareto optimal state.

Obviously, definitions are just definitions. While it is clearly desirable for society to seek Pareto optimality, we need to allow that optimality in this sense is not the only possible criterion for individual or social action. For example, only a few individuals in a society may be extremely happy or talented or wealthy, and yet the society may be Pareto optimal if there is no way of moving activities and resources to increase the happiness or talent or wealth of the many without hurting the few. Inevitably this brings certain qualifications to the definition.

Yet, however important such qualifications are in practical affairs, we must hold firm to our concept of progress as the movement of activities and resources to change society from a Pareto sub-optimal to a Pareto optimal state. I accept that this may not be, and even should not be the only workable definition of progress, but it is one that is always central, always important, and always capable of serving as a valid first criterion of what should be done by social action.

Differential Information

Market prices generate valuable information for those who have to make decisions as to what to buy and sell, and what to produce and consume. But prices can do more than that. In a competitive market, provided certain conditions are satisfied, price movements can bring about both a harmony between private and public interests and Pareto optimality.

More than that, provided the market is competitive, self-serving behaviour of buyers and sellers may well promote social progress more effectively than altruism. This was indeed the central message of Adam Smith in *The Wealth of Nations*:

> Every individual endeavours to employ his capital so that its produce may be of greatest value. He generally neither intends to promote the public interest, nor knows how much he is promoting it. He intends only his own security, only his own gain. And he is in this led by an invisible Hand to promote an end which is not part of his intention. By pursuing his own interest he frequently promotes that of society more effectively than he really intends to promote it. *(Smith, 1776)*

Thus did Adam Smith introduce to the world the role of private interest and competition, of the 'invisible hand', in moving society to progress. However, the conditions to be satisfied are not trivial. Amongst the conditions are that the buyer in the market can predict accurately the satisfaction to be got from acquiring a commodity. Here, as shall be seen, is the rub.

In modern times, there has been a renewal of faith in market competition as a means for universal progress. In this faith, there is the assumption that buyers do know what is good for them, more precisely, that they do know and can measure the consequences for themselves of acquiring a commodity. However, this assumption is not valid in respect of those commodities where there is differential information in favour of the producer (or seller) as to the outcome for the buyer of a sale. Here, faith in the market is confronted by reality. It is a matter of simple fact that there are highly important categories of commodities where conditions of differential information exist and, moreover, exist on a massive scale.

Differential information in favour of the producer as to the consequences for the consumer of the acquisition of a commodity is a characteristic of those services which are so complicated in their nature, and about which there is such uncertainty as to their effects for the recipient, that the producer has to be carefully trained over a lengthy period on the characteristics of the services. Because of this training, the information possessed by producers concerning the most likely consequences for a particular client of acquiring the service is very much greater than that of the client. In such circumstances, a price relationship is not a valid basis for an optimal level of transactions, particularly in relation to those services the proper distribution of which is deemed important by society for a sense of community to be maintained.

In this argument, it is assumed that information is difficult to transfer. The problem is in the receiver. Learning takes time and effort. The effort required can be very great in respect of certain services that are of social importance.

In health care, the doctor is not merely a provider of medicine, but also, necessarily, an agent of the client in providing information. In the decision to acquire health care, the sick cannot stand alone. Quite simply, they do not have the information needed to make an informed choice between the various medical options that are open, still less to make informed decisions about trade-offs between the cost and quality of medical service in relation to each option. They need the doctor to advise them, to be on their side, to wish them well. Certainly the sick cannot themselves predict the likely consequence of acquiring a particular programme of treatment. They rely upon the doctor to advise them not just what medicine to have, and how much and what and where, but also on the total programme. Thus, the doctor has two roles: provider and agent. This duality of roles has important consequences. The doctor, historically, is bound by society not to seek to maximize personal profit, but to seek to maximize client welfare. The doctor is also bound to consider the consequences of medical efforts for society as a whole and not just for particular clients. And society over the generations has developed powerful institutions to regulate the relationship between doctor and client.

Duality of role of the producer also characterizes, in greater measure or less, the areas of education, welfare and security, including the law, because here too there is differential information, and here too the producer needs to be the agent of the client. The essential characteristics of the market system, arms-length negotiation between willing and knowledgeable buyers and sellers, is lacking. The argument being made here is based on my field research, but the point about differential information is not original.

The consequences for the citizen–client arising from the existence of differential information are examined in chapter 3. It will be seen that service delivery in core public services has to be adapted to take account of this feature, including consultation with citizens, the provision of appellate systems and survey of citizen satisfaction. However, much recent change in service delivery is based on a market model that seeks to ignore the central characteristic of core public services – differential information between provider and client.

Yet governments, particularly of English-speaking countries, continue to promote reforms in the public sector on the assumption of the universal validity of market competition, and continue to search for ways to introduce market competition in the supply of welfare services from the public sector. It is as though the problem of differential information was swept under the carpet.

For example, in seeking to simulate a market mechanism in public service management, governments in the United Kingdom and New Zealand have separated the functions of purchaser (i.e. who pays) and that of supplier (i.e. the school, hospital, etc.). They thereby hope to stimulate competition between different parts of the delivery system so as to increase the efficiency and effectiveness of service delivery. However, in discussing these structural changes in New Zealand in respect of health care I was told that 'we don't know if the new system will work', and that 'we ploughed into areas of social policy because of our earlier success in financial changes'. In the UK (discussed in chapter 5) I saw no evidence that competition in health-care provision has yielded any additional benefit to clients. In Sweden the reformed health-care allocation system was described to me by Professor Borgenhammar as a 'Calcutta market' (i.e. chaotic) which showed no signs of rationality.

The data from many countries in this text support the argument that many changes made in core public services were not very well thought out or planned. Implementation was a rushed affair, little consultation took place with providers, managers or the citizen–client. There was little evidence of piloting of change or systematic evaluation of the often dramatic change in organization and delivery. A 'one best way' of managing was introduced based on unsupported evidence and reliant on private sector models.

In my fieldwork I was particularly struck by the fact that many professional groups felt threatened by government reforms in public service management. This feeling was especially the case where the reforms were based on legislation prescribing in close detail the activities of professionals. In the UK, reforms of education, including the introduction of a national curriculum and standardized testing, have had the effect of curtailing professional judgement and replacing it with a mechanistic assessment framework. New Zealand's reforms of education have sought to strengthen parental control of schools and to strengthen the external inspectorate function to ensure compliance with government policy. In New Zealand's case, however, there was co-operation between the professional associations and parents – a collaborative alliance – in seeking to moderate government changes which they viewed as inimical to the traditions of New Zealand schools. The New Zealand Education Institute (NZEI – the professional association for primary teachers) instituted an effective promotion and publication strategy that drew attention to the attainment standards of New Zealand primary schools.

At the same time, training courses in effective management were developed for school principals by NZEI so as to prepare the ground for the reforms which placed particular emphasis on effective management of the school as an institution.

In Germany, by contrast, with its decentralized tradition of federal autonomy in education, the emphasis is on increasing partnership between the school and its community. Central government does not feature highly in school activities. The individual school and teachers, at secondary level, have autonomy in setting and grading the final examination – the *Abitur* – thus granting a great degree of professional autonomy to the schools and teachers. The German notion of *beamte*, a professional salaried civil servant (which developed over one hundred years) is viewed as a basic building block for public services management to ensure quality professional service to clients. This can be put in another way. Educational standards are set by the education profession and the autonomy of professionals is supported by the *beamte* concept. Consensus and participation characterize the management of schools through legislation which specifies the roles of headteacher, teachers and parents.

The German education system (which does not display the scale and scope of New Zealand reforms) has remained largely a highly structured and decentralized partnership between the State (or *Land*) and the professions. The highly regulated nature of the German model where laws and regulations prescribe large areas of the education system (teacher training, the division of responsibilities between the inspectorate and headteachers, outlining the scope and extent of teacher–parent decision-making) the effect is to leave the task of education to the professions themselves. The *Abitur*, whilst examined by the school itself, is highly regarded by pupils, parents and employers. Thus there is a seeming paradox in the German bureaucratic model: the system is effective because of the laws and regulations which grant sufficient autonomy to the professionals. The system does not seek to make headteachers into financial or maintenance managers; it seeks, instead, to give them legal autonomy to do the task they were trained for – educational and pedagogic leadership.

The decentralized framework, which is dictated by the Federal Constitution and Basic Law, thus prevents the Federal Government (even if it so desired) from centralizing an activity like secondary schooling, which is, by its nature, a decentralized one based on the school. The most often used terms in the German fieldwork interviews were 'consensus, openness and transparency' to describe the activity of the headteachers.

The field data that I report on the collaboration of public service professionals and managers in the context of appropriate strategic legislation are important and they are examined at length in later chapters. For present purposes we can begin to see the importance of the SLPO in its environment, where conflicting forces are acting upon it and where the management task is to balance appropriate control (via legislation, organizational structures, measurement systems) with the requirement of professionals to meet client needs. My research indicates that, in the UK especially, there is antagonism between the professionals and the state whereby in their view operational and mechanistic controls are applied in the absence of appropriate legislation. (This aspect of management control is dealt with in chapter 7 of the text.)

■■■ Agenda of Government ■■■

Historically, for the provision of important services, government has been explicitly or implicitly held out as the institution which is an alternative to the market for the allocation of resources. That society will seek to achieve optimality by government (or other social) action if it cannot achieve it by the market is amongst the oldest traditions of behaviour in western civilization. However this behaviour occurs in a time frame. Government has stepped in at one time for one purpose and another time for another and, perhaps, quite different purpose. In the result, the public sector, or government, contains a wide variety of activities which have only two aspects in common, first, each activity is socially important, and, secondly, the market is seen as not being able to develop the activity properly. Table 2.1 classifies the various activities of government by reason for inclusion in the public sector.

The figures in table 2.1 for percentage of public employment is the average for all modern (i.e. OECD) countries in the period 1985–90. On the same

Table 2.1 Government activities classified by reason for inclusion in the public sector

Reason for public sector	Issue	Government activities	Percentage of public employment
Political	Sovereignty and identity	Defence; law and order; foreign affairs; taxation; roads; trade and industry; postal services	25
Economic	Natural monopolies	Telephones; electricity; water supply; gas	25
Social welfare	Differential information and merit distribution of goods	Health; education; welfare (law and order aspects)	50

Source: Wrigley and McKevitt, 1995.

basis, the proportion of total labour force in public employment was about 20 per cent, and government expenditure (which includes transfer payments) was about 40 per cent of gross national income. Clearly, government is not just widespread but also big. What is enormously important is that activities are in the public sector for very different reasons indeed. Of course, one can ascend to those happy uplands where simple generalizations explain everything. 'Market failure' is one such generalization. Ideology is another. For operational purposes, distinctions are needed.

In table 2.1, three quite different reasons are presented for activities to be in the public sector.

- *Sovereignty and identity*: a political reason which holds sway in all countries, everywhere, at all times, but in modern times, on average, only in respect of 25 per cent of government employees.
- *Natural monopolies*: an economic reason which holds sway in many but not all modern countries and, on average, for the western world today accounts for 25 per cent of government employees.
- *Differential information*: a social welfare reason, which now holds sway in all modern countries, but not equally for all the relevant services, and which on average accounts for 50 per cent of all government employment.

As mentioned, these reasons are very different from each other. This fundamental difference is relevant to arguments for revolutionary changes in the public sector. None of the arguments recognize the fundamental differences between types of government activity. To that extent, we might say, these arguments would be invalid. There is no reason to believe that problems in the political sector will be similar in kind to problems in the economic or the social welfare sector. But there is more than that. Most of the examples presented in the arguments as evidence of the need for revolution are taken from the social welfare category, but without reference to the problem of differential information. Social welfare is one particular category of government agenda, but it is not the whole of government.

At the same time, social welfare, that is the general area of health, education, welfare and security, is by far the largest in the public sector. This general area grew rapidly in the 1950s and 1960s but then governments everywhere felt obliged to set limits to the relative size of the area. Powerful forces were at play. The very differential information which ensured these activities were in the public sector in the first place, also ensured continuous pressure for growth.

Of course, resource allocation is also influenced by the demands of citizen–clients. Where such demands are articulated and heard, the resources are allocated by government bearing in mind the views of citizens in the role of taxpayers. But, in resource allocation for social welfare, professional standards do play a significant role – as I noted in my field research – along with the demands of citizen–clients, and the priorities and workings of government. The question arises how these three bodies, professions, citizen–clients, and government, do in fact relate to each other in the allocation of resources. After all, it is very easy to say that the market does not make for progress, and has been superseded by government in the areas of health, education, welfare and security, where differential information obtains. But how, in relation to the demands from citizen–clients, and the professional standards of the welfare workers, does the government step in? This is a very important question. It has indeed both inspired and centred my and others' research over time and across space. But before looking at it we need, as it were, to construct a platform to observe government in a particular way.

▬▬ Core Skills ▬▬

Since the mid-1970s, there has been great interest in the problem of government efficiency. The concern of 'think tanks', political parties, and academics has been to change the role and scale of government, with much discussion of efficiency audits, value for money, competition and, of course, privatization. However, there is a peculiar aspect to all this. The focus of the concerns and such associated studies as are made have been on the extremes: on the one hand, on decisions by high-ranking ministerial policy makers, and, on the other hand, the case studies of individual officials dealing with individual citizen–clients. These are very particular viewpoints. Moreover, they are viewpoints which can lead the observer away from operational matters. We need to switch the focus towards the middle, where middle management actually ensure the service delivery.

Figure 2.2 Creation and development of core skills

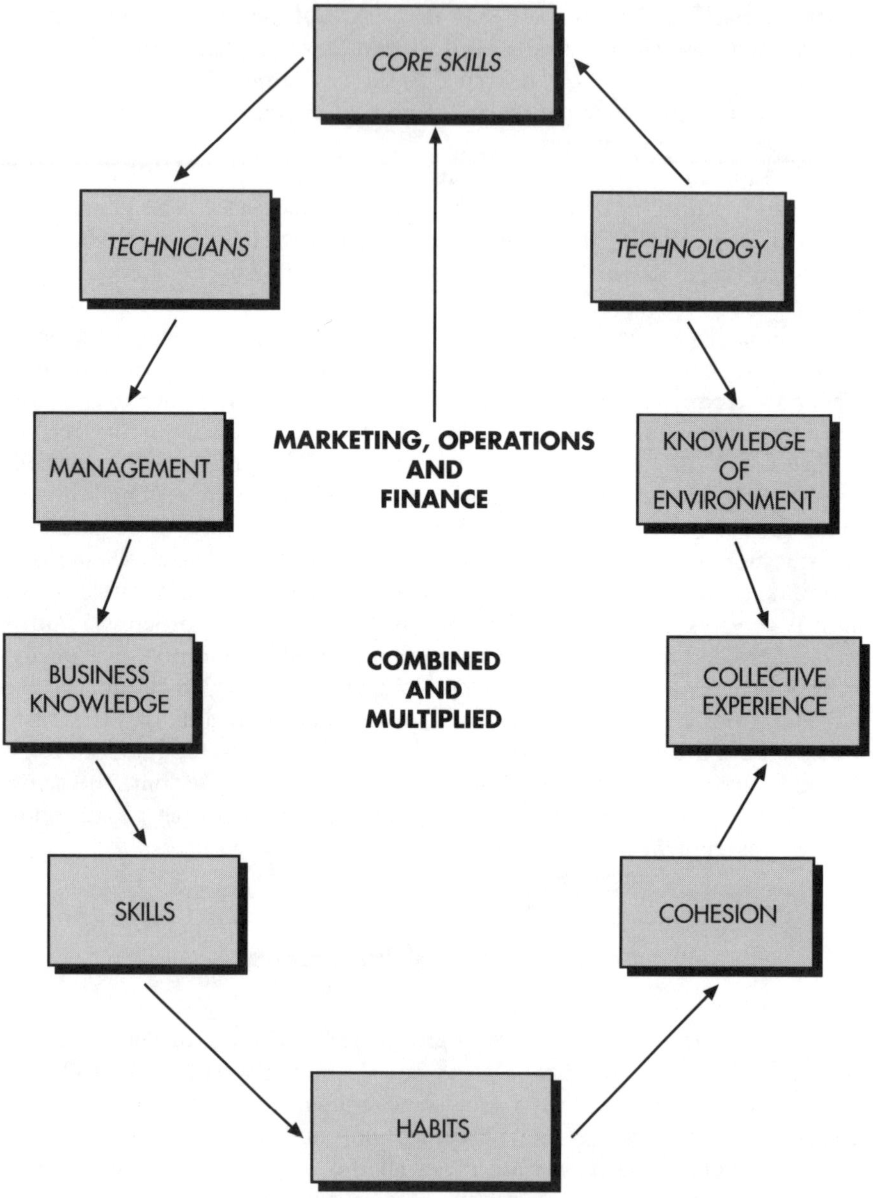

The Creation of Core Skills

Source: Adapted from Wrigley 1970

For this, we need surely to concentrate on where the action is, that is, in the hospitals, clinics, schools, colleges, welfare offices and police stations. It is at this level where professional specialists, government officials, and citizen–clients deal with each other face to face and it is here where service delivery actually takes place. However, to enable the switch in focus we need to deploy the concepts and categories of another discipline, namely, management theory, as developed originally for the private sector.

In the private sector, the analogy to the hospital, school, welfare office or police station is the department store or manufacturing enterprise or mining company. Here is where the service is created, the product is made, and the crucial process of service delivery is carried out. Here also is where the mass of workers are employed, the mass of financial assets are invested, and the mass of innovations are created and developed, and here too is where the supplier deals face to face with the buyer. And it is most significant that here is where the greatest studies of business administration, from the writings of Fayol and Taylor to the writings of Drucker and Porter are focused. Over the years it is in relation to the workings of such enterprises that the most powerful and robust management concepts have been developed and refined.

Since 1970, with the development that year of the notion of 'Core Skill' by Wrigley, at the Harvard Business School, these private sector enterprises have been conceptualized as in figure 2.2. It will be noted that marketing, operations and finance are presented as the basic functions that have to be performed by a private enterprise if it is to survive and prosper in a competitive environment. But these functions cannot effectively be performed in isolation. They have to be and are connected in a useful and profitable way. Here, the core skill comes into play.

The core skill, according to Wrigley is:

> the collective knowledge, skills, habits of working together, as well as the collective experience of what the market and technology will bear, that is required in the cadre of managerial and technical personnel if the firm is to survive and grow in a competitive market . . . It is a collective knowledge not just of a market or of a technology, but of one in relation to the other. *(1970)*

Since 1970, the concept has been in general use, though in the early 1990s under slightly different names, such as 'core competence', or 'core capability'.

In the event, with this concept, the firm is seen as a living entity, an occupational community which possesses an inner structure, an inner dynamic force, the core skill, which makes it and enables it to function. The firm possesses organic arrangements that reflect and embellish the forces in the external environment, the competitive market. Whether we call it core skill, core competence, or core capability, does not really matter. What really matters is that core skill is a robust concept which can be employed to explain the workings of hospitals, schools, welfare offices and police stations. While the impetus that shapes the birth of all collective enterprises may and probably does lie in the needs of environment, it is the internally developed core skill that becomes, over time, the central force shaping all undertakings where it is necessary and habitual to get things done through people.

However, events do not always occur suddenly. The time element is important in developing and maintaining core skills. The pace of reform, for example, in New Zealand's programme of public service change has been such that 'institutional memory' has been lost, thus robbing the institution of knowledge of how things were handled in the past.

An instructive example of this pace of change might be found in New Zealand, where the reforms in education were described to me as 'a big bang model of reform' – the regional educational boards were abolished, the inspectorate system was disbanded, there was devolution of finance and industrial relations accountability to individual schools, and the training of school principals was contracted out from the Ministry of Education. These changes happened in a five-year period and were clearly aimed at radically altering the structure of education delivery and control. With the abolition of a national inspectorate, it is more difficult to identify and support the diffusion of good practice throughout the system. (An extended examination of New Zealand's reforms are discussed in chapters 5 and 6.)

In the early 1990s Sweden sought to adapt its system of public management to meet the immediate constraints of its budgetary situation. When I had observed the Swedish system in the 1980s I was struck by its then careful attention to the process of legislation, including wide preparatory investigation and piloting of change prior to full scale implementation. It was remarkable how, in the 1990s, this incremental, emergent, process had been changed. One observer remarked that the 'pace of change is too fast', while another said that 'today you don't have experts, interest groups or pilots' prior to legislative change and 'that the old co-operation philosophy is gone'. Clearly, when major changes in legislation are envisioned it is important to consider the views of the major stakeholders. In this regard I would observe that Sweden has, perhaps, lost some of the coherence required between attendance to the 'rules of game' and the requirements of the client/community. Furthermore, when major changes in the nature and workings of public enterprises are planned, the time needed for the development of the core skills needs to be kept in mind. We are talking about the time needed for the development of collective habits and values and skills, for the emergence of an occupational community, for the emergence of an enterprise culture. The relationship between core skills and the environment of core public services is set out in figure 2.3.

The adaptation of public managers to a new legislative or organizational environment does, as discussed above, take time. New skills, new co-operative or consensual ways of working have to be developed, new relationships forged with providers and clients. I will go on to report examples of appropriate and inappropriate forms of these relationships throughout the text. Here it is sufficient to note the importance of time frame in changes within core public services, and the requirement for new skills by public service managers.

Figure 2.3 Core skills and the environment of core public services

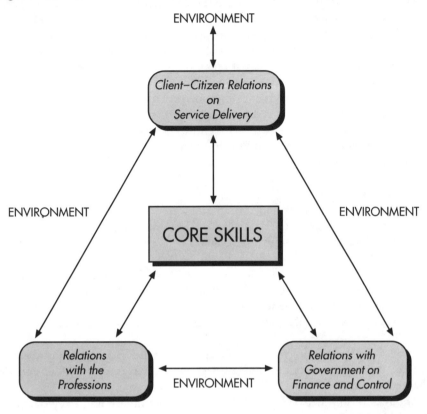

Source: McKevitt 1996

■■■■ Street Level Public Organizations (SLPOs) ■■■■

At this stage, I will offer a description of the institutional character of the public sector. In the private sector, we may use the notion of the 'firm' to describe the huge variety of enterprises that transact for profit with the environment. For the public sector, we need an analogy. One is to hand. The MIT political scientist, Michael Lipsky, in describing public enterprises such as hospitals and schools and police stations, coined the phrase 'street level bureaucracy'. This was a most remarkably useful innovation. However, on the basis of field research, I would reject the term 'bureaucracy' because of its connotation of a closed system. But the term 'street level' is most helpful. Accordingly, I have developed and given the term SLPO to those public enterprises like hospitals, clinics, schools, welfare offices and police stations, where government officials, professional specialists, and citizen–clients meet face-to-face and deal with each other.

These SLPOs cannot be seen in a void. They relate to and are affected by their environment. It is only in that perspective that they can properly be seen. The state of the environment is very important for their internal relationships. If the environment is stable, the internal relationship tends to be mechanical, placid and undemanding. But in an unstable environment, as has been common in recent decades, the internal relationship tends to be organic, dynamic and uncertain, and needs to be managed skilfully. The question presents itself, what is out there in the external environment that is so important for SLPOs?

On the basis of the field research, and in tune with the famous model of Richard Caves and Michael Porter, I identify and categorize five key aspects in the environment common to SLPOs in the areas of health, education, welfare and security, as follows:

1 central government, in the shape of politicians, central departments, Treasury, law courts and central auditors;
2 citizen–clients and their families and communities;
3 professional associations that contain the career ladders and loyalties of the professional specialists in the SLPOs;
4 related SLPOs, for example, clinics which refer clients to hospitals; or primary schools which feed students to secondary schools;
5 suppliers of equipment, which may also be involved in product research, for example, drug companies in the area of health care.

The key relationships are conceptualized as figure 2.4. Structures for effective service delivery and purposeful professional behaviour are discussed in chapters 6 and 7.

The relationship between the SLPO and its community was a key component of my field work. I sought to track how schools, for example, related to their community and how headteachers could evaluate their effectiveness in this regard. I found that in Germany, which has a long tradition of legislation prescribing the roles of teachers and parents in school governance, the relationship between the school and the community was a close one. The School Board can decide on the school's assessment strategy, the length of the school week (within an agreed State total of hours) and the selection of text books. Schools do not have autonomy on their budgets (which they receive direct from the local community), and the headteacher sees him/herself as the pedagogic leader within the school, the official job description of a principal is someone 'who has to implement the decisions of the School Board'. In my discussions with German school principals I was struck by their attendance to the internal processes of their organization rather than the need to concentrate on financial issues such as school maintenance and budgets. The legislative and structural supports allowed the principals to concentrate on educational issues and leadership, and so to enhance relationships with the community.

The different strategies pursued in the United Kingdom, New Zealand and Germany to try to modernize educational organizations are discussed in chapters 5 and 6. Government steps into the area of health, education, welfare and

Figure 2.4 The street level public organization in its environment

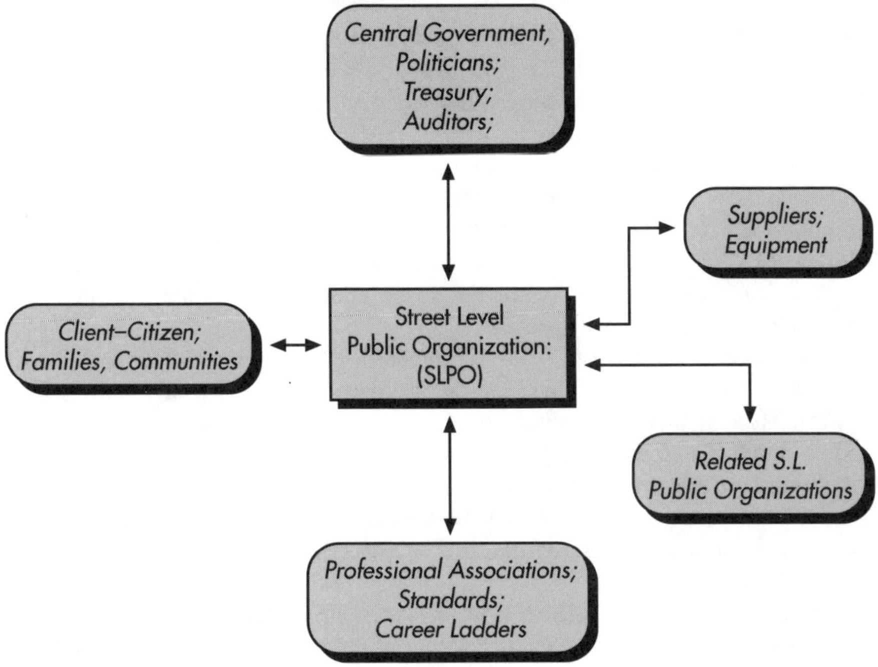

```
                    ┌──────────────────┐
                    │ Central Government,│
                    │   Politicians;    │
                    │    Treasury;      │
                    │    Auditors;      │
                    └──────────────────┘
                             ↕
                                        ┌──────────────┐
                                        │  Suppliers;  │
                                        │  Equipment   │
                                        └──────────────┘
┌──────────────────┐    ┌──────────────────┐
│  Client–Citizen;  │↔   │   Street Level    │
│Families, Communities│  │Public Organization:│
└──────────────────┘    │     (SLPO)        │
                        └──────────────────┘
                                        ┌──────────────────┐
                             ↕          │   Related S.L.    │
                                        │Public Organizations│
                        ┌──────────────────┐ └──────────────────┘
                        │Professional Associations;│
                        │      Standards;      │
                        │    Career Ladders    │
                        └──────────────────┘
```

Source: McKevitt 1996

security through the method of creating and developing and supporting SLPOs. It does this in a relationship of greater or lesser harmony with the professions and with the community in the persons of citizen–clients. There is in the result no monolithic organization, as presented by 'think tanks', no rational bureaucracy, as shaped along the lines of Weber, no dominance of individual interest, as portrayed by Niaskanen. What is created and developed and supported are living institutions, collective entities containing the hopes and fears, affections and loyalties of a whole mass of people and institutions. In that light, as a model for the setting up of SLPOs, government, ideally, is a partner, a partner of the past, the present and the future, a partner of the professions and of citizen–clients. That is to say, SLPOs, like hospitals, schools, welfare offices and police stations, need to be set up and developed as part of a community by a government which itself is part of the community. Of course, as I have reported above, reality is at some distance from models and ideals. Nevertheless, ideals and models are important for sustained endeavour and success. SLPOs are organizations which have amongst their mission a complex and difficult job to do, particularly in hard times, when demand is great and resources are scarce. That mission is rationing resources to those most in need. This particular job is done in large part by the professional specialists. Rationing resources to those most in need merits special attention.

▬▬ Rationing Public Resources ▬▬

Generally, street level social services are free to the citizen–client, but paid for out of taxation. The trend in recent decades is for public demand to increase disproportionately to the resources that society as a whole in the shape of the government has been willing to make available. The result in practice is a shortfall of supply. This brings a complicated problem. In relation to the need for social services, people are not homogeneous. They differ greatly. They cannot be treated as though they have identical needs and circumstances. A McDonald's hamburger store approach is not appropriate. Standardization is not a realistic possibility. Account has to be taken of the differences in needs and circumstances between people.

Consequently, each SLPO has to develop a rationing system to allocate resources to the various individual clients in their various individual circumstances. SLPOs, such as hospitals, schools, welfare offices and the law, have all had to develop a complex system of rationing to allocate in a sensitive manner the limited supply available to them. This is no simple task. It is professional judgement on priority, not customer affluence, nor simple rules, say, of 'equal shares', which determines, within the relevant legislation, the allocation of resources between clients.

Typical street level professionals are doctors, health visitors, teachers, child-carers, social workers, social security officers, citizens' lawyers, and police and fire officers. In the rationing of resources, those professional specialists exercise discretion. They do this to allow for the differences between people. Because of the exercise of discretion in dealing with citizens, these street level professionals have considerable policy-making powers. Bob Hudson has described the circumstances:

> Unlike lower level workers in most organizations, street level bureaucrats (professionals) have a considerable amount of discretion in determining the nature, amount, and quality of benefits provided by their agencies. Policemen decide who to arrest and whose behaviour to overlook; teachers make subtle decisions on who is teachable; social workers on who is socially salvageable; health care workers on who has a life worth preserving; housing letting officers on who gets accommodation and so on. The discretion is therefore largely brought to bear in the rationing of resources in a situation where demand for them exceeds supply. *(1989, p. 388)*

Professor A. H. Halsey, writing on change in British society, looks at the phenomenon from another viewpoint, namely, the authority of street level professionals to decide which citizens get what from whom.

> when we come to the service of more subtle and varied human needs in medicine, education, or social security, difficulties multiply. The open space activities are not 'proved' right or good because they are in command of a charismatic leader, or because of tradition, or because they can be subsumed

under some general rule, but because they are so certified by the trained members of the organization whose special function it is to evaluate the particular issue. This is professional authority. Decisions, characteristically in the form of advice, are made by those who have been appointed to a 'sphere of competence' on the basis of qualifications attested by a professional group of peers. *(Halsey, 1987, p. 169)*

In a parliamentary democracy, where the doctrine of public accountability holds sway, the question immediately presents itself how this discretion, this professional authority is constrained and controlled in the public interest. This question is addressed later, under 'professional ethics'. Meanwhile we need to examine in more detail the environment of SLPOs.

▬▬ Conflicting Environmental Forces ▬▬

Professional codes of ethics are directly analogous to the 'rules of the game' which headquarters of large corporations in the private sector establish to ensure good order in the activities of the various subunits. Field research on the private sector highlights the context in which rules of the game are established. The headquarters unit which establishes the rules of the game also allocates resources, designs the organizational structure, and measures the performance of the affected subordinate units. This is a fact which is useful for an understanding of the endemic tensions of public organization in the area of social welfare, namely, uneasy relations between central government on the one hand, and professionals in SLPOs as well as the professional bodies themselves on the other hand (see figure 2.1).

To see the source of the problem, it is necessary to construct a model of the specific influences from the environment that play on service delivery of public organizations. For present purposes, I will adapt the 'Open Systems Model of Organizations', originally developed by Bruce Scott, at the Harvard Business School, because this particular model highlights the workings of 'subunits' (part/whole relationships), and contains the notion – important for my purpose – that each subunit is best understood as responding to the various forces in its own particular environment. In the words of Scott:

> Briefly, our model asserts that (1) any organization relates to its environment via a strategy for advancing its interests as it perceives those interests; (2) the interests of the various subunits of an organization often differ from those of the organization as a whole, and (3) thus the central or general headquarters of the organization must bring continuous influence to bear on the subunits in order to motivate them to act in conformity, not with their own divergent interests, but with the general or shared interest of the organization as a whole. *(Scott, 1962)*

Scott then goes on to highlight the forms of influence available, and here are matters of critical importance for this study.

Figure 2.5 Tensions in the SLPO environment

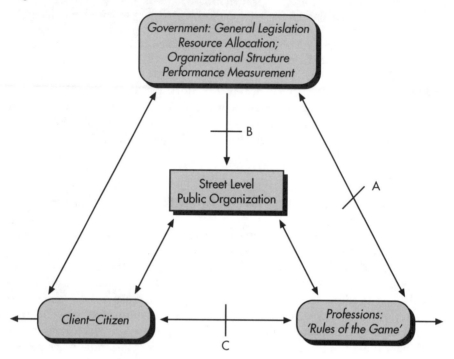

Source: Adapted from Wrigley and McKevitt 1995

Among the various modes of influence which the headquarters has at its disposal, four are of particular importance:

1 the ability to allocate resources;
2 to establish and alter organizational structures;
3 to measure and reward individuals and subunits;
4 and to formulate policy limits or 'rules of the game'. *(Scott, 1962)*

I accept this model for my present purpose, but need to expand it to accommodate a key feature of the sector, namely, general legislation. Thus general legislation needs to be added to the list of the modes of influence available to headquarters. Legislation in its role of strategic control is examined at length in chapter 5.

On that basis, let us note from the field research that service delivery in the area of social welfare is a managed process. Let us also note that the essence of the management task involved is relating an SLPO to its environment. The question then is what are the key points in the environment itself.

Here we are scanning the environment for the recurring 'tension points' that are common to the environment of all SLPOs. It is in this respect that data from field research, over a period of time in a number of countries, is vital. Figure 2.5, as a model, represents the research findings of the recurring tension points in the environment of SLPOs.

It will be noted that the immediate source of recurring tension is point A, the relations between central government and the professions. The model enables us to see an essential fact. SLPOs are under a dual set of influences. From central government, there are four modes of influence, namely: general legislation; allocation of resources; organizational structure; and performance measurement, each of which is powerful, and the four together extremely powerful. But without established, accepted and enforced rules of the game, as we know from research on private enterprise, the effect of these four powerful modes of influence can cause the activities of SLPOs to run wild and undirected. Because each of these four modes of influence play mainly on individual self-interest, it is the rules of the game, the ethical codes, which are needed to harness the forces of self-interest to social goals. Rules of the game carry an importance that can hardly be over emphasized, in that these rules are established by a quite different kind of institution, namely, the professions. If there is a solid relationship between government and the professions, the inevitable tensions at point A can be resolved without adverse impact on the SLPO. If the relationship however, is poor, then the tension at point A will debilitate the whole system of service delivery, as my research in the UK makes quite clear. In the social welfare area of the public sector, good relations between government and the professions are important for success in quality service delivery.

However, government influence on SLPOs may be fundamentally impaired by problems in general legislation as at point B above. As mentioned, there are major differences in the reasons why activities are in the public sector. These differences should be reflected in differences in the construction of the relevant general legislation. But this is not always done. In my study of health care policy in Ireland I used a comparative approach whereby, in certain crucial aspects, Ireland was compared with other modern countries, including Sweden and Holland. In regard to the legislative framework of public health care, I observed:

> A central stance of the [findings] is that control in health care yields similar challenges to politicians, civil servants and health care professionals under different financial systems for service delivery . . . Control, *per se*, is rectificatory and not restorative: that is, it is about the maintenance of norms, the following of patterns and rules once these have been laid down. In Ireland, control was not seen in this way, largely because the legislative framework did not contain any explicit strategy.
>
> Decisions on resource allocation were not related to specific objectives, nor were the performance of health care professionals subject to any sustained scrutiny. As a consequence, the information data-base did not extend beyond that of functional cost accounting and it was inadequate to test for measures on the return on the investment in health care provision . . .
>
> The Swedish and Dutch systems, in contrast, share common features in their concern for explicitness in legislation, their attendance to the sovereign importance of measurement and control systems, and their willingness to adapt and modify their control system to refocus their investment decisions.
> *(McKevitt, 1989, p. 158)*

From this view, it can be seen that any defect in the legislative framework which impairs the process of resource allocation will lead to recurring tension of a fundamental kind between central government and professional association in the environment of SLPOs. But the central government may not be the only fundamental source of recurring tensions.

In public service delivery and investment decisions legislation is pivotal to any strategy that requires a change in the pattern of resource allocation to underpin new policies. Most public service managers instinctively understand the inertial force of a pattern of incremental resource allocation; this year's increment (or decrement) of resources is justified on the basis of last year's pattern of allocation. To move new monies to a policy priority area usually requires a change in legislation. The legislation we evaluated (see chapter 5), apart from the United Kingdom model, confirms this proposition: the pattern of investment in social provision, reflecting as it does consensus and compromise amongst many stakeholders, is built up over considerable periods of time. If countries wish to change these patterns then legislation is required to shift the balance of investment allocation: Treasury officials are unmoved by policy objectives without the backing of legislation. In parliamentary democracies legislation gives legitimacy and status to policy objectives and captures the high ground in policy decisions in investment priorities.

Indeed, the absence of a coherent legislative strategy to underpin some of the major UK policy shifts in education and health care probably accounts for their relative lack of success. I do not, of course, propose the view that legislation, even if it is cast in a strategic dimension such as found in Swedish health care, is a guarantee of strategic control. Policy makers have numerous and conflicting demands on their attention and legislation can also be viewed as partly a symbolic act which represents good intentions rather than administrative clarity.

The research indicates that another fundamental source of the tension may well lie at point C in figure 2.5 above, namely, a break in the natural relationship between the community of citizens and the professional bodies. In English-speaking countries, at least, the professions can and sometimes do in their practices go too far ahead of social sentiment, thereby essentially becoming isolated bodies in the environment. Governments cannot do this because of the democratic system. Professional bodies can, particularly in the Anglo-Saxon countries where the prevailing culture may feature individualism.

Thus, in the English-speaking countries, the 'rules of the game', the code of professional ethics, may evolve in ways that go too far off the boundaries provided by social sentiment, and therefore be a fundamental source of great tension in the environment between citizen–clients and the professions.

The most conspicuous example in the early 1990s of such tension in the United Kingdom is provided by the system of primary education. Professionals and their management in this context are examined in chapter 7.

In the event, the fact that for SLPOs the rules of the game are provided from a different source than the other modes of influence does mean there will be tensions, and these tensions will not go away.

▬▬ Institutions of Social Obligation ▬▬

Allocation of scarce resources in the market system is done by price. In the public domain, it is done within the limits set by central government by the decisions and authority of professional specialists in SLPOs. But decisions are not capricious. These specialists decide within an institutional framework of social obligations. And the efficacy of social service delivery activities is very largely affected by the strength and appropriateness of this institutional framework.

Exhortation and expectations of good behaviour have their place in public affairs. Nevertheless, to be effective in bad times as well as good, such exhortations and expectations have to be embodied in the specific form of social institutions, of which three are particularly relevant in respect of street level social welfare services, namely:

- legal regulations;
- civil law; and
- Code of Professional Ethics.

The legal regulations, essentially, the legislative framework, specify the right and duties under law relating to the specific services. Civil law enables the law courts to be brought into public service in respect of damages suffered by clients from defective delivery, as characterized by malpractice suits. While institutionalized codes of ethics prompt good behaviour not by an appeal to an individual conscience, but by well enforced and well understood and rigorously grounded definitions of good and bad behaviour and practice.

▬▬ Code of Professional Ethics ▬▬

Ethics is a broad term, designed more to catch the flow of life than to define it. Perhaps in essence, ethics mean there are certain things you must not do to other people. Ethics, therefore, refer to shared standards of behaviour in the particular circumstances of a particular environment.

Ethical codes appropriate to professional activities are, arguably, organically related to differential information in favour of the producers in respect of services which carry a high risk for the client. The prime purpose of the code is to protect the client in an arena where trust is crucial. The organic nature of this particular relationship has consequences of importance for the possibilities of progress.

In areas where there is a large difference in information in favour of the producer, strong ethical codes make for opportunities for progress, immediately in terms of greater economic efficiency, more fundamentally in strengthening the sense of community, through greater trust and transaction enhancing relationships.

But ethical codes developed to have an even wider role. All professions pre-suppose a large measure of differential information in favour of the producers. In the first place, ethical codes evolved to protect the client. This remains their prime purpose. But such codes, when strongly institutionalized in the form of widespread understanding and proper enforcement, provide, as it were, a 'level playing field' in which each professional can compete with his or her fellows without cheating either the client or colleagues. Moreover, the existence of such codes provide information and guidance to new entrants to the profession as to good and bad practice. Client protection, a level playing field for com-petition, and information and guidance to new entrants are major benefits of strong professional codes. But there is more than that, there is the problem of rationing.

Rationing is inevitable in public service delivery where there is, virtually, unlimited demand. Legal regulations may stipulate priorities at a general level for receiving service. But it is the strength of the ethical code which determines whether effect at street level is given in practice to the legal regulations, and whether the regulation is complied with in spirit as well as letter. The question arises of how the codes actually operate. How do professional specialists cope on the ground?

Michael Lipsky described the workings of SLPOs in really hard conditions, that is, where demand is great relative to supply in the general area of social welfare. We repeat below a passage from Lipsky because it reflects so accurately the position seen in the Cork regional hospital in month after month of field research.

> Street level bureaucrats (professionals) often spend their lives in a corrupted world of service. They believe themselves to be doing the best they can under adverse circumstances, and they develop techniques to salvage service and decision-making values within the limits imposed on them by the structure of the work. They develop conceptions of their work and of their clients that narrow the gap between their personal and work limitations and the service ideal. *(Lipsky, 1980, p. 383)*

It is here, in the development of these conceptions, that we see in street level operations in hard conditions the true significance of the codes of professional ethics. If the codes are good and properly enforced, then the conceptions of work and priorities for services make for progress, otherwise not.

A UK government 'position paper', published in November 1996, attempted to define the 'nature and derivation of competence at higher NVQ (National Vocational Qualification) levels' (Department for Education and Employ-ment, 1996). In other words, the writer(s) used expressions such as 'problem solving', 'dealing with the unexpected', 'ethics' and 'judgements' and tried to identify what professionals do that characterizes 'the professions' and sets them apart from others. The document noted, among the features of the higher occu-pational levels, those advanced problem-solving skills that distinguish profes-sionals and their exercising of considerable personal autonomy:

The customer or client, whilst possibly having a clear view of the outcome they hope a professional will provide, often has little comprehension of the precise nature of the service they are seeking or the standards to which it should be provided.

'A professional does not meet his patients or client on equal terms. He is consulted for his special knowledge and experience by people who are in no position to make an informed or valid judgement about his skill or ability or integrity.' *(Medical Ethics, Ormrod, 1967; quoted in Department for Education and Employment, 1996)*

It is thus the case that the customer is more likely to bring the professional a problem, often ill-defined, than a specific service requirement.

The document goes on to express caution where clients' expectations are concerned:

'Little, however, is provided to make clear to the public or employers what they can expect from members of the profession other than that they will be professionally qualified.' *(Assessing Competence in the Professions, Eraut and Cole, 1993; quoted in Department for Education and Employment, 1996)*

David Bartram, writing in *The Psychologist*, on the subject of 'dealing with the unexpected', notes that any description of professional 'competence' needs to include:

'an explicit representation of the notion that professionalism resides as much in what we know not to do as in what we know to do. The ability to be aware of one's competence and its limitations, to know where and how to call on other resources, and to operate *within an ethical framework*, have all been stressed as key issues.' *(Bartram, 1995; emphasis added; quoted in Department for Education and Employment, 1996)*

A case is clearly being made here for professionals to play the greatest part in specifying their own occupational standards. The question is – what part should be played by users of their service and other regulatory bodies? All jobs have an ethical dimension, and in HEWS this dimension is generally regarded to have particular importance. It is reasonable to expect qualifications to embrace knowledge of ethical codes and awareness of the sensitivities of ethical dilemmas. The position paper concludes:

A distinction might be drawn . . . between *ethical behaviour* and making *ethical decisions*, which may have a significant impact on others (sometimes extending well beyond the customer/client relationship). What is perhaps distinctive at higher levels is the degree of skill required by professionals in making *judgements* with a major ethical dimension in them. *(Department for Education and Employment, 1996)*

We look at the relationship between professional codes of ethics and management change in chapter 7.

▰▰ **Conclusion** ▰▰

This chapter has set out the conceptual framework for this study. It was developed from empirical fieldwork across a number of countries and integrated with general strategy models from the management literature. Thus, whilst the models will help to make sense of the data reported from a number of countries, those data are independent of any particular theoretical framework. As I am concerned to show best practice, as much as possible I allow the voice of managers and professionals to stand alone as evidence. The models help to place the evidence in an appropriate framework for managers to learn from the experience of other countries. The models presented will be applied selectively in the remainder of the text. The idea of the SLPO is central to this study; this is where services are delivered, where managers and professionals co-operate and where limited resources impose rationing decisions. It is a world you will recognize even if it is not yet managed in a way you would agree with; in the next chapter I focus on the design of responsive service delivery systems in a number of countries and apply the knowledge that has been gained of the environment of SLPOs.

CHAPTER
3

Service Delivery – Meeting
Citizen Needs

▬▬ Introduction ▬▬

This chapter describes and examines the relationship between the SLPO and
the citizen–client. A major issue in the SLPO/citizen–client relationship is the
problem of substituting priority or rationing by professionals according to
need in the public sector, for the price mechanism in the private sector according to income. I examine here the growing relevance of the marketing function in the public sector, the use and deployment of marketing techniques,
including customer satisfaction surveys, through an examination of service
delivery in a number of countries, that is, England, New Zealand and Ireland.
This examination includes the activities of central government departments,
executive agencies in the United Kingdom and local government. The role of
marketing is increasing within the public sector: as contracting-out of services
increases, including the contracting-out of 'white collar' activities such as legal
and career guidance services, the challenge faced by public service managers is
to retain citizen–clients in opposition to rival service providers. Whilst marketing in the public service does not have the same importance as in the private
sector, techniques of client satisfaction surveys, promotion of service availability and evaluation of service quality are all now part of the required general
competence of public service managers.

We saw in chapter 2 how differential information between provider and
citizen–client requires a relationship of trust between professionals and the
citizen. This chapter describes how public service managers can install and
monitor responsive delivery systems for non-marketable goods and services,
for example health care for the young and elderly. Through an examination
of different organizational contexts lessons can be drawn, from a number of
countries, as to the appropriateness of the marketing function in the improvement of service delivery to the citizen–client.

The manager faces particular challenges in developing responsive service delivery systems, as across much of the core public services the citizen–client has no

possibility of 'exit' from the relationship with the public service provider: this lack of 'exit' is what distinguishes the citizen–client in the public sector from the consumer–client in the private sector. Using Hirschman's (1970) well-known framework, it can be seen that the manager needs to set up mechanisms for hearing and responding to citizen 'voice': 'loyalty' is not an available strategy for the citizen across most of the core public services: for example, the citizen has to attend state schools, comply with public health regulations, register for tax returns. The opportunity to 'exit' public service provision is not an option available to the majority of the citizenry in most countries. These restrictions place particular responsibility on managers and service providers to install responsive and flexible delivery systems, and mechanisms for citizen-redress, for example ombudsman and appellate structures, and build performance measurement systems which give attention to 'citizen-voice'.

This chapter examines three central aspects of service delivery:

1   the relevance of using consumer models of service delivery in core public services;
2   the design of service systems for the provision of core public services;
3   the rationing of public services and the importance of appellate structures.

Citizen, Client, Consumer: the Language of Service Delivery

Chapter 2 examined the relationship between differential information, professionals and the SLPO and how such relationships constituted the environmental context for service delivery. It identified the influence of professional codes of practice on the SLPO, and how ethical frameworks can help shape the context and content of SLPOs' operating procedures. The influence of such ethical frameworks is particularly felt in the rationing of public service delivery, an issue discussed later in this chapter.

Rationing brings into focus the distinctiveness of managing core public services and, indeed, of the value of the marketing function in such an environment. The purposes of marketing include the objective of raising consumer demand (in some instances, indeed, of creating a demand) and such an objective uneasily fits the rationing context of many SLPOs. Service marketing has, in its strategic objectives, obvious resonance for the management of public services – that is, the creation and maintenance of a valued relationship with the citizen–client. For example, customer complaints in the private sector are an important source of management data for the improvement of service quality: the traditional public sector attitude has been to ignore complaints from service recipients, that is, citizens. Public organizations faced with complaints regarding service delivery tend to defend their reputation or that of their professionals delivering the service rather than learn from the patterns of such complaints. Disregard of citizen 'voice', the inflexible stance of service providers – 'we know what is best practice' – has led to growing demands for organizational and structural change in service delivery systems, ranging from privatization through compulsory competitive tendering (CCT) to the creation of NHS Trusts: the organizational effect of these changes is examined in chapter 6.

The focus here, however, is on the implications for managers connoted by the terms citizen, client and consumer. A central feature of New Right thinking, which found expression in the political campaigns of Ronald Reagan in America and Margaret Thatcher in the United Kingdom in the 1980s, is the language of consumerism – 'the customer is king' – and the minimalist state is the *leitmotiv* which drives radical change in delivery (and cost) of public services.

The arguments for consumer sovereignty – 'the customer is always right' – were translated into exhortations to the public sector that it must respond to consumers of services in the same way as the private sector was portrayed as doing, that is, responsive, flexible and customer-driven.

Leaving aside this idealization of private sector responsiveness, the New Right agenda was a powerful engine for public sector reform: the writings of Peters and Waterman, *In Search of Excellence* (1982) became required reading for any self-respecting local authority manager. Similarly, in the 1990s, Osborne and Gabler's *Reinventing Government* captured the attention of President Clinton and Vice-President Gore and its prescriptions of 'steering not rowing', in respect of government provision of strategic leadership for service delivery, was the stuff of many a newspaper editorial enjoining public sector managers to be more like their private sector counterpart. Managers were encouraged to adopt the concepts and practices of re-engineering, Total Quality Management (TQM), empowerment of staff and, more generally, to 'enable' service provision rather than be a provider of services *per se*.

The purchaser–provider split in health care, the imposition of CCT in local government, and Local Management of Schools (LMS) were the organizational and structural expressions of the intent to bring public services 'closer to the customer'. Countries as diverse in their history and culture such as Sweden, the UK and New Zealand were seized by the *zeitgeist* of consumer sovereignty – I examine the strategic and operational effect of such change in chapters 5 and 6. The language of consumerism, moves towards greater decentralization of services and the attendant panoply of business planning, customer segmentation and customer surveys can, if pushed, obscure the importance of citizenship and its relationship to the modern social democratic state. In a speech in 1993, William Waldegrave, when Secretary of State for Health, said:

> Our 'customers' do not come to us because the price of beans is less . . . they come because they are ill, not seldom frightened, and they want help and expect care . . . without remitting for one moment the pressure to get a better management system, borrowing what is useful from business, let us watch our

language a bit. It just bears saying straight out: the NHS is not a business; it is a public service and a great one.

The emphasis on restraint of government expenditure, exemplified by the hypnotic fascination in the political mind with the size of the Public Sector Borrowing Requirement (PSBR), establishment of monetary targets, European Monetary Union convergence targets, can paradoxically lead to an overvaluing of the State's role in everyday life. The New Right sought to redefine and reduce the State's role (see Chapter 4 on the investment aspect of this debate), through the application of management principles which were aptly expressed in the purchaser–provider contract. The use of a purchaser–provider contract as a means of strategic control is examined in chapter 5.

Potter (1988) suggests five principles that could guide our thinking about the nature of responsiveness in public services:

1 *Access.* Deciding who shall have access to a particular public service is a political responsibility, and citizens have a right to know what criteria their political representatives have agreed should be applied and why. Citizens' political representatives are advised by managers. Once the criteria are clear, however, concern moves on to the issue of accessibility and how it can be improved.

2 *Choice.* The quasi-markets being introduced in education and health are apparently aimed at extending parents' choice of schools and patients' choice of GPs and hospitals. There are also services in which this type of choice is almost certain to be absent (for example, the compulsory services that deal with child abuse). Potter suggests that a number of partial substitutes may be possible, including: complaints systems that are easily available and/or independent external inspections of the service in question, the publication of 'performance indicators' to show the public how well service units are providing the services that users want; the formal recognition of mentors or advocates who are given rights to speak for users and who exercise some degree of choice on their behalf.

3 *Information.* Potter indicates that users of services need information about:

- the existence of the service;
- the objectives of the service;
- the standards or quality attained by those offering the service;
- their rights to use the service and to complain if it is not satisfactory;
- the way the service and its decision making are organized;
- the particular decisions that are being taken or have been taken;
- the reasons for those decisions.

4 *Redress.* A survey in the late 1980s showed that many local authorities in the UK had departments with no proper complaints procedures,

failed to give their procedures much publicity, or failed to analyse the pattern of complaints in order to inform service managers.

5 *Representation*. Potter suggests that 'the views of consumers should be adequately represented to decision makers at all points in the system where decisions are taken concerning their interests'. (1988, p. 154)

Given evidence of rigidities within a service and indifference to consumers or citizens, the perennial, crucial question for many experienced managers would seem to be 'So what can be done about it?' Before answering that question it is necessary to explore the language of citizenship and consumerism. It will come as no surprise that the language is the subject of considerable debate and that it has much hidden meaning. This has serious implications for managers in the public services and their values.

The dispute over terminology is not only there to liven up dull moments in boring meetings. Behind the different terms lie models or stereotypes of the people being served. Some of the language so easily confirms the traditional 'You take what you're given' attitude that is typical of producers and can still be found in parts of the public services. The word 'consumer', on the other hand, tends to conjure up a picture of someone shopping, moving from display to display, choosing the goods, then paying for them at the check-out. The word 'client' is redolent of a professional relationship in which the provider of a service is ethically committed to serving someone's best interests. Another popular term in public services, 'student', suggests a context of learning in which the subject, although in a sense a consumer, does not necessarily know best.

Several writers, including Hambleton and Hoggett (1990), have argued that models of private sector consumerism are not easily applied to the public services. There are several reasons for this argument. Here are a few:

■ Some public services are, *de jure* or *de facto*, compulsory. Their consumers cannot choose to go elsewhere. This is the case for claimants of income support from the Social Security Benefits Agency. A public service may be supplied against consumers' expressed wishes: for example, prison services.
■ Even large numbers of public service users may have little effective choice, in so far as they face a monopoly supplier or provider. The village that has only one general practice and a local school typifies this situation.
■ Citizens who want to use public services may be prevented from doing so. Access to council housing or NHS services are examples. Many public service managers are concerned with rationing or prioritizing their services. In the NHS or local authority housing department, expenditure or staffing limits or capital projects may preclude any increased provision.
■ There are diverse community needs – for instance, access for disadvantaged groups such as blind people or non-native speakers of English.

- In health care, the personal social services, education and the proba-tion service, providers commonly communicate with consumers dis-cursively, face to face, and over long periods. These are developmental relations in which the maintenance of trust is essential to the effect-iveness of the service being provided. Arguments that such consumers may secure the best buy on the basis of good information are ser-iously inadequate.
- In leisure and the arts, there are social and cultural markets in which the exchange of value is measured in more than economic terms. Many local libraries and opportunities for sports and the arts would not exist without public subsidy. The rationale for their provision is that local quality of life should be expressed in the physical and mental well-being of local citizens. Consider, for example, the in-volvement of local authorities in the development of local theatres to express civic pride and, more important, to foster local identity. It is notions of local culture and local identity that tend to transcend the individualistic ethic of consumerism.
- There is a different balance between 'voice' and 'exit' in the private sector (Hirschman, 1970) in favour of 'voice'. People who want to signal their dissatisfaction with a product or service have two main options: 'exit' and 'voice'. Voice is about expressing judgements and preferences, and participating in decision-making processes in an effective way. Exit allows people to vote with their feet.

Citizenship is often portrayed as an individual property, although with strong overtones of collective responsibility. The tension between the individualistic and the collective ideas of citizenship is real, and there is disagreement over the boundaries of citizenship.

The consumerist model, in contrast, is essentially individualistic, and has the market, not the state, as the principal focus for its transactions and values. Public services, such as the erstwhile British Rail, that have moved towards a sharper market focus, have sought to escape the traditional requirements of full public service consultation where they can and rely instead on market research to make the wants of their customers compatible with the provision of a profitable service.

The rights that have featured in the long historical struggle to expand the notion of citizenship include justice, representation and participation – not normally part of the vocabulary of the supermarket. While participation has not featured in all models of democratic theory it is to be found at the heart of twentieth-century concepts of citizenship. You will probably find that an important test of a service's meaning of the word 'citizenship' lies in the extent to which its concept of citizenship is compatible with community participation.

One model that may help you to review the consumer–citizen debate is pro-vided by Gyford (1991) who identifies three basic fields of activity – economic, political and the use of services – and two dimensions for each activity. The combination of fields and dimensions produces six different ideal types of role.

Within Gyford's model, voters are passive providers of political legitimacy, but do not have the opportunity to take part in the political process. In contrast, citizens develop a more active role, having a chance to express particular opinions and control the decision-making process. The client is passive and very dependent on service professionals. The consumer wishes to determine the nature of a service and the way of providing it. These ideal roles may be performed in a variety of ways. Gyford describes three different types of relationship between a local authority and its public – participative (taking part), consultative (the right to be heard) and informative (access).

Some would argue that the active citizen ideal is essentially individualistic itself and tends to minimize differences in competence. An active citizen tends to be a middle-class citizen who will certainly have needs but will rarely be the most needy. Active citizenship – as a meaningful concept that can be applied across society – raises important and awkward issues for managers. This is particularly true when the concept involves advocacy and the empowerment of users in the community by making professional and other resources available outside the local authority.

Gyford's ideas of taking part and of the right to be heard also bring into play the idea of empowerment. The citizen cannot be assumed to be a passive recipient of services from the state and local authority, but what power does she or he have and who is the primary actor? Pfeffer and Coote (1991) contrast responsiveness and empowerment. Empowerment is about a consumerist approach to quality focused on the desire of the customer to be satisfied.

A significant element of the current debate about empowerment and citizenship is whether a citizen should be empowered at the expense of central and/or local government, or whether this is an area for partnership between the citizen and the state. Legislation – such as the Education Reform Act 1988 in England and Wales – has made a direct correlation between a smaller role for the local authority and more citizen empowerment.

Politicians and managers in public service have used the term 'empowerment' with increasing latitude, undoubtedly seeking to make the word theirs alone. Within the notion of creating markets in the public services, for example, the Right has argued that a vital feature of the market is the empowered consumer. Pirie (1991) suggests that by giving people certain consumer rights, including the right to receive compensation, they will attain real and measurable powers over state servants and so make them provide the level and quality of services that they think they ought to receive.

The consumerist approach to public management values uniformity of technique over diversity of response. This is because increased efficiency in service provision is seen as a single 'best way', to meet citizen needs. Foucault describes and captures this debate:

> The excessive value attributed to the problem of the state is expressed, basic-ally, in two ways: the one form, immediate, affective and tragic, is the lyricism of the *monstre froid* we see confronting us; but there is a second way of over-valuing the problem of the state, one which is paradoxical because apparently

43

reductionist: it is the form of analysis that consists in reducing the state to a certain number of functions, such as the development of productive forces and the reproduction of relations of production, and yet this reductionist vision of the relative importance of the state's role nevertheless renders it absolutely essential as a target needing to be attacked and a privileged position needing to be occupied. But the state, no more probably today than at any other time in its history, does not have this unity, this individuality, this rigorous functionality, nor, to speak frankly, this importance . . . Maybe what is really important for our modernity – that is, for our present – is not so much the *étatisation* of society, as the 'governmentalization' of the state. *(1994, p. 23)*

This book describes the growing governmentalization of the state across a number of countries and analyses the role of the public sector manager in this process. It is, however, more concerned with the practical problems of the citizen–client than the abstruse problems posed by the delineation of the min-imalist state or, indeed, the functions of the 'New Welfare State'. Delivery of core public services to the citizen–client transcends the concepts and categor-ies of the consumer model – the needy, the old and the sick require stronger medicine than that provided by the ideologues of the right and left.

Universality of provision of social services such as welfare entitlements (for example, child allowances), education and health means that entitlements are distributed to all citizens, thus giving rise to the world-wide phenomenon of middle-class capture of the benefits of the welfare state. Articulate middle-class recipients of such services exert pressure on professional providers and gener-ally gain proportionately higher shares of the universal benefits on offer. For example, *Social Trends* (1997) in the UK showed that the top fifth of house-holds by income receive almost £4000 in care from the NHS, education for their children and payments ranging from pensions to child benefit. Govern-ments, in seeking to restrain expenditure, propose 'cut-backs' in the growth in welfare entitlements that proportionately hit the working class or unemployed harder than the middle class. Voucher schemes have been suggested for ser-vices such as pre-school education, and university education as a means of giving 'equal chance' to all recipients. Whilst ignoring the geographic diversity of existing supply of such services (largely a pattern of unequal shares based on existing middle-class dominance), no government has seriously sought to im-plement such schemes.

In one sense, therefore, techniques of performance evaluation and quality assurance of services may help to redress the imbalance in service provision by drawing attention to its unequal distribution. All too often, however, such im-balances are utilized to stigmatize the service provider, for example the debate on 'failing schools' and incompetent teachers in the UK. Quasi-independent measures of outcome become instruments of critique rather than sources of renewal.

Chapter 7 examines the performance measurement of professional providers and explores the concept of custodial relationships between providers and clients. It also examines how inappropriate institutional controls can disrupt the relationship between professionals and the state.

Table 3.1 Relationships with customers

Nature of service delivery	'Membership' relationship	No formal relationship
Continuous delivery of service	Insurance Telephone subscription College enrollment Banking American Automobile Association	Radio station Police protection Lighthouse Public highway
Discrete transactions	Long-distance phone calls Theatre series subscription Commuter ticket or transit pass	Car rental Mail services Toll highway Pay phone Movie theatre Public transportation Restaurant

Source: Bateson, 1995

▬▬ **Marketing of Public Services** ▬▬

Bateson (1995) provides a helpful categorization of the relationship between service organizations and customers (table 3.1): he identifies that no formal relationship exists between supplier and customers of 'public goods' – broadcasting, police and lighthouse services – where no charge is made for consumption of services that are continuously available. There is, of course, a formal relationship in a civic sense between professional providers of public services and the citizen–client. In marketing terms, however, the lack of a formal relationship and the absence of price in public service transactions does make it different from service transactions in the private sector. The key aspects of services which are relevant here are:

- intangibility;
- heterogeneity;
- simultaneous production and consumption;
- lack of ownership;
- perishability.

These characteristics pose challenges for the management of productivity (which is internal to the organization) and for the management of quality (which is external to the organization). The question of service quality is addressed later in this chapter and the management of professionals is examined in chapters 6 and 7.

Table 3.2 Classification of service systems by extent of required customer contact in creation of the service

High contact	Pure service:	Increasing freedom in
	Health centres	designing efficient
	Hotels	production procedures
	Public transportation	
	Restaurants	
	Schools	
	Personal services	
	Mixed service:	
	Branch offices of:	
	Banks	
	Computer companies	
	Real estate	
	Post offices	
	Funeral homes	
	Quasi-manufacturing:	
	Home offices of:	
	Banks	
	Computer companies	
	Government administration	
	Wholesale houses	
	Post offices	
	Manufacturing:	
	Factories producing durable goods	
	Food processors	
	Mining companies	
Low contact	Chemical plants	

Source: Bateson, 1995

Services can also be classified by evaluating the extent of customer contact required in the creation of the service: Bateson provides such a classification (table 3.2). It will be noted that many of the services with which this study is concerned – health, welfare – require high contact with service providers. Understanding the dynamics of these contacts including the requirement of systematic evaluation of professional performance is a key to appreciating the marketing contribution in public service management.

It requires some imagination on the part of public sector managers to simulate a relationship with citizen–clients so as to allow the techniques and frameworks of private sector service marketing to be applied to core public services. How can this be achieved?

One way is to be realistic in assessing how much relevant technique can be transferred from private sector practice. Chapter 2 identified the genericist school of management literature which, at the extreme, claims that there is no substantive difference between public and private management. Clearly, however, the absence of a price mechanism in service transactions in the public sector, added to the lack of 'exit' from the public sector market means that 'responsiveness' to the citizen–client is of a different character in the core public services.

Additionally, the presence of differential information together with professional gatekeeping of services means that public service managers have to develop and deliver a service relationship that is not dependent on a price relationship with the client.

An example of direct marketing of schools can be seen in New Zealand, where education reforms (discussed in detail in chapter 5) have made the individual school the cost centre for government expenditures. Schools actively compete for students and use marketing techniques to assist them in this effort.

A Charter Framework for Hutt Valley High School, running to some twenty-five pages is distributed to all parents and prospective parents: it covers areas such as mission statement, specific goals and objectives of the school, personnel, finance, property through to school procedures, board meetings and codes of conduct. A brief extract from the Charter follows:

The Educational Purpose and General Goals of the School

Mission Statement
We aim to allocate our resources so all students will learn and can confidently grow towards their full potential.

General Goals
1. This school should be the school of preference for those secondary age students living in the local community.
2. The nature of society today is such that this school has an added responsibility in nurturing and socialising young people. We are still committed to the belief that it is the primary responsibility of the home and the community to ensure that students are adequately cared for in their basic physical and emotional needs. It is the school's aim that each student who leaves will have:

- Basic academic ability and skills
- A striving for high standards of performance
- Confidence and high self-esteem
- Self discipline and respect for authority
- Flexibility of thinking
- Cultural awareness and sensitivity
- The skills to co-operate and also to be independent
- A desire for life-long learning
- A healthy lifestyle

Specific Goals and Objectives of the School:
1. New Zealand Curriculum Goal and Objectives
Goal: To enhance children's learning.

Objectives:

(a) At all times accept the obligation to meet New Zealand curriculum objectives prescribed by the Minister of Education and the requirements of all syllabuses prescribed under the Education Act or relevant regulations.

(b) Every year decide what optional subjects are to be offered in the school. (Note: This objective applies only to secondary schools).

(c) At all times accept the obligation to prepare every learner to make the transition to full membership of New Zealand society.

(d) Specify local curriculum goals and objectives that take into account the needs and interests of the students, the special skills and qualifications of the staff and the aspirations and resources of the local community.

(e) Every year approve a policy statement that details how the school will deliver the curriculum. This policy will include time allocation, resources, staff preparation, and options and progressions available to students.

(f) Every year ensure that the curriculum is implemented through the learning and teaching programmes developed by the staff. These programmes will be attached and read as part of the charter but are not part of the approval process. They will include specific learning objectives and outcomes realistically stated in terms of a range of achievements.

(g) Each year review ways in which the school consults with individual students and their families on matters of personal and academic progress. Schools should continue to formulate their programmes within existing New Zealand syllabuses, prescriptions, guidelines and course statements. *(Hutt Valley High, 1993)*

The School Charter is used as a marketing device to attract students, or more precisely to encourage parents to send their children to the school. Hutt Valley High, set in a prosperous middle-class area does not need, as the principal agreed, to fight for students. Similarly, in the UK the league tables of school performance in state examinations faithfully reflect the social and economic intake of their pupils. In some measure, therefore, marketing in the sense of creating and responding to demand is largely a function of successful SLPOs; the techniques do not address the more fundamental issue of meeting the needs of all citizens.

Later chapters examine the application of structural devices that purport to increase SLPO effectiveness, for example decentralization. Schools are obliged by law in New Zealand to have charters so Hutt Valley High has one; it could be argued that the Charter increases openness to parents and students and is to be welcomed; that the Charter gives 'voice' to the parents and is consonant with increasing participation through membership of the School Board (see chapter 6). As shall be seen in later chapters, the reform of New Zealand schools succeeded in so far as there were partnerships between trade unions and parents, the profession and the client. In this regard the SLPO was not in conflict with its external environment; this was a situation not found in the UK reforms.

Service transactions can be managed as a process which shapes the provider–citizen relationship to countervail the distinctive character of differential information and the informal, albeit powerful, gatekeeping role of the professional

Table 3.3 Categories of quality developments in European public services organizations

Reception	Improving the conditions of direct client/provider contact
Information	Improving the availability and nature of information for clients about public services
Simplification	Reducing complexities related to rules, procedures and official forms
Co-ordination	Cutting across administrative divisions or departments to promote more co-ordinated delivery of services to clients
Marketing approach	Conducting surveys of consumers to find out their opinions, needs and preferences
Complaints procedures	Setting up agreed and publicized mechanisms to provide for customer redress
Culture change	Ensuring that there is a commitment throughout the organization to consumer–service quality values
Setting standards	Developing quantifiable performance measures and targets
Decentralization	Breaking down large, centralized services into smaller, more accessible units, to be closer and more responsive to clients
Personnel practices	Introducing training and incentive schemes specifically to promote consumer responsive services
Two-way staff communication	Setting up mechanisms to encourage staff to communicate more effectively 'up the line' to management
Accountability and autonomy	Giving staff in closest contact with the consumer greater influence in decision making
Competition	Enabling consumers to exercise some choice in the services they receive
Consumer participation and representation	Involving customers directly in decisions that affect them

Source: NESF, 1995, p. 20

provider. A recent National Economic and Social Forum (NESF, 1995) report in Ireland examined the issue of quality delivery of social services through a comparative survey of best practice in OECD countries. Table 3.3 sets out the report's findings on the categories of quality developments in European Public Services Organizations. Clearly the categories set out are just that, categories: to operationalize them requires incremental, piecemeal, adjustments. It is important, as noted in chapter 2, that the time taken to adjust the performance of SLPOs is recognized and that core skills are not destroyed through precipitate change. I report later in chapter 5 on changes in New Zealand's education system whereby widescale and untimely change removed the 'institutional memory' of the Ministry of Education. Conversely it also has to be recognized that the building up of new skills, such as appropriate professional performance measures, also takes time; the application of micro-management techniques in a professional context will not attract loyalty or compliance.

The issue of productivity in service delivery is internal to the organization and is reliant on a balance between operational control and freedom for

Table 3.4 Proposed charter of rights under the supplementary welfare allowance scheme

Access	The right to have applications dealt with in decent comfortable surroundings; access for disabled people, women with children etc.; prompt service; clear advertising of times and locations of service
Courtesy	The right to be treated with courtesy and respect; the right to be listened to
Honesty	The right to be presumed to be honest, unless there is reason to believe to the contrary
Information	The right to full information on the Scheme – the procedures, policies and standards; the right to have this information readily available in plain and simple language
Non-discrimination	The right to full access to services and fair treatment irrespective of political, religious, cultural or sexual beliefs or behaviour
Privacy	The right to have all personal dealings with the service conducted in a manner and place that is conductive to total privacy
Confidentiality	The right to ensure that all information supplied by the client is not transmitted to a third party without the client's explicit consent; the client's right to have access to all information contained on his/her file
Refusals	The client's right to full and written reasons for the refusal of any application
Appeals	The right to have appeals heard in a speedy manner consistent with the principles of natural justice
Complaints	The right to an explicit and transparent system for making complaints and the right to a speedy response to such complaints
Representation	The right to make comments and suggestions in relation to the quality of the service received; the right to client representation on bodies which are considering proposals in relation to the nature of the service or the delivery of the service

Source: NESF, 1995, p. 78

professionals to make their own professional judgements. The organizational component is examined in chapter 6 when evaluating the type of controls appropriate to a professional bureaucracy.

The NESF report, in a move reminiscent of recent changes in the United Kingdom and New Zealand, proposes a charter of rights for social welfare recipients (see table 3.4). There is a simplicity to the list of issues identified: who would dispute its relevance? However, managers have to be acutely aware of the difference between customers and citizens, in framing their service delivery strategies and in designing evaluation mechanisms to ensure service quality. Similarly core public services such as health, education and welfare demand different strategies as shall be seen in chapter 7 when examining the different approaches towards evaluation of educational standards in the United Kingdom and New Zealand.

Marketing of public services requires attention to issues such as citizen access, information, appeals and complaints. It also requires attention to the management of professionals and the design of appropriate organizational structures and controls for delivery of services. Moreover, the appraisal of service quality needs to include the active participation of providers, including trade unions, which is examined below. The consumer model, whilst inappropriate for core public services, does address a core aspect of service delivery – citizen 'voice' which is examined later in the chapter.

Public service trade unions, notably in Sweden and New Zealand have sought to adapt their traditional defensive attitudes to calls for greater efficiency (often a polite way of seeking job cuts) to a pro-active stance that works with the grain of government thinking whilst still seeking to prevent job losses. A good example of such attitudinal change is provided by Kommunal (Swedish Municipal Workers Union) in their strategy document of 1993 *Facing the Future – Now*. An extract from that strategy statement is shown below. The Kommunal strategy recognizes that the old way of managing an SLPO, the hierarchical model (management decide, workers comply) is no longer relevant or appropriate. The focus on customer needs, shared benefits, performance measurement may seem strange to a UK or Irish readership.

Clear measurement of results

(1) Vigorous decentralization of responsibility and authority as far down in the organization as possible.

(2) Utilizing and developing the employees' competence. Building up a learning organization from within and from below.

(3) A holistic view. Each part of the operation must be pulling in the same direction, every employee must participate.

(4) Concentration on results. The concentration on results is interesting. Here a new picture of Kommunal emerges. Gone is the trade union which only concentrates on distribution of wages. Now we are also involved in creating efficient and competitive production of care and service. And the benefits are to be shared by the members in the form of higher wages. 'We need to develop clear measurements of results in all municipal operations. This is solely to enable us to determine competitiveness in comparison with the alternatives. When we know which resources are needed for achieving a certain result, we will have an important basis for discussion as to how we can become more efficient. Correctly designed measurements of results also bring to the fore the importance of the work which the members of Kommunal do. It is important that the measurements of results are linked to the users' and customers' needs. The measurements should not only measure sums of money but also take quality aspects into account. It is only the occupational groups who are working with each respective operation who can draw up meaningful measurements of results'.

Kommunal – a movement for freedom

Freedom and freedom of choice have up to now not been concepts which have dominated the labour movement's organization, notes the group. 'It is important for us in Kommunal to realize this and give freedom and freedom of choice a constructive content which is based on justice and solidarity. Unless we succeed in this the members will turn their backs on the union'. Kommunal must also adopt a positive attitude towards diversity in services offered and in management of operations in the public sector. The group notes that unfortunately there have been cases where the union has opposed new forms of operation, in spite of the fact that the members have seen the change as positive. *(Kommunal, 1993)*

In part, such trade union flexibility represents a new way of organizing to the new environmental pressures on the SLPO; equally important, it represents a custodial vision of the core public services (also exemplified, as we shall see, in New Zealand) whereby social benefits are shared consistent with a dignity accorded to the professional base of the service providers. Let us now examine more closely the design of service quality systems in core public services.

▬▬ Design and Delivery of Service Quality ▬▬

Delivering consistently good service quality is difficult; most of the factors underlying quality revolve around communication and control processes and the consequences of these processes such as the role of professionals and potential role conflict between citizen–clients and providers. The focus here is on the delivery of service quality; the benchmark being the experience in New Zealand, and the United Kingdom. Zeithaml, Berry and Parasuraman (1988) provide a model which identifies the 'gaps' in service quality delivery. It can be seen that provision of service quality is highly dependent on employee perform-ance including an understanding of what the clients' needs are: performance of professionals is a resource which cannot be as easily controlled as quality can be in manufacturing goods.

A service delivery strategy, therefore, depends on an organization-wide implementation: it is not something which can be left to the providers them-selves: for example, raising educational attainment targets cannot solely rely on teacher performance, it is closely associated with the resource base of schools, teacher training and the socio-economic variable of student intake. It is also, as we have seen, dependent on the co-operation of service providers.

The gaps on the service provider scale are as follows:

Gap 1   Difference between citizen–client expectations and management/ provider expectations;

Gap 2   Difference between management/provider perceptions of citizen–client expectations and service quality expectations;

Gap 3   Difference between service quality expectations and the service actually delivered;

Gap 4   Difference between service delivery and what is communicated about the service to the citizen–client;

Gap 5   Difference between perceived service and expected service.

The same researchers later identified five determinants of service quality which are ranked in order of importance to customers:

1 Reliability – service dependability;
2 Responsiveness – willingness to help customers;
3 Assurance – courtesy, trust and confidence;
4 Empathy – caring, individualized attention;
5 Tangibles – appearance of the physical environment of the service provider.

As we have seen in chapter 2 the existence of differential information between provider and client makes the management of core public services a consensual process; it is reliant on co-operation between provider, government and the citizen–client.

One measure that can be used to assess quality and access is a sustained communication strategy between the organization providing the service and the recipients of the service. Such a strategy, however, has to be a genuine 'open' communication; it cannot be, if it is to be effective, a one-way information giving exercise on the part of the organization.

New Zealand, which has undergone radical and sustained change in the management, financing and legislative basis of its public services over the last decade, has certainly adopted a sustained communications strategy with the citizen–client. Throughout the public services, across both central government departments, reaching down to the individual school, a sustained communication strategy has been adopted. Communication is not one-way, that is, the government 'informing' the citizenry; it embraces a wide two-way communication as the evidence from the National Advisory Committee on Core Health and Disability Services (1993) demonstrates. It is clear from the example shown in the extract below that issues of access, assigning priority to service investment and facilitating two-way communication are important features of service quality delivery. Those issues also reflect quite closely the determinants of service quality (Zeithmal *et al.*, 1988) set out above.

Consultation in New Zealand Health care

The Consultation Process
The Committee's public meetings have been well attended. They provide an important mechanism for the Committee members to hear the concerns of people directly. Attendance by representatives from the Regional Health Authorities and Crown Health Enterprises has also added a valuable dimension to discussion in the public meetings.
The Committee has been asked whether the consultation mechanism of public meetings will remain an avenue for public input.
　We recognize that every method of consultation has its drawbacks. We have been challenged at the meetings about how we know we are getting a representative viewpoint and not just the viewpoint of those motivated to turn up. One response to this, which we are considering, is to shift the emphasis in our public consultations towards more formal, qualitative methods such as smaller

focus groups and surveys. We remain committed to systematically hearing the views of the community and accurately reflecting them in the advice we give to the Minister.

We would like to acknowledge the detailed submissions we have received on adult dental services, fertility services, sexual abuse services, complementary therapies, drug and alcohol counselling and rehabilitation, gambling addiction services, services for people who are deaf or who stutter, and access to treatments for people with haemophilia who have developed inhibitors to current treatments, among others. These issues have not yet been considered in detail by the Committee. Many of the proposals, if adopted, would require major reallocation of existing resources from other services.

With respect to dental services in particular, we note that the Minister of Health has referred the matter of access for low income adults to basic dental services to the Core Services Committee. The Committee has heard from multiple sources that people in some parts of New Zealand do not have access to basic urgent dental services such as emergency repair of painful teeth. In some areas, public hospitals have provided such services for those who cannot afford private dental care.

The Committee is developing a process for making decisions about the relative allocation of resources between services. This is no easy task. When little, if any, additional funding is available for health and disability support services, more of one thing inevitably means there will be less of something else. A process to determine relative resource allocation will be a major focus of our work programme in the remainder of the 1993/94 year. *(Report of National Advisory Committee on Care Health Services, 1993)*

A recent study (McKevitt and Lawton, 1996) reported on the role of performance measurement in securing adequate representation for the citizen 'voice'. The study, which has now been updated with two further years of data, looked at the relative weight given to different stakeholders (political, managerial, consumer) in designing performance measures and the role each stakeholder had in influencing the form and content of the performance system. The data, drawn from over one hundred organizations, offer a valuable insight into how public organizations in the UK implement performance measurement systems. Unlike the data reported from New Zealand, it is clear that citizen 'voice' does not feature highly in the design of delivery systems. In part this could be due to the top–down nature of implementation, with legislation and senior politicians being the primary impetus for installation of performance systems; in part, neglect of the citizen could be explained by the lack of openness by UK SLPOs to citizen voice.

The typology developed by Kanter and Summers (1987), in which they identify three major functions of performance measurement systems, was used. Kanter and Summers take the view that performance measurement systems should reflect the interests of a multiplicity of stakeholders:

- Institutional functions which are concerned with legitimacy renewal and resource attraction, that is, is the organization meeting the expectations of external stakeholders?

- Managerial functions which centre on structure and process corrections and internal allocation; the central stakeholders here are the
  various levels of managers and professionals in the organization.
- Technical functions which are concerned with the effectiveness and
  quality of services and products; the main stakeholders here are the
  customers and clients of the organization.

Kanter and Summers view organizations as temporary alliances of different
groups pursuing multiple and inconsistent objectives. They argue that ambiguous operational objectives create opportunities for internal politics and goal
displacement 'for loose coupling between official or stated mission and operating goals' (p. 163). Stakeholders are likely to be in conflict with each other as
they pursue their own goals:

> For non-profits, these are exaggerated because of two kinds of loose coupling:
> between sources of legitimacy and standards of management and between
> those providing resources (donors of funds or time) and those receiving ser-
> vices (clients). In between are the managers and professionals, who have their
> own view of what the organization should be doing. *(Kanter and Summers,
> 1987, p. 159)*

Three key issues are examined: the source of impetus behind the development
of measurement systems; the role played by major stakeholders in their development; and the extent of user involvement in the development of measures of
effectiveness and quality of service delivery.

1   Where did the impetus for performance measurement come from?
Managers identified, overwhelmingly, top–down external forces as the most
important driving force behind performance measurement. These included
legislation, the Audit Commission and individual politicians. Senior management was identified as the next most important source of impetus in all
organizations. The consumer, client or patient had the least impact, along
with field staff. In the NHS, professionals had some impact on the introduction of performance measurement. Clearly, then, the citizen–client ranked low
in priority in many UK organizations.

2   Who devised the criteria?
In all organizations, senior managers and politicians were identified as making
the largest contribution. Consumers, clients and patients made a negligible
contribution. In the NHS, professionals made a significant contribution.

*3   Which group of stakeholders were best represented in your organization's per-
formance measures?*
The data clearly showed that the primary orientation of the measurement systems was on institutional measures of performance, the next major emphasis
was on managerial measures and the data showed that technical measures were
prominent in eight organizations. These included a community health unit,

a health promotion unit, a health authority pharmacy department, a chiropody services unit and a local authority environmental services department.

The primary impetus behind the development of performance measures was legislation or central government initiatives and senior management were the most important stakeholders involved in the design and implementation of the measurement systems. Managers reported on the difficulties encountered in implementing performance measurement systems: the most frequent response was that there was not enough consultation with staff; the second most frequent response cited insufficient time given to systems. Other responses included lack of information, the financial bias of the indicators, insufficient training, and that the performance measures were not linked to the overall strategy of the organization. Respondents indicated that the motivation and commitment of staff was thereby lowered, leading to scepticism and a sense of fear about the use to which the measures would be put. Such a finding would indicate that attention to the needs of the staff delivering the service was not a priority.

A manager reported that:

> Genuine concerns are expressed that the changes are disadvantaging the under-privileged, homeless and poorer members of the community. The caring public sector orientation which many staff have is being seriously challenged and questioned. This has unforeseen consequences at all levels as we adopt and develop new 'bottom lines' including that of profit.

The unintended consequences of such a strategy are, however, considerable. Middle managers now find themselves uncomfortably 'close to the customers' to the extent that they now have to take responsibility for what they perceive to be inadequate levels of resources. This shifting of responsibility, from the political to the organizational, has given rise to significant pressure on middle level managers which is explored later in this section.

Technical functions

Top–down implementation, combined with middle manager disenchantment with the process, can mean that organizations show consistent inattention to the users of the services. Potter (1988) viewed the appropriate criteria to evaluate user responsiveness as access, choice, information, redress and representation.

Managers reported the need to attend to these issues:

> What is important here is that the correct information is provided to fulfil the individual stakeholder's need for understanding performance assessment. There needs to be, therefore, an explicit system for obtaining service user's views about the services received. *(NHS trust hospital)*

A district council manager indicated that:

When considering assessment criteria and how they reflect stakeholder needs, it is acknowledged that originally the requirements of the customers of the service were not catered for. This group are such obvious and significant stakeholders that their omission is an issue which needs to be addressed as a matter of urgency.

Consistent with my earlier observation that implementation of performance measurement systems is largely one of compliance to external stakeholders, is the comment that:

> there is no way of appraising the success or otherwise of this structure in terms of responsiveness to local needs; success remains a function of satisfying con-tractual targets with government departments.

However, despite entreaties to recognize 'voice', many of the organizations in the study did not appear to have developed mechanisms for the expression of voice or convinced users that the organization was seeking to respond to their needs. For example, a Community Health Care unit manager stated that: 'The users' perception is of a paternalistic style which is resistant to change' and 'Managers are comfortable with measures of throughput, cost per in-patient admission, for their efficiency PIs. However, a lot of development work is required in assessing quality of service from the participants' viewpoint'. Con-sistent with a producer-oriented approach is the observation of a manager in a local authority that 'while the performance measures as presented are intelligible to managers, I doubt that they would be particularly meaningful to consumers' (McKevitt and Lawton, 1996).

A manager in Social Services reported that:

> consideration needs to be given to ensure that the voice of the end-user is heard, and ways examined to decide how to overcome 'built-in' social disadvantage.

A manager in the Benefits Agency stated that

> customer and customer representatives cannot influence performance measure-ment directly and only have influence if they are allowed to have a voice.

The manager went on to report that technical measures have the lowest prior-ity within the Benefits Agency.

Where procedures are in place:

> Although this area [complaints] could be fruitful in measuring equity and outcome, in practice there is likely to be a defensiveness [sic] by the organ-ization, its politicians and major fund holders, which will interfere with the process of discovering service deficiencies.

One health authority manager indicated that:

> the organizational performance measures used within the health visiting ser-
> vice reflect mainly institutional and managerial functions, which are there to
> satisfy the interest of purchasers, the Department of Health, levels of manage-
> ment and professionals. The significant stakeholders whose interest is not
> really served are the clients. However, they also have their own priorities and
> have to respond to other influences. The technical function of performance
> measurement is more problematic but is a crucial indicator of effectiveness
> and quality. Attention should be given to these issues.

Attempts to ensure that organizations are more responsive through, for example, 'charters' or through Audit Commission performance indicators have
been only partly successful.

Managers' responses to these approaches were as follows:

- They have no regard for different stakeholder interests.
- They are input based with no measures of outcome or quality.
- They are control rather than development oriented.

The Audit Commission (1993), in an examination of quality delivery, argued
that users of public services should be more widely defined than consumers of
the private sector: it argued that indirect recipients of the service, including the
wider community, should be included in stakeholder analysis of quality. Its
own checklist for quality communication includes:

> *Customers and Users:*
> Have you determined who are your 'customers'. If there are multiple cus-
> tomers, have priorities been established?
>
> *Listening and Understanding:*
> Have users been asked about standards, satisfaction, problems? Do you ana-
> lyse the complaints? Have you used the knowledge and experience of front-
> line skill to assess satisfaction? *(Audit Commission, 1993, p. 4)*

The data reported above suggest quite strongly that the users of services are
given the lowest priority in assessing quality delivery and that public organizations in the UK are primarily concerned with resource usage and legitimacy.

The Citizens' Charter Complaints Task Force (1995), in its investigation of
how public organizations in Great Britain respond to complaints from users
concerning service quality, advocated that complaints systems should be
'accessible, simple, speedy, fair, confidential, effective and informative' (1995,
p. vii). The Task Force reported that there have been improvements in recent
years in the capacity and willingness of public organizations to receive and act
on complaints, to provide internal procedures for handling complaints, and to
provide greater public information on complaints. On the negative side, the
Task Force found that many people were still dissatisfied with the complaints
system:

- complaints were still regarded as bad news and resisted (this was still a major barrier);
- some lack of senior management commitment was noted;
- there was a restrictive ethos of rules and regulations concerning complaints handling.

Clearly the inattention to citizen–client views is a feature of UK public organizations. However, as the data from McKevitt and Lawton (1996) above show, the neglect of citizen voice is a feature of the type of performance systems which have been put in place, rather than simply a function of provider neglect of this voice. That is, government has placed a higher priority on institutional and managerial measures (broadly those of efficiency) than it has on technical measures (those reflecting effectiveness). The public organization has, therefore, responded by installing performance measures which reflect the interests of its most powerful stakeholder, that is, government.

Clear communication between providers and clients, including clarity in specifying expected standards of service delivery are two strategies which help to close the 'gap' in quality delivery of services. New Zealand has adopted such organization-wide strategies albeit, as we shall see, that the effects of some of the New Zealand reforms are questioned by commentators in that country.

An area in the UK where organizations are active in the promotion of service quality can be found in Next Step Agencies, an organizational device to promote efficiency and effectiveness. The Child Support Agency, an organization which has occasioned passionate and virulent protest and loathing (from some of its clients!), has clearly and cogently set out, in information packs designed for its clients, its aims and objectives (see below). As with other Executive Agencies, some commentators wonder whether its aim to 'make the efficient and effective use of available resources' is not operationally translated as 'reduce government spending'.

Child Support Agency: aims and objectives

The Agency's primary aims are to deliver on behalf of children a consistent, effective and efficient service for the assessment, collection and payment of child maintenance, so as to ensure that parents maintain their children whenever they can afford to do so.

The Agency will also help people with care of children to make informed choices about whether to take up employment.

To achieve these aims, the Agency's objectives are to:

- implement successfully the Child Support Act under agreed plans for the phased take-on of clients, ensuring that maintenance assessments and payments are accurate and regular;
- in keeping with the principles of the Citizen's Charter, provide a service to clients which is accessible courteous, prompt, consistent and efficient and seen by them as such;

- provide clear and accurate information to clients and the public about the child support system and services and benefits available to clients who are in work;
- establish and maintain an effective working relationship with the courts, advice agencies and other organizations with an interest in the Agency's business;
- contribute effectively to the Department's evaluation and development of policy and ensure the Agency can respond effectively to change;
- make the most efficient and effective use of available resources. *(Child Support Agency, 1994)*

The inherent (some might describe it as inescapable) tensions between cost and operational efficiency and the needs of the citizen–client in core public services can be seen in this case.

I recall meeting the managers of the Child Benefit Agency (CBA) at MBA programmes at the Open University: there was no doubting the vigour and enthusiasm that the managers brought to the implementation of their mission statements and 'core values'. Such vigour contrasted with the bemusement (and sometimes anger) of social services staff seeking to implement 'care in the community programmes'. In some measure the CBA staff were applying the technology of managerial efficiency (information systems, etc.) in a mechanical way to an environment where empathy, responsiveness, reliability were required. The emphasis was one of machine bureaucracy in an environment where it was inappropriate.

The 'test' of appropriateness in the context of the Child Support Agency is not the Mission Statement of the Agency but rather the response of its clients. This is not to criticize the CSA managers but the operating remit they were given by government.

To help clarify these tensions in mission and stakeholder objectives, you could now turn to the case study 'The vision and reality of an executive agency' by Charles Ferguson and Deirdre McGill in the appendix. The case study explores a number of the themes covered in this chapter – performance measurement, stakeholders and accountability for performance in relation to the Social Security Agency (Northern Ireland). You should answer the questions set out at the end of the case study. You will find that the case study examines key issues in service delivery and it helps to demonstrate the inherent tensions in service delivery, that is, responsiveness to government and responsiveness to clients. The case study, one of five cases in this book, helps to provide a management context for the service and delivery issues addressed in chapters 3 to 7.

An additional resource contained in the appendix is an example of a patient satisfaction questionnaire, which has been pre-tested, to evaluate client satisfaction with accident and emergency services in hospitals. The questionnaire can serve as a helpful tool for evaluating service quality in a hospital environment. You can see from the questionnaire that all aspects of service are covered from a client's perspective. You could use the questionnaire to develop other surveys of client satisfaction for your own organization.

Rationing of Core Public Services and Appellate Structures

Core public services are everywhere rationed so as to constrain public expenditure. The rationing process has, hitherto, been implicit rather than explicit; the doctor has always 'restricted treatment', ostensibly on personal grounds – 'for the good of the patient' – but, in reality, the process has as much to do with constrained resources as with professional ethics. The impetus, across many OECD countries and elsewhere, to constrain expenditure and increase efficiency has resulted in a more explicit and public rationing process, albeit that it is usually described as 'targeting', 'focused strategies' or, more prosaicly, 'customer driven'. The professional has in the implicit rationing of services been rewarded by the State through the granting of large professional autonomy, self-regulation under legislation and quite significant financial reward. Harrison identifies the symbiotic relationship between State and professionals in the UK:

> The autonomy enjoyed by professionals is partly illusory: their judgements are, in fact, heavily influenced by the socialization they have received through training. This socialization is oriented towards the perception of illness as an individual pathology rather than one which is socially, politically or economically created. Such a view is non-threatening to the state because it places the illness either in biological contingencies for which no one can be held responsible, or in individual lifestyles for which the victim can be blamed . . . Because [the] rationing decisions are highly fragmented into individual transactions between patients and professionals, they are politically invisible. *(Harrison, 1993, p. 18)*

In recent years public sector organizations have sought to increase delivery quality through two general strategies: by increased efficiency seen in programmes such as the Financial Management Initiative (FMI) in the UK, the contractor–provider model in New Zealand, which is discussed in chapter 5, and the development of performance indicators.

The phenomenon of organizational slack identified by March and Simon (1958), which buffers an organization in 'bad times', is now under threat. In addition, the programmes of micro-management of professional behaviour utilizing mechanistic performance measurement systems to curtail and monitor resource usage have, as a consequence, resulted in doctors, teachers and others reviewing their 'psychological contract' with their organizations. The unintended consequences of such micro-management programmes has led to professional 'exit' from the public service value-system. New Zealand has developed a targeted marketing strategy for social welfare recipients (based on a segmentation model – discussed in chapter 4) that illustrates the growing importance of using rationing techniques for public service delivery.

An 'alternative' view of health care reform in New Zealand is argued in *Health Reforms – a second opinion* (Wellington Action Committee, 1992), an extract from which is set out below. Whilst the views expressed are quite strident, it does demonstrate that access and citizen voice are not simply terms which can be taken for granted by government reformers. One of the key ways access can be facilitated is through appropriate organizational structures, an issue I return to in chapter 6.

The case for local voice

The abolition of elected area health boards in July 1991 was an extraordinary political act. Extraordinary because it was announced in a Budget, making a mockery of the parliamentary process. Extraordinary because it was in stark contrast to [the National Party's] election policy. Extraordinary because it reversed, without public discussion, the way in which our public health system had been organized for decades.

Governance through locally elected boards was not beyond criticism. Some decisions made over the years were ill-advised. But the same criticism can be made of other democratic institutions. And there are those who argued that the dual accountability of boards – to their local constituency on the one hand, and to central government, the paymaster, on the other – was fatally flawed. In their view, the attempt to apply a notion of 'partnership' was at the centre of the perceived problems in the public health service.

This is too simple a view. First, it sets aside the way in which boards, supported by general management and the evolving relationship with the Crown, were grappling with difficult issues. Less than two years was a very short time in which to test the new area health board system.

Secondly, it gives no weight to the democratic arguments for local participation in decision-making about the public health service. In brief, these are:

- decisions are best made close to the point of action (the principle of 'subsidiarity');
- there is a sense of ownership so often reflected in community support for local health facilities and services;
- there is a local voice to countervail the centralist, Wellington domination – the checks and balances argument.

These democratic values have not cut much ice with the economic rationalists who have restructured the New Zealand state in recent years. With what alternative are we now presented in the Health and Disability Services Bill? Mr Upton's reforms are essentially centralist, ministerially driven and lacking in local voice. The Minister for Health will appoint members of four regional health authorities (RHAs). The Minister of Finance and Crown Health Enterprises (the 'shareholding Ministers') will appoint the boards of directors of crown health enterprises (CHEs). The powers of ministers to direct these agencies are numerous and significant. How they are to be exercised is crucial.

So far as the responsibility of ministers is concerned, we have ample experience with State Owned Enterprises (SOEs) to question the claim that accountability has been enhanced by legislative provisions in the Health and Disability Services Bill (Clause 4) which are substantially repeated from the State Owned Enterprises Act (Section 6).

To the extent that RHAs and CHEs are to have varying measures of 'autonomy' – discretion to act within the boundaries of ministerial directive – other questions arise. At a practical level there are clearly real difficulties in the Dunedin RHA (covering most of the South Island) exercising responsibility for, say, the mental health services of the West Coast. There has been no regard to the community of interest which is so important in local government and education. Area health boards shared regional council boundaries. They manifest the concepts of 'recognition of the existence of different communities', 'recognition of communities of interest' and 'effective participation of local persons' emphasized in Section 37k of the Local Government Act 1974.

We are told that the network of complex contracts cascading down from the RHAs will more adequately translate local needs into effective services. That is an act of faith which is contradicted by experience internationally and in New Zealand with contracts in other areas of social policy. Contracts, especially in respect of quality, are very difficult to specify; they are costly to monitor; and remedial action (often the termination of the contract or the sacking of the board) is unsatisfactory and too late. We are told, too, that the RHAs will be 'customer-driven' – that the statutory requirement to consult 'from time to time' (Clause 22) is crucial. This is, however, a weak formulation: there is no equivalent to the provisions in the Area Health Boards Act for consultation via service development groups and community committees. It would be futile to look at CHEs as the voice of the community. They are to operate as a 'successful business . . . as profitable and efficient as comparable businesses not owned by the Crown' (Clause 25(c)).

Above all, the question to be asked is: Who is responsible when something goes wrong 'on the ground'? Is it, for example, the management – or the directors – of the CHE? Is it the RHA (or the PHC [Public Health Commission]) who purchased the service, and who was charged with monitoring performance? Is it the Department of Health, which is to monitor RHAs' purchasing function? Is it the Ministers of Finance and CHEs-the owners? Or the Minister of Health? The accountability problems of area health boards appear minuscule in the face of such complexities. To sum up: whatever their faults, area health boards provided for local voice through the electoral process; they were a countervailing force against central dominance; and there were statutory mechanisms for consultation. The proposed reforms will replace these democratic institutions with ministerially appointed boards, weak provisions for consultation, and a complex network of contracts which will confuse, rather than clarify, the location of responsibility for public services.
(Wellington Action Committee, 1992)

In Sweden the recent reforms of health care delivery (discussed in greater detail in chapter 5) have seen a reduction in the number of hospital beds from 4.4 per 1000 inhabitants in 1985 to 3.1 per 1000 inhabitants in 1993. Patients now have a guarantee, in force since 1992, for in-patient hospital treatment after consultation with a specialist, that they need wait no more than three months for treatment. If the waiting time is expected to be longer, the patient has the right to have treatment in another hospital – be that in another county or in a private hospital (Hakansson and Nordling, 1997). The changes in Sweden's health system reflect general changes in the political agenda, from a concern with equity issues in the 1970s/80s, to concerns with efficiency and cost containment in the 1990s. Table 3.5 sets out the major issues of Sweden's

Table 3.5 Tentative connection between reforms and health-sector changes during the 1990s, aggregate level for all county councils in Sweden

Measure	Effect	Association with reform
Efficiency	Substantial increase in 1992 and 1993, moderate increase in 1994	Can be associated both with national and county-council reforms
Volume of services	Substantial increase in 1992 and 1993, moderate increase in 1994	Most likely to be associated with health care guarantee, freedom of choice for patients and per-case payments for providers
Expenditure	Real decrease of hospital expenditures between 1992 and 1994	Associated with enhanced cost awareness among hospital providers, but mostly the result of political decisions to reduce costs
Waiting times	Reduced especially in 1992, are beginning to increase again	Most likely to be associated with health care guarantee, freedom of choice for patients and per-case payments for providers
Consumer orientation	Anecdotal and survey evidence of changes in provider attitudes; the public is probably less influenced	Most likely to be associated with health care guarantee, freedom of choice for patients and per-case payments for providers
Quality of services	No proven change in medical quality; possible decreased quality of care due to reduced length of stay; improved access	Can be associated both with national and county-council reforms
Equity	No proven change; possible distortion in favour of the elderly	Associated with the reforms that increased volume of services (same as for volume of services)

Source: Anell, Rosen and Svarvar, 1996

health care system as it struggles to cope with economic and political change in the 1990s.

One source of redress for the citizen–client is the existence of appellate or review procedures in the public sector exemplified by the ombudsman system, which is of Nordic origin. The pressure on service providers is given concrete expression in the quality (or lack of it) of service provision. The Health Service

Commissioner for England, for Scotland and for Wales in his report for 1993/94 outlines the dimensions of service quality:

Dimension of service quality

- rudeness (though that is a matter of degree);
- unnwillingness to treat the complainant as a person with rights;
- refusal to answer reasonable questions;
- neglecting to inform a complainant on request of his or her rights or entitlement;
- knowingly giving advice which is misleading or inadequate;
- ignoring valid advice or overruling considerations which would produce an uncomfortable result for the overruler;
- offering no redress or manifestly disproportionate redress;
- showing bias whether because of colour, sex, or any other grounds;
- omission to notify those who thereby lose a right of appeal;
- refusal to inform adequately of the right of appeal;
- faulty procedures;
- failure by management to monitor compliance with adequate procedures;
- cavalier disregard of guidance which is intended to be followed in the interest of equitable treatment of those who use a service;
- partiality; and failure to mitigate the effects of rigid adherence to the letter of the law where that produces manifestly inequitable treatment. *(Health Service Commissioner, 1995)*

In the report he pays specific attention to the effects of purchaser–provider arrangements in the National Health Service (NHS) and the relationships between NHS Authorities, Boards and Trusts as regulated by the Hospital Procedures Act 1985. He found that:

> all too often my investigations (quarterly reports of Boards and Trusts) show that such a provision is absent from local procedures or that, even though it is there, it is being ignored. A quality service is about devoting personal attention to individual patients. Policies and procedures are useless if that essential human element is missing. *(1995, Section 1.6)*

The Health Service Commissioner found occasion to rebuke management (as distinct from doctors) in trenchant terms:

> In many of the cases which I investigated I was obliged to criticize what can only be regarded as an abrogation of responsibility and neglect of management. Far too often I have to deplore the treatment of patients which shows disregard for the needs and care of fellow humans. Far too often nothing has been done to manage patient care properly until I have completed an investigation. In cases such as that those responsible should feel a sense of shame.

Table 3.6 sets out the Health Commissioner's list of grievances investigated and upheld, 1984/85 to 1993/94: an upward trend is evident in this table. Such data would appear to indicate increasing citizen–client dissatisfaction

Table 3.6 Number of grievances investigated and upheld, 1984/85 to 1993/94

Year	Number investigated		Number upheld	
	Total	No. of grievances per report issued	Total	% of (ii)
(i)	(ii)	(iii)	(iv)	(v)
1984/85	443	3.54	209	47.18
1985/86	526	3.84	302	57.41
1986/87	483	3.69	290	60.04
1987/88	525	3.94	321	61.14
1988/89	556	4.00	322	57.91
1989/90	345	3.88	177	51.30
1990/91	487	3.50	236	48.46
1991/92	442	3.37	243	55.00
1992/93	476	3.09	287	60.29
1993/94	426	2.58	275	63.07
TOTALS	4719	3.51	2662	56.41

with the 'New NHS'; it would also indicate a disregard for citizen voice in the rationing process.

Conclusion

So how relevant is marketing and the language of consumerism to the core public services? Clearly the concepts and categories of service marketing have a relevance. Walsh states:

> If we apply the ideas of marketing simply by adjusting its definitions, for example dropping the notion of profit, we will not capture what is specific to the public service, namely the conflict and ambiguity of values and purposes, the need for collective choice, and the mutuality of commitment and responsibility. Marketing for the public service will need to develop a psychology of citizenship to match the psychology of the consumer. *(1994, p. 70)*

The SLPO is, as noted in chapter 2, under a number of environmental forces which greatly impact on its effective working. We have seen evidence in this chapter that public organizations, especially in the UK, do not give attention to citizen voice in the design of delivery systems; much more effort is devoted to issues of organizational legitimacy and managerial issues. As rationing of resources becomes more explicit in core public services so too does the attendant requirement that managers should become more alert to the design of delivery systems that, as in New Zealand, give attention to citizen 'voice'. An example has been provided in the appendix in Case Study 1 of such evaluative surveys. The manager is 'caught in the middle' between government pressure on resource usage and citizen need for effective services. Marketing, in the sense of creating and sustaining a valued relationship with the client, does have a role within core public services. That role, however, must be explicitly extended to include specific organizational devices for the collection and evaluation of citizen voice in the context of rationing decisions.

Mission statements and statements of 'core values' are inappropriate and redundant devices unless, as the Health Commissioner for England reports, they are accompanied by 'a quality service that is about devoting personal attention to individual [patients]'. It is that personal relationship between manager, provider and client that has to be sustained in core public services.

The implications of this chapter for managers and professional providers are:

1 to be aware that consumer models of service delivery do not meet all the requirements of the citizen in the provision of core public services;
2 to design delivery systems and performance measurement frameworks with the active involvement and participation of the citizen–client;
3 To provide timely, relevant and flexible systems for redress of citizen complaints on service quality.

The organizational structures, including strategic control, that support such strategies, are examined in chapters 5 and 6. Let us now examine the role of investment planning for the delivery of quality services.

CHAPTER

4

Managing Resources for Social Gain

━━━ **Introduction** ━━━

Core public services form a large part of government expenditure and there is constant pressure on managers and providers to restrain the growth in their expenditure. There are large capital projects associated with the provision of such services, for example hospitals and schools, and they require skilled decision-makers when deciding on the priorities for such capital projects. This chapter discusses the techniques and models which can assist the public service manager make these priority decisions and evaluates how these decisions are taken in a number of countries. It is concerned, therefore, with major capital expenditure rather than with the operational, day-to-day, resource management of SLPOs. There will, however, be a discussion of important aspects of operational decisions – review and calculation of service demand – in so far as they impact on the estimation of future demands which go to make up the capital allocation decision for new projects.

Investment decision-making and the allocation of scarce capital resources to support government policy priorities in health and welfare services constitute the main focus of this chapter. In examining this important area of the public manager's job, I draw on the mainstream models and techniques of investment decision and resource allocation – by authors such as Bower, Simon, Hayes and Wheelwright, Schmenner – which are proposed as constitutive of best practice. I evaluate recent experience in the UK and New Zealand and consider how the models and techniques help our understanding of whether public investment decisions can be better structured to yield social gain for the citizen–client. The implementation of such decisions is an important part of the activities of the SLPO.

The chapter examines:

1   a framework for analysing the environment to assess investment needs in the core public services;

2   a framework for the investment decisions for capital projects in the
    core public services;
3   the need for specialists in operational decision-making in managing
    the capital allocation process.

Strategic control of publicly funded services can be achieved through a range of
frameworks and policy instruments – legislation, statutory regulation of standards, professional self-regulation and, in the UK, through auditing and regulatory bodies such as OFWAT (for water authorities) and the National Audit
Office and the Audit Commission (for local authorities and health authorities).
The creation and control of the regulatory process also has a strong European
dimension through the activities of the European Commission and the European Court of Justice and the growing convergence of the supra-national
standards that flow from their decisions. Changes in the domain of public
management of service delivery including organizational change, responsiveness to the citizen–consumer and the attendant performance measurement
frameworks, are discussed in chapters 6 and 7.

I have described in chapters 1 and 2 the guiding characteristics of core
public services as:

■ the non-marketability;
■ the existence of differential information between providers and
   consumers;
■ the attendant framework of accountability that arises from their publicly financed status.

I will examine in chapter 5 one of the central 'means of influence' open to a
government wishing to exercise strategic control over its investment decisions'
legislation. In the UK, the Rayner scrutinies, the value for money (VFM)
studies of the National Audit Office and the work of the Audit Commission
are also directed at the issues of control, efficiency and effectiveness of government programmes. Indeed, the 'performance measurement' movement has
been a growth industry for the consultancy firms, the computer suppliers and
academics!

If you accept the proposition that strategic control in the public services
requires attention to the legislative framework that guides the public investment decision, then much of the performance measurement movement is
centred on operational control. It is, however, a very large part of the technology of control available to the government and to public service managers. It
has an important role to play in enabling the consumer–citizen to gain a
'voice' in the regulation of public services and a say in improving their responsiveness. (Citizen voice in service delivery was examined in chapter 3.)

Much of the apparatus of control is centred on the rational model of economic decision-making; that is, the formal specification of rules of the game at
the operational level of management. The Hogwood and Gunn policy process
model which is set out in table 4.1 provides a useful framework of analysis. In

Table 4.1 Conceptual stages in the policy process

Stage	Description
1 Issue search	What are the issues which demand or need (or will soon demand or need) attention from policy-makers?
2 Issue filtration	Given that time and attention are finite resources, which of the issues identified in the issue search are most consequential for the organization? And which are most amenable to available analytical techniques?
3 Issue definition	What is the nature of each of the key issues chosen at the previous stage? What kind of problems or opportunities do they offer?
4 Forecasting	What can be predicted concerning trends relevant to these key issues (e.g. demographic or technological change)?
5 Objectives and priorities	What should be the organization's objectives with respect to each key issue, and what relative priorities should the different objectives be assigned?
6 Options generation	What alternative ways are there of achieving the specified objectives?
7 Options analysis	What are the costs and benefits (including political costs and benefits) attaching to each alternative route for achieving the specified objective? Options analysis has the aim of identifying the route with the highest benefit-to-cost ratio, subject to any specified cost or political constraints (e.g. that such-and-such a social group must be no worse off as a result of the new policy). Note that to choose between options logically implies that some criteria of choice (e.g. efficiency, effectiveness, impact on priority groups) have been specified.
8 Implementation	Carrying out the chosen route/method.
9 Monitoring and control	Checking that implementation is running to plan: learning from any changes or adaptations which have to be made: making any necessary or advantageous tactical adjustments.
10 Evaluation	Evaluating the results of implementation, and possibly re-evaluating priorities and objectives.
11 Policy succession and policy termination	Planning the transition from one policy to the next (e.g. is the original problem actually solved? Have new problems appeared? Are new methods becoming available?) Return to issue search?

Source: adapted from Hogwood and Gunn, 1984.

terms of the model, this chapter is concerned with stages 4 to 7, forecasting, objectives and priorities, options generation and options analysis, for capital projects. It examines how a number of countries approach this policy cycle and how the public service manager can draw on a range of models and techniques to achieve this end. Clearly, though, the policy process model is just that, a model, and it cannot be taken as representative of all policy decision processes in the core public services. Thus, for example, when examining strategic control (stage 9) in chapter 5 we will be very aware that defects in early phases, for example issue definition, can hinder any attempt at control if the original mission or strategy is flawed. Similarly, when we examine in this chapter the idea of cost/benefit analysis (stage 7) we will observe how, especially in the core public services, imprecision in specifying benefits can render such techniques ineffective or inappropriate.

The central thrust of the 'technology' of control is the post hoc examination of activities; it does not tell us whether we should be engaged in these activities or whether the consumer–citizen is to benefit from them. Kanter and Summers (1987) in a study of performance measurement in not-for-profit organizations make a convincing case that the problem in the public services is not how to measure but what to measure; their argument is driven by the existence of multiple stakeholders in the public services which requires multiple measures of performance assessment. They see performance measurement as serving three distinct functions:

1   The institutional: the issue here is the attraction of resources from the environment and the renewal of organizational legitimacy that results from continued funding.
2   The managerial: the issues here are largely concerned with internal allocation decisions and corrections to the structure and processes of the organization.
3   The technical: the issues here largely centre on the efficacy and quality of service delivery.

Kanter and Summers argue that there is a loose coupling between the sources of legitimacy and the standards of management, between those providing resources and those receiving the services. The weak influence of the consumer–citizen, combined with the ambiguous operating objectives of the organization, can lead to goal displacement on the part of the organization. Mintzberg (1983) contends that 'bureaucratization of the administrative components of the organization drove a further wedge between mission and the organizational goal system, which became increasingly based on system goals'. Mintzberg's argument will be taken up in the next chapter when examining the 'agency-capture' model that drove the reform programme in New Zealand's public service reforms. The point to note here is the proposition that public agencies, over time, will serve their own interests and agenda to the exclusion of the real interests of their clients. This argument, sometimes labelled 'provider interests' or 'producer interests', lies behind the growing development of performance frameworks that purport to control professional providers, an issue examined in chapter 7.

We should also be alert to the possibility that operational control and performance measurement systems may be incapable of resolving the dilemmas of efficiency and effectiveness in government programmes. It has already been seen in chapter 2 that the context of government decisions is influenced by many variables: economic, political and social. The decisions of governments to act (or to do nothing) are constrained by the realities that such action may itself be ineffectual: Baier, March and Saetern are leading proponents of the 'non-rational' school of public policy and their observations on the process are worth repeating:

> Policies are frequently ambiguous: but their ambiguities are less a result of deficiency in policy makers than a natural consequence of gaining necessary support for the policies, and of changing preferences over time. Conflict of interest is not just a property of the relations between policy makers on the one hand and administrators on the other; it is a general feature of policy negotiation and bureaucratic life. *(1986, p. 168)*

The idea of public good as the end of organizational activity in the public sector is itself open to debate and conflict: it is dependent for its expression on the interplay of social, political and economic forces, which can vary from country to country. Brunnson, in a review of politics within and between public organizations, puts the case as follows:

> Every organization [then] has to reflect in itself the inconsistencies in the conception of the public good, becoming more self-sufficient and possessing greater autonomous legitimacy . . . According to this hypothesis, politics at the organizational level could be expected to be particularly strong in countries such as Scandinavia and West Germany where state ownership, national planning and capitalistic theory are particularly weak. *(1989, p. 217)*

How then, given this uncertainty and ambiguity in the policy environment and consequent organizational politics at the operational level, can the public service manager make capital investment proposals that will reduce uncertainty in the environment? One way is to have a method for analysing the environment, a topic which will be discussed at length in the next section of this chapter. In the case of organization politics, as raised by Brunnson above, we need to look at how wider social forces and values impinge on the SLPO; this is an issue examined in chapter 6. The ambiguity and trade-offs in the policy environment are examined in chapter 5, where I argue that legislation is a key policy device in the core public service for strategy formation and implementation. The interplay of these important influences – legislative, organizational and policy – impact quite strongly on the SLPO as it seeks to deliver services in the society of which it is a part; this impact on the professionals delivering the service is examined in chapter 7.

It is apparent, therefore, that the SLPO is part of a systemic relationship between its institutional environment (where it gets its funding), its technical environment (from which it derives its rules and procedures) and its managerial environment (from which its rules and norms on internal allocation are derived). A central proposition of this book is that governments have to be aware of the complexity of environmental forces acting on the SLPO and that no one single 'best way' is available to manage this complexity. There are numerous examples of the unintended consequences of applying a single model of reform to the SLPO, for example, decentralization or purchaser–provider contracts. Let us now examine the nature of the external environment that provides the context for investment decisions in the core public services of the SLPO.

The Environment for Government Investment Decisions

How are the activities and programmes for resource allocation selected and translated into spending decisions by public managers? I begin here with a study of the environmental context. However, before doing so, I need to make some general observations as a basis for selecting a particular system for segmenting the environment.

The ends (or goals or mission) of the public services are to be found in the environment. However, the environment is not a simple or fixed thing. It contains many elements that are constantly changing. For my purposes I will employ the STEP framework to characterize the environment – social, technical, economic and political. For convenience of exposition I will place the users, clients and customers in the political area, along with politicians and single interest pressure groups (SIPGs), as described below. The problem of timescale immediately presents itself. Core public service managers must place their objectives and strategy for resource allocation in a temporal framework.

Short term	Resources for service delivery today.
Medium term	Resources for investment in facilities like hospitals, schools, roads, which may take five years from plan to construction.
Long term	Resources for the development of the necessary skills and collective habits, which may take twenty years from the moment of impetus.

This chapter examines the models and frameworks for medium term strategies of investment.

However, as the years since the end of the Second World War have shown, the resources of democratic states, even when such states are acting alone, are not exhausted by hand-to-mouth activities. To offset the tendency towards 'short-termism' among politicians, democratic states have developed institutions (such as Royal Commissions) where established authorities, with expert advisers, concern themselves with medium-term and long-term public needs. In Sweden the tradition of 'Consensus Statements' evaluating proposed new technology or treatments in health care are a similar device. Similar consensus statements on health care priorities have been developed in New Zealand. Correspondingly, in relation to the short-termism and narrow focus of SIPGs, there has evolved, almost spontaneously, the 'think tanks' of professional bodies, which like the Royal Commissions (and their equivalent) are concerned

Figure 4.1 Life-style changes: classification of customers by class and life-style

Class	Young singles	New nest	Early nest	Full nest	Empty nest	Old singles
A						
B						
C1						
C2						
C3						
D						
E						

Source: adapted from Rowntree, 1901

with the medium and long term. Thus, public service managers are provided with the authority to make medium and long-term investment proposals. In the UK, there has been a near twenty-year abandonment of Royal Commissions; the think tanks of the Right and Left have now substituted for this source of 'independent' advice. It is noteworthy that in the UK, unlike Sweden and New Zealand, there is no tradition of consensus statements which can help determine a professional or provider benchmark of good practice. The SLPO, in the UK, therefore lacks an important guidance mechanism (consensus statements) that can help direct and focus its investment strategies.

To aid them in their thinking in specific ways about changes in public needs over time, the Royal Commissioners and think tanks use a classification system like that described in figure 4.1. This is an adaptation of a classification system developed for, and employed by, marketing specialists in the area of consumer goods. You will note that consumers or customers are classified by both class and life style. In his famous study on poverty in York, Rowntree (1901) developed and used this system to show that the greatest needs for public welfare did not flow in a simple line from the rich (class A) to the poor (class E); account had to be taken of life style, from 'young singles' to 'old singles'.

In their analysis, the 'independent' commission or committee can, in the political domain, will the ends, if not the means, of core public services; and in their deliberations they can offer solutions which rely more on ideology than the needs of the citizens. In New Zealand, the National Interim Provider Board (1992) did just that in its report on providing better health care for New Zealanders. We will examine in chapter 5 the legislative basis of New Zealand's reforms; here we pause to look at the analysis underlying health care reform. As in all facets of core public service reform New Zealand adopted the contract model, splitting financing of the service from provision of the service, a model (as we shall see in chapter 6) that sharply differentiates between provider and management of the service. In designing their reforms, the Interim Board recommended that the following effects should be seen:

- liberate the innovative initiative of health care personnel at every level to combine excellence and economy in more creative and construct- ive ways;
- balance that new freedom with performance based accountability;
- tie the interests of managers and staff more closely to the success of their organizations;
- make the success of those organizations directly dependent on serv- ing their patients at least as well as alternative providers;

In a rather bizarre mixed metaphor, the *Interim Report* continued:

> It is important to understand that, within this framework, competition is not a matter of ideology, nor does it serve any dog-eat-dog purpose. No one believes that the teams on a football ground play worse because they are competing against each other. *(1992, p. 30)*

Chapter 3 examined the rationing decisions that resulted from the New Zea- land reforms in health care and social welfare which would seem to run coun- ter to the philosophy of a 'rising tide rises all boats', expressed in the report of the Interim Board. The ideological attitude in New Zealand to health provi- sion is captured in the words of a senior official in the Ministry of Health:

> for right or wrong a community of interest does not exist; we will 'see this in spades' as times goes on.

The organizational and structural reform of New Zealand's core public services is examined more closely in later chapters. Here it is noteworthy that reform which is predicated on the market model alone runs counter to the idea of social cohesion and interdependence which is a primary characteristic of core public services.

Of course, in the political environment, the problem of short-termism in resource allocation can never be completely resolved. In the short term, the public service manager is dealing with real numbers, on which all can agree if a proper method of calculation can be employed. By contrast, in the medium and long term there is uncertainty; the numbers are conjectural, leaving room for political patronage to intrude in making forecasts. Hence, there is a great need for those who deal with the medium to long term to be seen as 'object- ive' and authoritative if allegations of political patronage are to be avoided in decisions on medium and long-term investments in the area of core public services.

However, short-termism is not the only problem in assessing public needs in the environment of core public services. Equally fundamental is the problem of defining and assessing public needs in a way that is operational for public service managers. Since the time of Rowntree, a century ago, much has been written on the problems of defining and assessing needs in the public domain.

Stewart and Ranson (1988) make the point that demand for, and the price of, products and services are the principal criteria for allocation in the private domain. By contrast, need is the most appropriate criterion for allocation in the public domain. It is necessary, therefore, to define and contrast these two terms: needs and wants.

Taking the latter first, wants may be expressions of desires which may not reflect a rational assessment of what is required. For example, a heroin addict may want more heroin but need treatment. However, need is not a simple concept. Cuyler (1976, pp. 13–19) makes the distinction between expressed, felt and normative need. Expressed need is perhaps the easiest to conceptualize. It is indistinguishable from a market demand. If you were to say, 'I need a new car', that would be an expressed need. It is a clearly felt and communicated need by a consumer who knows the consequences of the purchase of a new car.

A felt need exists prior to communication or action. In a society where access to power and influence is unevenly distributed, many felt needs may go unarticulated. For example, language problems, lack of confidence, or lack of knowledge, skills or mobility may mean that a felt need for, say, better street lighting may not be communicated to those who are responsible for supplying the service. In this regard, look at figure 4.1 again and consider the felt needs of those in the bottom right-hand sector.

Normative need involves a judgement made by a professional, such as a medical doctor. Such a judgement may conflict with the subject's felt need. A patient may have a felt need for a good meal, while the normative judgement of the doctor may be a programme of exercise combined with a planned diet. At the same time, conflict in the decision-making process can revolve around competition for scarce resources and a lack of consensus about what is to be achieved and how. In other words, value judgements have to be made as to what are desirable ends. Moreover, many of the desirable ends are not compatible with each other and may, indeed, be in conflict. Politicians tackle this difficulty by attending to individual problems in turn and by creating slack resources in the system through economic growth.

Le Grand (1982) in a study of social service provision found that:

■ Almost all public expenditure on the social services in Britain benefits the better-off to a greater extent than the poor. This is not only true for services such as roads where, due to the insignificant role played by a concern for equality in determining policy, such an outcome might be expected: it is also true for services whose aims are at least in part egalitarian, such as the National Health Service, higher education, public transport and the aggregate complex of housing policies (see the *Social Trends*, 1977, figures in chapter 3).

- As a result equality, in any sense of the term, has not been achieved. In all the relevant areas, there persist substantial inequalities in public expenditure, in use, in opportunity, in access and in outcomes. Moreover, in some areas (though by no means all) there is evidence to suggest that the policies concerned have failed even to reduce inequality significantly.

At this point it is useful to refer again to Stewart and Ranson, who argued that generic approaches to management in the public domain are inappropriate because of the distinctive characteristics of this domain:

> In the public domain need has to be assessed. It is a task for government with its own purposes. In the private sector need is established, in order to establish demand. In the public domain need is assessed as a condition of government. Choices have to be made . . . Scarce resources have to be fitted to unmet need. This involves collective choice both in the definition of need and the allocation of resources to need. *(1988, p. 16)*

Hence resource allocation is, at least in part, a task that involves allocating scarce resources to meet needs that are significant but are, of their nature, not met by the market economy. This, in turn, means that political and social values are at play. Different families of values compete for influence, and the resource allocation process itself is perhaps the most common locus of this competition. Hence resource allocation is an intensely political process. This is a factor in the environment of the first order of magnitude.

The Economic Environment

Four key periods in UK public expenditure trends can be identified. They are:

1974–5 to 1975–6:	dramatic real spending growth
1975–6 to 1977–8:	dramatic fall in real spending
1977–8 to 1984–5:	small rise in real spending
1984–5 to 1988–9:	marked decline in real spending

In 1979, real government expenditure in the UK accounted for 42.5 per cent of GDP, almost exactly the same as in 1995–6.

These are overall figures. Even in periods of growth there were departments that suffered a reduction in real resources: and in periods of cutback some enjoyed an increase in real resources. Since our concern in this chapter is resource allocation, it is not necessary to be specific about the global financial environment. Our approach will be focused on the circumstances that the organization faces at a particular point in time.

However, it is worth recognizing the overall pressures that have come to bear on public service managers. The stated aim of economic policy in the

United Kingdom, Sweden and New Zealand, was both to reduce overall spending and to open up monopolistic services to the forces of competition. A central theme was an attack on patterns of service provision that, it was perceived, were dominated by the interests of producers – be they trade unions or professional bodies, which are discussed in chapters 5 and 7.

In central government in the UK, the Rayner scrutinies aimed to produce lasting changes in the way that civil servants went about their work. These scrutinies were followed by the Financial Management Initiative, which aimed to introduce more accountable management, with responsibility for resources exercised closer to the point at which services are delivered.

The Next Steps programme, together with the Citizen's Charter, aimed to raise the overall standard of public services. However, it is possible to detect a changing emphasis in the Efficiency Strategy – its early focus was on reducing overall costs (inputs), while later initiatives have devoted greater attention to service quality (outputs).

This was an issue highlighted in the Efficiency Unit report which led to the Next Steps initiative in the UK. In their report to the Prime Minister, the authors noted that:

> the pressures on departments are mainly on expenditure and activities; there is still too little attention paid to the results to be achieved with the resources. The public expenditure system is still the most powerful central influence on departmental management. It is still overwhelmingly dominated by the need to keep within the levels of money available rather than by the effectiveness with which the money is used. (*Jenkins, Caines and Jackson, 1988, p. 4*)

The same basic thinking underpinned approaches to the reform of local government. The key features were:

- increase of control over grant payments to local authorities;
- greater reliance on local authorities generating their own income;
- introduction of the community charge to widen the tax base and enhance accountability;
- abolition of certain authorities, including the Greater London Council and the metropolitan counties; and
- greater circumscription of the powers of local authorities.

Competitive tendering for local authority services was introduced in 1980 for a small range of services, including office cleaning and refuse collection. The value of such services rose dramatically from less than £100m in the late 1980s to almost £2 billion by the end of 1992. The Audit Commission (1993), in a review of the experience within local authorities, noted the following issues that needed to be resolved:

- poorly defined and, in some cases, over-defined specifications;
- unenforceable contract conditions;
- inadequate tender evaluation procedures;

- inefficient contract monitoring;
- bureaucratic contract administration.

The Commission saw most of the shortcomings stemming from a single source – the failure to adequately involve the consumers of the service in the contract process. Indeed such an observation is consistent with the discussion of client involvement in chapter 3 and it is a topic I return to in chapter 6 in the context of decentralized administrative structures. The Educational Service is one of the largest local government services and schools receive some £750m (1993 prices) of services that are subject to CCT. The Audit Commission set out their advice on how to overcome the problems identified (see below); whilst this area relates to day-to-day expenditures it is helpful as a guideline to public managers in the general area of contract management.

Solutions to the problems

Authorities should take a range of actions to remedy identified problems. Determine realistic service direction and appropriate contract strategy:

- balance priorities
- obtain market intelligence
- package contracts to maximize interest
- plan for contingencies

Write specification to:

- reflect consumers' views
- define contract outputs as far as possible
- allow flexibility for changing circumstances
- take account of experience with first-round contracts

Ensure contract conditions are comprehensive:

- define responsibilities of parties to the contract
- spell out how variations should be made
- clarify alternatives if things go wrong
- set out administrative arrangements

Make contract letting procedures as transparent as possible:

- define and adhere to timetable
- provide relevant information to all potential tenderers
- carry out tender evaluation fairly
- utilize mobilization period to resolve anticipated difficulties

Involve consumers and contractors in contract monitoring:

- understand the purpose of monitoring
- utilize complaints systems, and encourage consumer feedback
- encourage contractor quality assurance
- provide monitoring information to interested parties

Streamline contract administration:

- set out clear responsibilities
- hold regular meetings between client, contractor and consumer

- resolve problems at the local level if possible
  apply defaults fairly
- use arbitration procedures where appropriate
  Source: Audit Commission, 1993

Competitive tendering has now been extended to a wide range of services:

Architectural Design
Quantity Surveyors
Grounds Maintenance
Computing Facilities Management
Supplies
Building Cleaning
Catering
Vehicle Maintenance
Reprographics
Corporate Training Delivery
Music Tuition
Forestry
Highways and Ancillary Maintenance
Highways and Planning Consultancy
Financial Services
Estates and Valuation
Building Maintenance (Part)
Source: *Financial Times*, 1994

Further competition is in the pipeline for professional services. The stated aim is to reduce costs and increase quality. Table 4.2 shows the range of services subject to CCT/market testing in the NHS.

The Audit Commission, created in 1982, acts as a watchdog in this area. Half of its work extends beyond traditional auditing, for it conducts value for money studies which aim to improve economy, efficiency and effectiveness. These values, known as 'Thatcherism', are reflected in the dominant norm in UK government strategy during the 1980s – 'keep it lean and purposeful'. This approach presented a particular challenge for managers. Since the mid-1970s, there has been a demand for managers of public services to be conscious of the resource constraints within which they operate and to optimize the utility derived from their deployment.

Tyson argues that management in an environment dominated by this type of approach may lead to problems of motivation:

> Neither abstruse notions of efficiency, nor incantations about value for money, are likely to prove inspirational to hard-pressed middle ranking civil servants, many of whom will have seen their promotion chances dwindle and their pay fall behind their private sector friends and neighbours. *(1990, p. 28)*

I examine the effects of the environment on performance measurement of managers and professionals in chapter 7.

Table 4.2 Market Testing in the NHS

Range of services market tested up to March 1993	Courier	Microbiology
Admin, information and financial	Creche	MRI – Mobile Resonance Imaging
Advertising and recruitment	Domestic	Nursing home
Agency staffing	Facilities management	Occupational health
Audit	Gardening	Occupational therapy
Banking	Hotel services	Opthalmology
Clerical and secretarial	Laundry/linen	Orthoptics
Computer	Pest control	Pathology
Consultants	Portering	Patient appliance
Financial	Security	Pharmacy
Human resources	Supplies	Radiation protection
Insurance	Switchboard/reception	Speech therapy
Legal	Transport	Sterile supplies
Management services	Waste disposal	Training
Micro-filming	Clinical and clinical support	Education
Hotel and non-clinical support	Biochemistry	Fire
Accommodation	CSSD	Staff
Car parks	HSDU	
Catering	Medical physics	

Source: Financial Times, 1994.

▬▬ The Social Environment ▬▬

Christopher Hood sets out three families of values that figure in debates about organizational design (see table 4.3). Although he describes them as 'core administrative values', they do have a more general application in that they may underpin the thinking of both politicians and tax-paying citizens when making decisions. He calls them sigma, theta, and lambda-type values. Sigma-type values stress the importance of matching resources to specific tasks. As Hood puts it:

> Such values are central, mainstream and traditional in public management. From this point of view, frugality of resource use in relation to given goals is a criterion of success, while failure is counted in terms of instances of avoidable waste and incompetence. *(1991, p. 12)*

Theta-type values are concerned with high ethical standards, probity and rectitude. Concepts such as public accountability, public scrutiny and public trust are emphasized. Hence, the concern is that activities are carried out in a procedurally correct manner. For example, the District Audit scrutinizes the

Table 4.3 Social values in the core public services environment

	Sigma-type values	Theta-type values	Lambda-type values
	Keep it lean and purposeful	*Keep it robust and resilient*	*Keep it honest and fair*
Standard of success	Frugality	Rectitude	Resilience
Standard of failure	Waste	Malversation	Catastrophe
Currency of fairness and failure	Money and time	Trust and entitlements	Security and survival
Control emphasis	Output	Processes	Input/process
Slack	Low	Medium	High

Source: Adapted from Hood, 1991, p. 11

financial probity of local authorities. Lambda-type values concern the resilience of the service, its ability to survive and adapt to a changing environment. For example, a fire brigade is expected to respond effectively to every emergency – which involves large amounts of resources lying idle for long periods of time.

One of the recurring themes of this text has been the changes that have taken place in the way in which public services have been delivered and the demands that are made on public managers. Hood's argument is that the so-called 'new public management':

> can be understood as primarily an expression of sigma-type values. Its claims have lain mainly in the direction of cutting costs and doing more for less as a result of better quality management and different structural design. *(1991, p. 13)*

During the 1990s, these concerns have been particularly influential in the process of resource allocation in public service organizations. Primarily, the aim was to reduce public expenditure in order to enhance the role of the private sector. However, this has not been entirely at the expense of the remaining families of values. The role of institutional values in SLPOs is examined in chapter 6.

The Technological Environment

For core public services, technology operates in the environment in two quite different ways. First, it enlarges the possibilities open to provide a better service. For example, a new medical technology may enable a formerly incurable illness to be cured. Secondly, it enlarges the inequality of information between the providers and users of a service as to the consequences for the patient of a particular course of treatment.

Technology, therefore, embraces the need for public service managers to become not just more skilled but also more professional in their approach to the needs of the public (an issue that was examined in chapter 3). Indeed, in the area of core public services, with its concern for basic human needs, the public may gain more through the development of a stricter professional code for public service managers than through more competition between those providing a public service. I return to the issue of professionals in chapter 7. Be that as it may, technological innovations can now be transferred very easily between nations provided that public service managers are able and willing to learn from foreign practices and absorb new information.

Differing abilities to absorb new technological information may well explain the significant differences that continue to exist between nations in terms of the effectiveness of their core public services for a given outlay of public funds. By definition, in conservative nations, major change can only take place slowly. And if those responsible for the design of capital investment in the core public services are conservative, then the provision of out-of-date services is perpetuated.

In this light, foreign technological innovations in the core public services are most likely to be assimilated if capital investment is in the hands of the most up-to-date and professional of public service managers. Here, indeed, may be the key to great improvements in the delivery of core public services. It also follows that the technological environment is important because capital investment is important.

For present purposes, I have taken the environmental context in terms of the STEP framework. This framework is useful for an understanding of complex processes. I now turn to the process involved in major capital investment decisions, which can have a critical effect on the delivery of public services. Capital investment in one direction means that capital investment in another direction is forgone. For that reason, the decision to invest public funds in such facilities – hospitals, schools, bridges – is strategic, for it determines what the public sector is to be in the long term.

Capital Investment Facilities

An essential condition in core public services is a lack of competitive markets to allocate resources effectively and efficiently. Consequently, in all countries of the modern competitive world, core public services are, to an overwhelming extent, in the public domain. The onus is on the public service supplier to determine the volume and quality of services to be made available to society today, and to determine the capacity of capital facilities at particular times in the future.

Table 4.4 provides examples of capital facilities commonly found in the area of core public services. It will be noted that the facilities are fixed, specialized, durable and a central element in the provision of services in their field. By their nature, they tend to be very expensive – like their counterparts in the private sector, such as steel mills, factories and aircraft – and hence, an investment in such new facilities constitutes a strategic move of the first order of magnitude for the particular sector involved.

Table 4.4 Capital facilities in core public services

Area	Capital facilities
Health	Buildings and equipment for clinics, hospitals, hospices
Education	Buildings and equipment for primary, secondary and higher education
Welfare	Housing for the homeless, welfare offices for benefit distribution
Security	Buildings and equipment for police stations, fire stations, prisons, army depots

To relate capital investment facilities to public sector strategies, we need to develop a set of categories which, in generic language, describes both the strategic objectives and the exact criteria against which the performance of the facilities will be assessed. To construct such a set, two dimensions most obviously present themselves because of their everyday familiarity:

- costs and benefits;
- supply and demand.

Along the first dimension – costs and benefits – the strategic objective giving rise to a capital investment programme can be either cost minimization or benefit maximization. Clearly, at the margin, there is a fundamental difference between these two objectives. A strategy calling for both cost minimization and benefit maximization is a logical absurdity, impossible to achieve. In practice, a new capital facility might reduce the unit costs of the services provided, while increasing the volume and improving the quality of the services. Costs and benefits are basic criteria according to which the performance of capital investment facilities is audited, and anticipation of this necessarily influences those who propose a new facility. Simon (1994), in discussing criteria for allocation decision, makes the very important point that:

> in actuality, administrators in reaching decisions commonly disclaim responsibility for the indirect results of administrative activities. To this point of view we oppose the contrary opinion that the administrator, serving a public agency in a democratic state, must give a proper weight to all community values that are relevant to his activity, and that are reasonably ascertainable in relation thereto, and cannot restrict himself to values that happen to be his particular responsibility. Only under these conditions can a criterion of efficiency be validly postulated as a determinant of action. *(p. 46)*

Florio (1990) has reviewed the British experience of using cost-benefit analysis in the control of public expenditure and he argues that, because of increased pressure of selectivity on their departments, the technique has had limited application. An important impediment in the use of cost benefit analysis was, Florio found, that there was no agreed or accepted measure to quantify benefits to the consumer; consequently, quantity rationing was used. It is difficult to get information on the demands of clients for services (see chapter 3 for a further discussion of this topic) and hence spending departments relied on information supplied by intermediate agents or 'quasi-clients', for example, doctors, magistrates etc.

Thus, Florio observes:

> The preferences of the millions are then substituted by the preferences of the thousands under the control of the departments. These people are in close contact with the 'end-of-the-line' needs the departments are committed to satisfy, but as these needs are regularly observed and measured, there is a fundamental area of uncertainty within each agency and differences among agencies may arise in relation to their attitude to an uncertain environment . . . Policy makers' and their consultants' preferences may simply be the only available ones. *(1990, p. 127)*

Later in this chapter examples of how agencies can improve on the capturing of client preferences are examined. The point made by Simon (1994) above is, however, paramount; it is the benefit to the community which must be weighed in the decision – not simply individual utility. This community aspect of the decision is particularly relevant in core public services because of their aim of increasing (or sustaining) social cohesion and interdependence.

Along the second dimension – supply and demand – the strategic objective could be to meet an increased demand (or want, or need) arising from a change, say, in population – perhaps on the condition that the overall quality of service is not to be lowered. Or it could be to take advantage of a techno-logical innovation in the method of service supply, perhaps on the condition that the overall unit costs are not to rise, or not to rise beyond a specified level. Supply and demand are also basic categories.

Internal Stages in the Process of Public Capital Investment

I come now to the process involved in allocating resources for public capital investment. In identifying the constituent elements in the process, I begin with those elements, or stages, internal to the public sector.

Bower, in his study *Managing the Resource Allocation Process: A Study of Corporate Planning and Investment* (1970), identified three internal stages to the capital investment process: definition, impetus and capital appropriation. Although the Bower study was a landmark, it related to private enterprise, and his stages need to be modified to take account of the conditions of public sector capital investment. Hence, I retitle the stages:

1 strategic and financial assessment (definition)
2 operational judgement (impetus)
3 technical definition (capital appropriation)

These terms are defined below. You will note that the definitions are in line with the comparable terms that Bower uses, but imply a kind of organizational structure that is more centralized, featuring more top–down planning than the organization he took for study.

Major elements can be seen in terms of the roles played by management in the process overall, particularly in activities that influence the process. All field research agrees that, in capital investment decisions, the role of top management includes the strategic and financial assessment of proposals. However, studies by Hayes and Wheelwright (1984), as well as others, demonstrate that the role tends to go beyond that to include:

- the establishment of policy guidelines to direct subordinates in their consideration of investment in capacity expansion, specifically in the consideration of new facilities;
- setting the organizational context within which the long-term process of resource allocation takes place, in order to influence the decisions of the operational managers and functional specialists involved in capital investment proposals. (This particular role was emphasized in the Bower study.)

▬▬▬ Strategic and Financial Assessment ▬▬▬

Top management policy guidelines for capital investment in a new facility are set out in table 4.5. This set of guidelines is adapted from an original in Hayes

Table 4.5 Top management policy guidelines for strategy-driven capital investment decisions for a new facility

1 The capital investment proposal for a new facility is to be related directly to the major elements in the environment.
2 Alternative proposals are to be made and defined creatively. They must represent a broad variety of options compared with past practices.
3 The proposals must address issues of focus and mission, long and short term, as well as size, location, specialization, the amount of capacity to be added, and its timing and cost.
4 A facility investment proposal is to be evaluated in terms of its impact on the performance of other comparable and related facilities within the institutional domain.
5 Specific recommendations are to reflect changes in the long-term strategy of the institution, particularly in regard to how public needs will be accommodated in terms of capacity reserves.
6 Proposals are to be opportunity-created, especially in relation to new and anticipated future public needs, and technological innovation.
7 Protection of the service's focus and the cost effectiveness of the facility are to be specifically provided for.

Source: Adapted from Hayes and Wheelwright, 1984

and Wheelwright (1984) which summarizes 'best practices' in successful enterprises in the USA, Germany and Japan. Account has also been taken of field studies in public enterprises in the UK. The table, therefore, is more than an idealization, for it is rooted in reality. At the same time, few, if any, institutions have followed the guidelines in all respects. They are to be seen as an account of what should be done to improve the effectiveness and efficiency of long-term resource allocation for capacity expansion. The table may also be seen as a formal expression of a capacity strategy.

In the majority of institutions, public and private, capacity strategy is not formally established, and can only be inferred from the pattern of decisions on individual facility proposals. This observation is in line with March's (1976) contention that 'one of the primary ways in which the goals of an organization are developed is by interpreting the decisions it makes'. However, this lack of coherence has negative results. Bower, in his study, showed the impact on subordinate managers of the lack of a formally structured capacity strategy. Many subordinates were discouraged from submitting proposals for new capital investment because they did not know the criteria on which these were judged, with the result of loss of market share in those enterprises facing a growing market, where capacity is the key to success. Thus, the guidelines are best seen as providing an encouraging framework for highly talented operations managers and functional specialists to push their proposals for new capital investment.

It is worth observing here that decisions on capital investment or on formula based funding for core services can be subject to both audit and parliamentary review. A relevant and appropriate example of the latter is the House of Commons Health Committee's (1994) report on the care of mentally ill in the community. The Committee noted the breakdown in communication between hospitals and those charged with support of mentally ill in the community and it recommended that purchasers of mental health services required:

> specific instructions . . . to require providers to implement . . . adequate hospital discharge procedures; clear local operational policies on the management of acute beds; annual reports by providers on the number of service contracts by patients with serious mental illness and by other patients.

In other words, the House of Commons was calling to account the investment decisions made by managers in this important area of core public services. The Committee (1994, pp. 220–1) went on to criticize the existing funding formula used by the Department of Health and recommended:

(a) an urgent review of metropolitan health services;
(b) that a social deprivation score be included as a weighting factor in resource allocation formulae for mental health funding;
(c) that this review address the priorities and funding practices of health authorities and fundholding general practices in relation to the seriously mental ill;

Figure 4.2 Capital investment process in a new facility-two concept: 'top down' and 'bottom up'

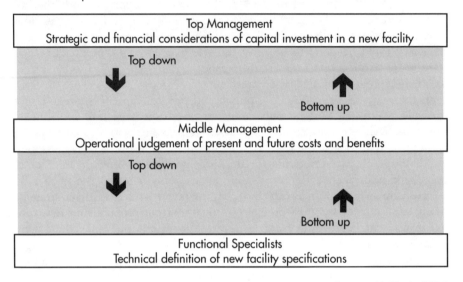

Source: McKevitt 1996

(d) that the specific requirements of the homeless mentally ill be prop-
     erly taken into account in purchasing local mental health services;
(e) the standard spending assessment formula for supported residential
     places be revised properly to allow funded placements for inner-city
     residents on a basis proportionate to need;
(f) that no further reductions in metropolitan mental health services
     budgets to be made until the review referred to in (a) above is
     completed.

This is a clear example of where funding and allocation decisions can be called into account by a higher authority. Whilst the Commons Committee does not have managerial responsibilities, its cross-party composition gives it an influential 'voice' in the review of allocation decisions.

Obviously, a set of guidelines without an appropriate organizational structure could lead to chaos. The function of the organizational context is to influence the rules for deciding the technical definition of new facilities. Ultimately, the purpose of the organization – as well as the performance measurement and rewards system, and the 'rules of the game' – is to align the careers of managers, the job to be done and the flow of information. In this light, if top management feels that the individual proposals for capital investment submitted to it are consistently defective, then it can do something about the problem through changes in the structure, and immediately through changes in the organization. Figure 4.2 characterizes the essentials of an institution where capital investment is a central and important element in overall strategy, and where the process of capital investment is taken very seriously. The organizational structure presented is intended to show that the flow of decisions about capital investment is top–down for some aspects, and bottom–up for others. You will note from figure 4.2 that operations management has a critical role in translating general policies into specific instruction in the top–down aspects of capital investment. Correspondingly, its role is to bring judgement to bear on the technical definition of new proposals submitted by functional specialists.

This judgement is particularly needed given the uncertainties inherent in capital investment proposals. Top management has to structure the organization so as to facilitate the development of such judgement in middle management.

The importance of the organizational context in so far as it allows managers to effect change in the culture and attitudes of those professionals involved in the decision-making process should also be noted. Thus, it will be seen that, while the resource allocation process has a technical (or economic) content, the behavioural component is also important. I shall now consider how this component of the resource allocation process can be managed so as to secure an alignment between strategic goals and the technical operations involved in resource allocation decisions.

Operational Judgement

For present purposes, the operational judgement of present and future costs and benefits in the capital investment process is given to middle management. More exactly, middle management is defined as those charged to exercise such judgement. The reason lies in both the uncertainty of capital investment and in the particular skills and experience possessed by the 'men (or women) in the middle' – those managers who are near enough to functional specialists to understand fully the technical definitions in the proposals for a new capital facility, those who are near enough to the relevant part of the environment to understand the degree of uncertainty in regard to need or demand, and those who are near enough to top management to have an operational understanding of the goals of the institution. That is, those managers in the SLPO whose task it is to give operational definition and implementation to policy decisions which require capital investment. I shall deal first with the problems of uncertainty.

In capital investment for a new facility the problem of uncertainty can best be seen by middle management in two quite different dimensions:

- uncertainty of the value of the facility's services in future years;
- uncertainty as to the second-order effects of the existence of the facility in future years.

Kenneth Arrow was not optimistic that such uncertainty could be reduced. He noted:

Table 4.6 Top management policy on capacity expansion strategies; alternatives on costs and benefits; guidelines for operational managers

Strategy A	Capacity lags demand; maximize the utilization of capacity to meet goal of minimizing costs.
Strategy B	Capacity leads needs or demand; capacity used as 'cushion' to meet goal of maximizing benefits.
Strategy C	Capacity to match average level of need or demand, achieving balance in costs and benefits.

Source: Adapted from Hayes and Wheelwright, 1984

> There are some special problems in applying the price system to investment. The pay-off is in the future whereas the commitment is in the present: the efficiency check provided by prices is not the same as for a transaction for a current moment of time. The pay-off is only as expected, not an actual pay-off, and this is a serious problem for a firm deciding on investment. The accountability that would ideally be called for is not really there, because when the future comes, it is a little too late to worry about whether you should have made the investment: it is already there . . . The investment planner is never completely on the ground of currently known facts but rather on the grounds of conjecture. *(1985, p. 115)*

Uncertainty is no less significant in the public sector, nor is the problem of deciding how to cope with it. Managers with a high degree of judgement in this matter should be secured. Uncertainty enters capital investment as a threat to goal achievement. Because of economies of scale, a new facility tends to add 'chunks' of capacity when it comes on stream. Assuming for a moment that there is no uncertainty, a goal of cost minimization will relate the timing of capital investment to changes in need or demand in a quite different way than would the goal of benefit maximization.

This difference is demonstrated between Strategy A and Strategy B in table 4.6, which also includes a balancing goal (Strategy C) midway between cost minimization and benefit maximization.

Senior managers have to ensure the achievement of one or other of these goals – which, of course, in public enterprise are taken from the political environment – and therefore have to influence decisions throughout the institutions, including capital investment decisions. This means structuring the goals in an operationally meaningful way (as in Strategies A, B or C). However, uncertainty will threaten the goals.

The structure shown in table 4.6 enables top management to see the impact of uncertainty on the trend in the need of, or demand for, the services. If, say, need or demand turns out to be greater in the future than predicted, then the impact of having capacity expansion planned for a specified time period can be best assessed in terms of possible shortfalls in capacity at particular times, the effect of relationships with the environment, and the risks involved. In this light, proposals for new facilities can be more critically evaluated and, in the

Table 4.7 Operational management: decision guidelines on capacity expansion for service delivery

---

1   Predicted growth and variability (uncertainty) of public needs or demands by region
2   Estimated costs and building and operating facilities of differing sizes
3   Predicted rate and direction of technological innovation in the supply of services
4   Anticipated changes in behaviour of major elements in the environment as a result of a new facility, assessed by different facility capacities
5   Impact of the facility over its lifetime on existing and projected facilities in the region
6   Comparison of the projected performance of the facility with related facilities at home and abroad, and projections over time

---

Source: Adapted from Schmenner, 1982

first instance, sharper proposals can be developed from the submissions of the functional specialists.

A good and pertinent example of this review by functional specialists is to be found in the internal document produced by the New Zealand Ministry of Health (1992) on the government's proposals for services to the disabled. In this case, demand for future services was a key issue as it was in the case of the UK example earlier in respect of the mentally ill. The New Zealand document draws attention to the proposed formula for funding services and observes that:

(i)   Attention is drawn to the fact that inaccurate statistics on the number of people with disabilities who require support for daily living were presented . . . It is suggested that a better statistical base is required if funds are to be allocated to services for particular consumer groups in proportion to their numbers.

(ii) It is also pointed out that raw numbers do not necessarily correspond to the level of need within a consumer population. Nor is uptake of current programmes a reliable indicator of need. Many services are provided by informal caregivers with no outside assistance and it is felt that levels of unmet need are significant. Both of these are difficult to quantify.

(iii) It is felt that in the specification of core services, vociferous interest groups may gain considerable advantage at the expense of more vulnerable consumers and services. *(1992, pp. 63–7)*

These responses by functional specialists were given in the context of a published government discussion document, public consultation seminars, and receipt of some 426 written submissions. Further examples of New Zealand's consultation process in the field of education are examined in chapters 5 and 6.

To arrive at an operational judgement on the degree of uncertainty in a proposal for a new facility submitted by functional specialists, middle management has to develop rules for decision-making. These may take the shape of a set of guidelines, as in table 4.7, which was adapted from Schmenner's field studies (Schmenner, 1982). You should note where the major uncertainties are expected.

The operational judgement role of middle management was described by Bower in terms of whether or not a proposal from technical specialists should be given impetus, that is, be forwarded up the hierarchy.

Bower describes the calculation brought to this process as follows:

> Whether impetus is forthcoming depends on two kinds of evaluation made by the [middle] manager in question. The first is his [or her] evaluation of the project. In particular, the [middle] manager must believe the sales forecast justifying the income projected, otherwise a project is dead . . . [and] . . . must also accept the technical aspects of a project, but typically, he expects his subordinates to be technically qualified, either personally or in the support obtained during the definition process. It should be recognized that in employing the market judgement, the [middle] manager . . . is exercising the responsibility delegated to him by making a judgement on the basis of his local expert competence. *(1970, p. 58)*

Bower continues:

> The second kind of evaluation the [middle] manager makes is an estimate of the benefits of being 'right' and the cost of being 'wrong' . . . the manager's perception of these factors is shaped by the structure of the organization, the way his job is defined, how the performance of his business is measured, the kinds of information available to him, and the way in which his performance is evaluated and rewarded.

In ways of coping with uncertainty, middle managers do not differ greatly from one kind of institution to another. The effects of organizational structure on management decision-making are examined in chapter 6.

In the event, once middle management has decided in favour of a capital investment project, the proposal must be submitted in a much simpler form than that presented by the functional specialists. Table 4.8 shows the typical shape of a proposal for capital investment in a new facility submitted to top management by a middle manager. It will be noted that uncertainty is dealt with under the heading of 'sensitivity analysis'.

You should now read the case study 'Capital accounting case study: UK local government' by Geoff Jones, which is in the appendix. This case study illustrates a number of the themes in this chapter: the role of specialists, the influence of capital decision making and the role of stakeholders in the decision-making process. You could also answer the questions set out at the end of the case study. You will see from your reading of the case study that the issue of capital decision-making is not simply a technical function and that it has implications for wider values in the SLPOs. As we will see later in this book, the issues of values in decision-making extends to the management and measurement of professional activity and, indeed, it underpins the reorganization of institutions delivering core public services.

Table 4.8 Operations management: draft proposal to top management for capital investment in a new facility

1 General comments
2 Present
  Existing capacity
  Future requirements
3 What is proposed
  Services to be delivered
  Location
  Physical facilities needed
  Advantages
  Risks
  Costs
4 Financial analysis of the proposal
5 Sensitivity analysis
6 Recommendations
7 Timetable and implementation plan
8 Appendix as required

Source: Adapted from Hayes and Wheelwright, 1984

Table 4.9 Functional specialists: technical definition of a new facility

1 Definition of the services to be provided and desired delivery date
2 Facility capacity, size, location, cost and time on stream
3 Specific processes to be used and work flow/pattern within the facility
4 Number of workers, mix of skills and workforce goals
5 Human resource development policies to meet workforce goals
6 Control system to be employed to ensure desired service delivery
7 Interrelationship between this new facility and existing comparable and related facilities, as well as with clients
8 Overhead function and support staff to be provided – both core and peripheral
9 Consideration of subsequent expansion of the facility and development of its human resources
10 Capabilities not required of the facility
11 Events that would cause a change in the basic plan for the facility

Source: Adapted from Schmenner, 1982

▬▬▬ Technical Definition ▬▬▬

The third internal stage is the development by functional specialists of the technical definitions of the proposed new facility in terms mainly of capacity, scope, level of expenditure required, and the date of availability. An example of the content of a technical definition is given in table 4.9. However, as Bower has noted:

> One of the issues that must be examined is what happens to this definition over time as the investment process develops. *(1970, p. 53)*

Assuming the definitions are a response to signs of a particular unmet need, then, if it is believed that other issues should enter into the facility definition (such as facility plans for other regions), explicit steps must be taken to introduce them. In Bower's words again:

> Either other managers concerned with these issues must intervene in the process of definition or the framework of the original definers' perception must be changed. Unless one of these steps is taken the original perception will constitute the sole conceptual framework shaping the final investment project.

One example of how the technical definition can be altered is to be found in the work of the New Zealand National Advisory Committee on Core Health and Disability Support Services. This advisory body, set up under statute, uses Consensus Conferences to bring together expert, client and provider opinion to provide advice to policy makers when they are making technical decisions on the scope and level of funding for services.

In its report for 1994/95 the Committee (1993, pp. 38–9) noted the following principles for support services:

- participation in society
- improved quality of life
- consistency in the delivery of services
- empowerment of individuals with disabilities
- cost-effective services
- services which are affordable
- services which are secure
- people with disabilities are involved in designing services
- services are flexible and responsive
- services are minimally intrusive and restrictive

The Committee also noted: 'the realistic expectations held by people with disabilities. They do not want everything. But they want the services that are funded within available public resources to better meet their needs'. The work of the Core Services committee in the area of technical definition dovetails with my earlier discussion of the internal Ministry of Health document in the area of disability. Here there is a useful example of how operational judgement and technical definition can be combined to give a more sustained and defensible decision on both the scope and level of expenditure on services. It can now be seen that the decision-making required is both detailed and iterative along the lines of the policy process model that was set out in table 4.1. A failure to incorporate such detail, or to ignore the voice of consumers, can lead to the decision being criticized by outside bodies, as for example we saw in chapter 3 in the report of the Commissioner for Administration for England and Wales.

The question then is how to influence the conceptual framework in terms of the functional specialists' internalized rules of decision-making. This is a crucial question in shaping the capital investment process. As already mentioned, top management does possess levers to influence the technical expert's definition of an investment project, that is, the expert's perception of what is needed. Five decades ago, Herbert Simon (1947) identified the most important levers, namely:

- organization structure;
- measurement and rewards;
- 'rules of the game'.

Changes in these levers indicate to the functional specialist 'what is now expected of me'. They play an important role in shaping the internalized rules of decision-making used to clarify the demands of the job. If top management feels it necessary to change the decision rules, it can use the levers to change the structure within which the functional specialists do their work. For example, if top management in a department of education wishes to reduce the downside risk of excess school capacity when a new school facility comes on stream, it can relate the proposals of functional specialists to capital usage. The object is to ensure that the functional specialists will define the capital facility in relation to the overall strategy as articulated by top-management and middle-management guidelines.

Chapters 6 and 7 examine how changes in organizational structure and performance measurement have been used to effect changes in responsiveness and in the management of professional service providers.

For convenience of exposition, the major elements in the capital investment decision process have been presented sequentially. In reality, there is interdependence between these major elements, and, therefore, continuous interaction between the personnel involved. This is particularly true if the environment is turbulent or otherwise unstable, and the penalty of being wrong is far reaching. Capacity expansion through investment in a new facility is no small thing, and therefore the need for interaction is great. I examine in chapter 6 how different organization structures can help or impede interaction between provider, manager and client.

▬▬ Conclusion ▬▬

This chapter has presented a number of frameworks for analysis of the external environment, outlined the stages involved in the capital allocation process and argued the importance of having managers who are familiar with these frameworks involved in the expenditure decision. In looking at recent UK and New Zealand experience, it was found that a most noteworthy omission in the allocation decision was a failure to adequately ascertain the opinion and advice of the citizen–client. In the case of the UK, external bodies such as the Audit Commission can, in part, compensate for citizen 'voice', yet this avenue is not sufficient in itself, as we saw in the case of services for the mentally ill. In New Zealand we saw examples of how both official and statutory committees actively sought out the opinions of the citizen–client, both in the formation of policy decisions and in the review of the effectiveness of their adequacy and scope of funding. The techniques and frameworks in this chapter cannot, therefore, be read and applied in isolation. Whilst they are based on best practice in the private and public sector, they have to be augmented by appropriate channels for citizen-voice, an issue that was examined in chapter 3. Decisions on investment also have to take account of the internal structure of the SLPO, and how values other than the economic are featured in the decision; these important structural questions are looked at in chapter 6. Capital allocation (or indeed revenue) decisions also have to be placed in their strategic context; what services, for whom? – I now turn in the next chapter to an evaluation of the strategic framework for government services and how different countries have tackled the important issue of strategic control in the management of core public services.

CHAPTER

5

Strategic Control of Core Public Services

 **Introduction**

The last three chapters have examined important functions carried out by the public service manager: identification of citizen need, delivery of services that target these needs and the investment decisions that support the delivery process. In this chapter another important part of the public service manager's role is examined: control of the delivery process to ensure that broad policy objectives are translated into measurable and reliable services to clients. Strategic control is central to the success of any organizational activity: the broad policy objectives of government have to be translated into legislation and programmes, new organizational structures and relationships created and sustained if policy is to be implemented. Knowledge and understanding of the control function is important for the public services manager and this chapter examines the issue of strategic control through an examination of the strategic frameworks adopted by a number of countries to control their public service delivery systems – the UK, Ireland, New Zealand and Sweden. The chapter centres on the following key aspects of public service control:

- legislative frameworks that provide for control of public service delivery systems;
- the model of control adopted by New Zealand which has been seen as the most radical restructuring of public service control in modern economies;
- the process of strategic control that ensures compliance with governments' policy objectives.

This chapter, together with chapter 2, comprises the major theoretical part of the text. The data in this chapter are primarily concerned with strategy and, as a result, the discussion is centred on policy objectives (the 'mission') of core public services.

The strategic orientation of the chapter provides us with a platform for chapters 6 and 7 which are focused on organizational and performance aspects of core public services. Unless, however, service delivery is set within a strategic context, the reform programmes of the countries studied become simply a narrative of change rather than a structured scrutiny of purposeful public activity. Strategy provides a framework for analysis and supplies us with a comparative framework for the analysis of government activity.

In examining strategic control in public service delivery we acknowledge that many public service managers are not themselves involved in the strategy formulation phase which is usually the domain of the politician (see the Hogwood and Gunn model set out in table 4.1). The drafting of legislation is a very specialized task and is the preserve of legal specialists. However, in conducting the field research for this study I encountered numerous public servants across many countries who had to contend with the effects of legislation or changes in government policy. These street-level managers have an important role to play in implementing legislation, their advice and interpretation of government policies also have a profound effect on the citizen–clients who look to them for effective services. It will be seen later in this chapter that legislation embodying strategic control is itself an outcome of bargaining between major stakeholders – government, political parties, interest groups – and that outcomes can have consequences that run counter to the original intentions of the legislators. Such consequences as, for example, the UK government's modification of the national curriculum (post-Dearing 1994), remind us that government policy cannot assume compliance from the service providers; neither can the passage of legislation ensure that policy objectives are achieved.

It is this dialogue between the main players in the strategic control process that an open-systems model (discussed in chapter 2) incorporates in its assumptions – a government department cannot operate effectively by assuming its policy objectives were clearly understood and articulated to all interested parties.

The public service manager is one of the focal points for this two-way process of control: control downwards via legislative and policy frameworks and control upwards via the feedback which managers provide from the citizen–clients that the policy is intended to serve. An effective framework of strategic control requires this dual mechanism and the public service manager is an integral part of it. See figure 5.1 which is reproduced from chapter 2 for convenience. This chapter is, therefore, concerned with one of the primary instruments of strategic control in core public services – legislation.

▬ **Definition of the Control Function** ▬

We can view control as comprising a number of interrelated features. First, the processes involved in the control function – setting of objectives for service delivery and measurement of those objectives. These processes are usually

Figure 5.1 Tensions in the SLPO environment

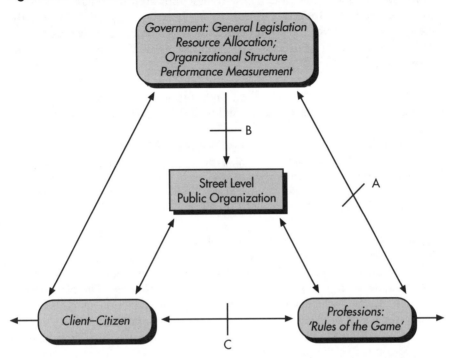

Source: Adapted from Wrigley and McKevitt 1995

described using the terms 'efficiency', 'are we doing things right?', and 'effect-iveness', 'are we doing the right things?' I will return to these processes in chapter 7 and observe here that, in areas of core public services, such terms can be very difficult to operationalize and measure. The measurement of objectives in social provision involves quite complex and demanding skills if it is to be effective. I examine later in this chapter the experience of New Zealand in its attempt to reorganize administrative arrangements in public service delivery to ensure professional compliance and service. New Zealand pursued its strategy through a relentless use of the purchase–provider model in core public services. New Zealand gives us an opportunity to examine a form of control which clearly articulates one of the central challenges in public management – the 'capture' model based on the premise that government workers will absorb incremental additions of expenditure through salaries and side payments that were intended for the provision of services.

What, then, is the nature of control in public service organizations and what is meant when people use terms such as 'the organization is out of control'? A good definition is offered by Peter Drucker who describes the function of control as bringing a 'social order' to the organization. In this perspective Drucker views control as a social process, seeing it as part of the organization's value system. Such a perspective is sympathetic to the public service manager where the act of service is part of a wider social transaction – the creation and maintenance of social cohesion. These transactions are the primary purpose of core public services. Indeed, Drucker in his later writings has identified the values of public and not-for-profit organization as integral to their effectiveness and he sees such control processes as having important lessons for the private sector organizations.

Another feature of control is that it embodies, in an overt or implicit manner, important assumptions regarding the motivation and incentive structures of managers and the citizen–client. Child offers the following description:

> Control within an organization is a process whereby management and other groups are able to initiate and regulate the conduct of activities so that the results accord with the goals and expectations held by these groups. Control, in other words, is aimed at ensuring that a predictable level and type of performance is attained and maintained. *(1984, p. 136)*

A primary instrument of strategic control in the public service is legislation which sets out the strategic objectives of government policy.

We are concerned here with a particular type of legislation: I examine later in this chapter examples of strategic legislation from Sweden, The Netherlands and New Zealand which seeks to guide the broad direction of government policies and which provides a focus for the measurement of performance against measurable objectives. Hence, legislation in this context is broadly similar to strategic control in the private sector which is a process that measures return on investment against strategic objectives.

Legislation, therefore, plays an important function in the control process. I acknowledge that legislation is not, in itself, sufficient to guarantee success; the committed participation of professionals in the delivery process is also necessary. I return to the theme of professional participation in chapter 7. The open-systems model described in chapter 2 provides for a fuller understanding of the management process for public service delivery; a 'two-way' process of control is outlined, and the open systems model, stressing as it does interdependency rather than competition, is capable of deepening our understanding of the control function. I return to the open-systems model in the next section.

The recent UK legislation in education provision is predicated on the assumption that public dissemination of school results ('league tables') will give parents more information and, hence, more choice in their selection of schools and that such league tables will provide incentives for school principals and boards of governors to bring their staff up to an acceptable level of service delivery. Leaving aside, for the present, the feasibility and acceptability of such measurement devices, it can be seen that control has to be congruent with the norms and values of the staff delivering the service. If it is not, then an immediate and pressing issue arises: how do you motivate and discipline professional staff who do not accept the validity of the measurement system? These issues are explored later in chapter 7, where I examine in some detail the relationships between professionals and performance measures and the defensive routines that organizations engage in when confronted by what they perceive to be inappropriate control.

The idea that public sector organizations are easily controlled through the importation of private sector techniques is not sustained by the evidence and data in this study. It is clear, however, that where public sector professionals and the citizen–clients agree with the broad intention of reform, then an increase in service effectiveness is attainable. Best practices in service delivery, strategic control and organization design from a range of countries support this partnership argument.

The control process is itself rectificatory and not restorative; that is, it is about the maintenance of service standards and the following of rules rather than the process by which such standards and rules are set in the first instance. How are service standards set in the public services and how can the control function contribute to their maintenance? There are three basic ways in which one can formulate goals or standards: by reference to the past – 'we are now investing more resources in education provision for special needs'; by reference to some other country – 'Sweden has clearly-defined legislative objectives which promote equity in health care resource allocation'; by reference to some social or political ideal – 'the UK clearly needs to invest more in the education of ethnic groups if it is to be regarded as a modern social democratic state'. The value of comparative research is that it helps to place such evaluation in a context that public service managers recognize – the allocation of attention and resources in an environment of conflicting stakeholder objectives.

The process of strategic control, therefore, comprises a number of related areas:

- legislative, the public statement of service and resourcing strategies;
- administrative, structuring of public organizations for effective performance;
- professional, the management and motivation of professional staff so that a responsive and dignified service is delivered to the citizen–client.

I examine administrative structures in chapter 6 and the management of professionals in chapter 7.

Legislation and Strategic Control

A corporate strategy model – 'An Open Systems Model of the Firm', briefly discussed in chapter 2 – is relevant and pertinent for the study of strategic control in public services. The model asserts that:

1   any organization relates to its environment via a strategy for advancing its interests as it perceives these interests;

2   the interests of the various sub-units of an organization often differ from those of the organization as a whole; and

3   thus the central or general headquarters of the organization must bring continuous influence to bear on the sub-units in order to motivate them to act in conformity with the general or shared interests of the organization.

The most important means of influence (according to the model) are the ability to allocate resources, to establish and alter organizational structures, to measure and reward performance and to formulate policy limits or 'rules of the game'.

The open-systems model seeks to explain how central government could direct the activities of its administrative apparatus whilst allowing for some degree of autonomy and initiative. The application of the model to strategic control of national health care systems is described in the next section. Central to the model's assumptions is that government has to apply a range of controls, budgetary, organizational and measurement of performance if it is to succeed in its strategic objectives. That is, given the diversity of stakeholder interests and the turbulent environment there is no single 'one best way' to organize for effective delivery and control. The diversity of government responses across a range of countries is examined closely to understand the importance of coherence of controls.

In New Zealand's case, for example, a coherent model was applied – that of agency capture – across all areas of core public services, an example of the application of a 'one best way' model in quite different environmental contexts, from industry regulation through to health care. The open-systems model, which stresses individual diversity within an overall strategic framework, is an appropriate framework for the analysis of core public services. Inattention to regulation of professionals, including their training, or an overemphasis on mechanistic regulatory prescriptions are examples of inappropriate use of strategic controls.

An important part of the control process is the setting of objectives and measurement standards whereby organizational success can be evaluated. It was noted in chapter 1 that a primary objective or outcome of core public service provision was the creation and maintenance of social cohesion and interdependence. I examine here how such processes can be translated into strategic objectives for managers and professional staff.

One of the most important instruments for setting objectives in the public service – and for trying to ensure responsive resource allocations to areas of greatest need – is through the passage of laws, which set out the objectives and intentions of public service provision. Critics of public service bureaucracy argue that organizations are stifled by rules and regulations which inhibit responsive service delivery. There is some validity to these criticisms and they will be examined in more detail in chapter 6. Legislation provides a basic mission statement or strategy for the provision of public services and provides a framework for resource allocation directed at specific and targeted citizen–client groups. Let us examine one of the largest public services, health care, both in expenditure and personnel, to understand the critical importance of legislation in the process of strategic control.

Official thinking on health care delivery in the UK is reflected in the re-structuring of health care management and delivery variously described as the 'purchaser–provider split' and the development of 'quasi-markets' in service provision with the establishment of NHS Trust hospitals and GP fundholding practices. These developments are based on a number of assumptions concerning the relationship between funding and management of health services delivery which are thought to provide greater efficiency and effectiveness in the overall system of care. These assumptions, largely untested and not based on detailed research, can be expressed as follows:

1 that there is benefit to be gained from separating funding of health care delivery from direct provision of services, that is, to establish hospital budgets for large acute public hospitals which are institution-ally separate from other sources of funding;
2 that administrative and managerial structures should be uniform throughout the system;
3 that further centralization of control will result in greater effective-ness, that is the abolition of Regional Health Authorities and the ministerial appointment of chairmen of Trust Boards;
4 that increased use of performance measurement systems will ensure greater accountability and responsiveness in the system.

In official thinking on health care a heavy reliance is placed on structural and budgetary arrangements which, though important, reflect a general propensity to seek solutions that are technical and operational in character. The problem is presented in narrow terms, for example, 'how can we reduce hospital waiting times' or 'how can we develop performance targets for some aspects of GP practice, rather than as an examination of the strategic framework required for health care management.

The introduction of GP fundholding, under the NHS and Community Care Act 1990, allows GPs who volunteer for the scheme to receive a budget to cover the costs of some hospital and community services, prescriptions for drugs and the salaries of non-medical practice staff. In a 1997 report, the Audit Commission noted that fundholding practices had, up to 1994/5, re-ceived some £232 million to cover the costs of staff, equipment and computers to manage fundholding, while £206 million in efficiency savings were made by fundholders in the same period. Increases in quality of care by fundholders, the Audit Commission argues, could tip the balance in favour of fundholding. It is not possible to compare the performance of fundholding versus non-fundholding practices because 'practices that join the scheme are self-selected and fundholders differ significantly from other practices in ways that make it impossible to tell how much observed differences in benefits to patients are caused by the fact that they are fundholders and how much by their other attributes' (1997, p. 9). In its review of performance, the Audit Commission makes a set of recommendations. Interesting from our perspective is the set of proposals on ascertaining citizen voice and accountability relationships.

Recommendations

1   Fundholders should learn from the best practice of their peers and:

- invest in high calibre management within the practice, involve their patients and the local community in decision taking, purchase a wide range of benefits for their patients and take up difficult challenges such as evidence-based purchasing.

2   The new health authorities should invest in training and develop support mechanisms for their fundholders. Specifically, they should:

- measure fundholders' performance against indicators of patient benefits including those listed in this report;
- use performance indicators to set individual targets for fundholders to improve their management of the fund and their approach to purchasing;
- identify leading-edge fundholders in their area and find ways of involving them in developing their peers;
- create opportunities for their own staff and GPs to benefit from joint learning; and
- make expertise available to fundholders in areas such as public health, IT and financial management.

3   The NHS Executive should consult further on proposals to change the Accountability Framework and the regulations governing the scheme. In particular, they should aim to make fundholders:

- provide evidence that they are taking account of their patients' priorities and consulting them about their purchasing plans;
- incorporate Health of the Nation and Patients' Charter targets into their contracts; and
- take account of local health priorities in their plans.

4   The NHS Executive should consider urgently the policy changes needed to improve fundholder purchasing. The options include:

- tighten – or expect health authorities to tighten – the criteria for entry to the scheme and require practices to show how they meet the scheme's standards;
- introduce contracts between health authorities and fundholders as a mechanism for making sure that fundholders use the fund efficiently and effectively; and
- introduce either an accreditation system or an inspectorate that will give an independent judgement on practices' suitability to become, and remain, budget holders.

(Audit Commission, 1997)

Here again, as we saw in chapters 2 and 3, is the evidence that reforms which are broadly institutional in character (top–down), ignore, or place less emphasis on, citizen voice. It is also the case that fundholding, because it is not a uniform nationwide phenomenon, opens up the argument of a two-tier level of service in a unitary NHS system. Since the NHS legislation does not, as in Sweden, specifically target equity in service provision, there is no impetus to measure and account for disparity in service provision. You have, therefore, a technical framework of reform which does not meet the needs of social cohesion and interdependence that characterize core public services.

It is clear that other countries, confronted by similar challenges in health care policy, have responded differently from the UK and that strategic legislation is a central component of this response. Legislation is also important in the context of the policy for the re-orientation of health care provision towards preventive, community-based care. It is difficult to see how such a policy could be implemented without a legislative statement of its aims and objectives. That is, without a clearly articulated legislative strategy for a new policy, the sunk investment costs pursued under the previous policy will prevent resource reallocation.

Indeed, we can reflect that the absence of a legislative strategy to underpin some of the major UK policy shifts in education and health care probably accounts for their relative lack of success. I do not, of course, propose to view that legislation, even if it is cast in a strategic dimension such as is found in Swedish health care, is a guarantee of strategic control. Policy makers have numerous and conflicting demands on their attention and legislation can also be viewed partly as a symbolic act which represents good intentions rather than administrative clarity. As Arnold observed:

> It is part of the function of how to give recognition to ideals representing the exact opposite of established conduct. Most of the complications arise from the necessity of pretending to do one thing, while actually doing another. *(1935, p. 34)*

It will be seen, for example, in chapter 7 that the rational model presented by New Zealand's Public Finance Act, 1989, in respect of government departments specifying their outputs and outcomes, comes face-to-face with the intractability of trying to specify in a numerate/monetary manner quite complex social relationships. The ambiguity of the policy process can, therefore, be carried over into the legislative function.

The process of strategic control embedded in the open-systems model reflects the complexity of the control process; legislation forms one part of the control function, administrative control together with professional regulation is also integral to the process. The field data in this study demonstrates one key attribute of the control function – beware the great simplifiers – the advocates of a 'one best way' to manage complex social and economic relationships. The countries examined in this chapter adapted and changed their legislation to take account of, and give effect to, changes in their health care investment strategies. Such changes have to take account of existing custom and practice and not seek to impose novel reforms which do not acknowledge the diversity and complexity of existing professional and client relationships.

▃▃▃ **Examples of Legislative Controls** ▃▃▃

How then can we understand recent developments in health care services in the United Kingdom for managers and professionals? One could do so by presenting the mission of the UK care managers as being concerned with the 'delivery of quality services at the lowest possible cost'. We could then examine relevant national and European indicators and try to understand how, and in what manner, different health care structures support effectiveness, citizen choice and responsiveness. We could then proceed to make some proposals for change in the UK arrangements. We are, however, prevented from such an enquiry by the absence of any formal legislative statement which specifies the strategic objectives of the UK health care system – that is, unlike a number of European countries, the UK and Ireland have no strategic framework that would guide the allocation process, provide for a control system responsive to agreed objectives and give legitimacy to the resource decisions of health care managers.

What does it mean to state that the UK lacks a clear legislative statement of its health care strategy? National health care systems which are primarily funded from taxation, rather than insurance based systems, are, in general, less costly and are subject to 'capping' by governments of their expenditure. Hence, it is easier to constrain the general level of health care expenditure in the UK, Ireland and New Zealand than in the United States where government expenditure accounts for some 40 per cent of total health expenditure, and where there is a large insurance-based private market in health care provision.

In this restricted sense, the UK can be seen as a cost effective system. However, the UK legislation governing health care (its most recent expression being the National Health Service and Community Care Act 1990) does not contain any explicit strategy that would help guide the allocation and investment decision. For example, there is near general agreement world-wide that hospital care is more costly and less effective for a range of illnesses (many hospitals have been used as a substitute for care in the community), yet the UK system of care is still primarily a hospital based one. While budgetary and structural adjustments, including activity based cost systems such as Diagnostic Related Groupings (DRG), have been applied to hospital care, there has been in the UK no clearly articulated legislative strategy for the redirection of resources to community based programmes. Nor has there been in the UK any formal recognition of the socio-economic and cultural inequities which underpin some medical and health care disorders. There was only one recent example of quasi-public investigation in this area, but it never received formal government recognition. The evidence strongly suggests that there is middle-class capture of health care resources. Any system of publicly financed social provision requires a clear articulation of legislative strategy to guide (or to redirect) the allocation process: in the absence of such statements, policy commitments are subject to a complex administrative and professional 'rent seeking' process whereby inertia and incremental change can severely inhibit a strategic refocusing of the investment decision. That is, without legislative impetus existing patterns of resource allocation and stakeholder relationships will be maintained.

The World Health Organization (WHO) strategy for health care in the year 2000 is primarily concerned with the socio-economic determinants of health status and the re-orientation of health service policy towards a preventive, community-based approach. The policy entitled 'Health for All by the Year 2000' was agreed in 1984.

The first target states: 'by the year 2000, the actual differences in health status between groups within countries should be reduced by at least 25 per cent, by improving the level of health of disadvantaged nations and groups'. In its suggested solution to this problem the WHO states: 'the target on health inequalities present a challenge; to change the trend by improving the health opportunities of disadvantaged nations and groups so as to enable them to catch up with their more privileged counterparts.'

> Within individual countries this policy implies above all a willingness in recognizing the problem, for initiative in actively seeking information on the real extent of the phenomenon, and for political will in designing social policies that go to the root of social group formation, in terms of guaranteed minimum income, assurance of the right to work, active outreach services to assist the groups in need, etc. *(WHO, 1984, p. 46)*

It is clear that if the UK was to seek to achieve these targets, which are primarily rooted in social, economic and resource considerations, then legislation would need to be altered, not only to change the organization of service delivery but to embed the equity statement outlined in the target above. Despite the many legislative and structural changes to the UK health care system no such legislative strategy has been enacted.

Thus, for example, the research programme adopted by WHO includes a priority to be given to research on inequities in health. The WHO document states:

> the two basic goals of health care are to raise the overall level of health and to increase equity; inequities may relate to social status or class, sex and gender, ethnic grouping or geographic location.
>
> Three areas of research are needed with regard to equity; theoretical and methodological work on concepts and indicators of health inequalities; a better understanding of the factors and mechanisms that create and maintain health inequalities and policy research and evaluation of programmes aimed at reducing health inequalities. *(WHO, 1984)*

To monitor progress, it is suggested that countries must carry out routine data collection that bears on health differences; it is clear that in the UK such data collection is not done on any systematic basis.

This contrasts with the Dutch and Swedish legislative responses to the challenge posed by the WHO strategy. This disparity also extends to the measurement system used in these countries where there is a clear concern to review the practical effects of health care policy. The following extract gives an outline of the Swedish health care system:

Sweden's Health Care: Legislative Provision and Administrative Arrangements

Swedish health care is decentralized with the twenty three County Councils having responsibility for health care provision and expenditure, based on local taxation. Swedish policy on health services, which is oriented to the implementation of the WHO 'Health for All' programme, began with a series of research programmes in 1978. These were published in 1982, and circulated to politicians, health care professionals and the public. The Act of Parliament, which was based on these research proposals and documents, was passed in June 1985. The guidelines underlying the Act HS-90 were:

(a)   health care must be characterized by active health policies;
(b)   the need of the population for care must determine the allocation of health care resources;
(c)   health care resources must be weighed against socio-economic and employment goals and limitations.

Discussion documents focused on socio-economic differences in health care utilization, social and occupational distribution of prevalent diseases, and correlation between health hazards and illness groups.
  Sweden's legislation states that health care on equal terms requires:

(a)   equality in the supply of resources available through out different parts of the country;
(b)   equality in the utilization of care between different groups of society;
(c)   equality in terms of access to care;
(d)   equality in terms of quality and efficiency of care.

The Swedish system provides a clear example of a nation that has attempted to achieve congruence between strategy, measurement and management. The social and political consensus in Sweden, relative to the aims and objectives of health care policy is in marked contrast to the UK situation. *(McKevitt, 1993, p. 312)*

  The economic climate of Sweden has, of course, changed quite significantly since the major health care reforms of the 1980s and Sweden has had to confront quite important social and economic priorities in order to adjust its health care system to the new economic conditions. For example, an analysis by SKTF (Swedish Union of Local Government Officers) of expenditure proposals of local authorities carried out, in 1994, showed there were projected job losses of some 25,000 to 30,000; that expenditure on child care services has decreased by some 10 per cent (in 1993) and that expenditure on elderly services, hitherto protected, are expected to be curtailed.
  An important feature of recent Swedish experience is the activity of public service trade unions in reaction to the economic cutbacks in all areas of social provision. On fieldwork for this study, I was struck by the initiative and innovation displayed by the trades unions as they sought to accommodate their member interests to the new strategic environment.

It was seen in chapter 3 how Kommunal, the largest blue collar trade union in Sweden, has recognized the need for strategic partnership with public service employers. Indeed, Kommunal has established a consultancy unit which advises local authorities on efficiency issues! The response of public service unions in New Zealand mirror, in part, those in Sweden. Such partnership can be accounted for largely by the tradition of social consensus in these countries; it is also the case that the unions, unlike their UK counterparts, perceive an advantage in co-operation rather than a continuation of adversarial roles. I return to this issue in chapter 7.

The Swedish health care legislation whilst outlining a clear legislative strategy of equality has had to contend with changes in the economic and political environment since its passage in 1985. In seeking to promote efficiency in its health care system, Sweden has encouraged a limit on national regulation and encouraged experimentation and change at the local level to increase responsiveness. The major changes have been:

- increased influence for the patient who will enjoy full freedom to choose health care provider;
- new methods of political control where the politicians shall act as purchasers and respresentatives of the patients;
- reformed payment systems for the health care providers;
- establishment of competition and development towards different forms of operation. *(Hakansson and Nordling 1997, p. 211)*

Raffel (1997) in a review of changes in the Swedish system noted that where decentralization happens, after a long period of central control, there is a risk of error as different approaches are tried in different parts of the country (county council). Decentralization, therefore, requires a level of tolerance and restraint on the part of the central authorities. I examine in chapter 6 the nature of decentralized structures as one way of increasing the responsiveness of public service providers. I can note here that Sweden has a tradition (see chapter 3 or 4) of consensus statements and measurement systems which seek to evaluate the impact of organizational and legislative change. Sweden has also sought to move incrementally towards new forms of provision whilst retaining its strategic objective of equality in service provision.

To develop a framework of enquiry let us examine the nature of health care resource decisions and the criteria that would have to be satisfied to ensure the development of a system of management that is accountable, responsive and professional.

Strategic Management of Health Care Resources

An OECD study of health care reforms in seven countries – Belgium, France, Germany, Ireland, The Netherlands, Spain and the UK – concluded that:

In several respects, the seven countries seem to be converging in their health care policies and institutions, This is evident in: the continuing moves towards universal public coverage; the strengthening of control over total health expenditure by government; the universal adoption of global budgets in hospital markets; and in the movements towards the contract model in several countries . . . Managed markets represent a new attempt to fulfil the adequacy, equity and efficiency objectives of health policy . . . however, certain trade-offs cannot be escaped: between responsiveness and equity, for example; and between cost containment and choice. All we can hope for is that, by raising the productivity of health care systems, the reformed systems will ease the pain involved in such trade-offs. *(OECD, 1993a)*

Control of health costs is high on the agenda for debate in every modern country. The specific characteristics of the debate vary from country to country and are related to the economic circumstances of the time, the organizational framework for the delivery of health services, the relative contribution of public and private revenues for health service provision and the role of the State in the organization of the service. Solutions advanced ranged from the strategic, a reduction of the health care system, to structural change, greater private provision of health services, through operational improvements, such as greater efficiency in the delivery of health services. At the core of health expenditures and the State's attempt to constrain their growth is the assumption that the money is being properly managed and that it is effective in achieving its objectives. The evaluation of effectiveness can take a number of forms. First, there must be effective financial control so that the money is spent and accounted for in accordance with legislative or regulatory policy. Secondly, the money must be used in a manner supportive of the policy of the legislature or control department to achieve specific objectives. For example, hospital expenditures must be properly managed so as to constrain overall costs and allow some reallocation to other areas of the health care system such as primary and community care. Thirdly, and most intractable, the money must not be diverted or captured by health care workers through wage increases or increasing sophistication of equipment to the detriment of patient care expenditure. This is the capture model clearly articulated in the reforms of the New Zealand public sector.

Research in the control of European systems of health care strategies (McKevitt, 1989) examines the management model utilized in three countries (Sweden, The Netherlands and Ireland) for evidence of convergence in management practice. The appraisal of health care systems uses the open-systems model to examine both the national policy process and its implementation from a perspective that acknowledges organizational diversity and the conflicting values of professional groupings within the system. That is, the study accepts the validity of different strategies that are themselves dependent on economic, social or political contexts. The research examines the national health care policies of Sweden, The Netherlands and Ireland to determine whether the management of their acute hospital systems formed part of a coherent and integrated national health care strategy. Historically, and world-wide, hospitals are the most cost intensive part of the health care delivery system and most countries have failed in their attempts to curtail expenditures in this area. Hospitals were seen as a sub-unit of the overall national health care system and government policies (the 'general headquarters') were assessed for coherence and consistency between the hospital system and other parts of the national health care structure.

Thus, the 'mission' or strategy was assessed at national level prior to a detailed examination at the hospital level. Given that health care control is a European-wide challenge for government, the different national strategies were evaluated for evidence of convergence in management practice.

Control in health care yields similar challenges to politicians, civil servants and health care professionals under different financing systems for service delivery. Ireland and the UK, unlike Sweden and The Netherlands, did not adapt to the challenge of control largely because their legislative framework did not contain any explicit strategy, nor were the performance of health service professionals subject to any sustained scrutiny. The Swedish and Dutch systems, in contrast, which differ quite markedly in their financial support for health care, share common features in their concern for explicitness in legislation, their attendance to the sovereign importance of measurement and information systems and their willingness to adapt and modify their control systems to refocus their investment decision. It is clear that legislation provides the basic control framework for investment decisions in public care provision ('the rules of the game') and that such frameworks need to be adapted and modified in the context of changing environmental conditions.

The theme of adaptation of legislative control frameworks to suit emergent environmental conditions is central to the development of appropriate strategic control at the national level. Thus, for example, the 'greying' of the population and the objective of care-in-the-community impose quite specific policy objectives for both hospital usage and the framework for service delivery. Both Sweden and The Netherlands, in their planning for health care in the year 2000, have looked to divert resources from the hospital sector to other parts of the health care system. Their legislative frameworks are quite explicit in this regard and, hence, operational control and measurement are directed to the implementation of such policy. There is in the public policy process in these countries an attempt to adapt strategy in the light of changing circumstances.

The process is emergent and dependent on collective expression of policy through legislative change. The reform process seeks to adapt to the decision environment of the public sector (macro level) rather than to impose additional pressure on the organization to achieve change at the micro level. That is, values are embedded in legislation as part of the process of strategic control.

We can now see that legislation is a primary instrument for strategic control in the public service environment. It is also used to establish a countervailing influence to professional providers and special interest groups. Indeed, the case of New Zealand is a good example of legislative reform based on the single premise of 'provider capture' of public resources.

At this stage in the discussion it is appropriate to turn to the case study in the appendix 'Implementing community care' by Alan Lawton. The case study highlights a number of the key issues in this chapter: acceptability of policy change to different stakeholders, the relationship between legislation and delivery of services and the complexity of managing in a professional environment. Please read the study and answer the questions set out at the end. You will see that some of the issues relate to themes covered in later chapters; at this stage, however, it is important that you see the intended and unintended consequences of legislation and the management task in a complex professional context.

Legislative Control in New Zealand

During the past decade New Zealand stands unique among OECD countries in the range and extent of its public sector changes (OECD, 1993b). The following extract outlines the main provisions of these changes:

New Zealand Administrative and Legislative Reforms

1986 State Owned Enterprises Act
Separation of commercial activities from government departments; commercial criteria would provide an assessment of managerial performance; board members to be primarily appointed from the private sector.

1988 State Sector Act
Personnel and industrial relations for civil servants to be placed on a par with private sector arrangements; increased accountability to be assigned to senior managers. The Act explicitly assumed that employers, unions and workers in the state and private sectors would be treated in the same way unless there was a compelling case for different treatment.

1989 State Sector Amendment Act
Extended the principle of management and accountability contained in the State Sector Act into the Education Service; the amendment conferred normal employer rights to employers in the Education Service, placed senior positions in secondary schools on contract and provided for national criteria for assessing teacher performance.

1989 Public Finance Act
Provided for new contractual relationship between heads of government departments (chief executive) and Ministers. Departments required to adopt accrual accounting, to give them more complete financial information and to enable costs of outputs to be more easily measured. Chief Executives appointed on performance-linked contracts of up to five years. The budgetary process was altered so that the two separate interests of government, as purchaser of the outputs of the departments and as owner of department's assets are separated.

1991 Employment Contracts Act
Employees of the state have the choice of whether to belong to any form of employee's organization (which may be a union) formed to represent their

interests. Employers and employees are free to negotiate over whether to have individual or collective contracts, and subject, to the Act and other legislation, their content. The number, type and mix of contracts to apply in a particular workplace is a negotiable matter. *(McKevitt, 1996, p. 43)*

The organizational changes in New Zealand where administrative and structural changes were implemented in education to refocus the role of central government and local communities in curriculum and finance are examined in chapter 6. In designing its strategic control framework, the authors of change in New Zealand adopted a consistent model of control: the role of central government departments was one of policy advice and the role of local communities was implementation and delivery of services. The contract framework was widely diffused in all of the core public services; that is, the centre specified what services were to be provided from general taxation and it was the responsibility of providers, for example the 2700 schools, to deliver services.

Regional education authorities were abolished and the local community became the sole provider. The national inspectorate system was disbanded and a new audit agency, the Education Review Office, was established to audit, under statute, school effectiveness. At the heart of the New Zealand model is a distrust of providers (agency theory and the capture model are very real in New Zealand official mind) and the problem of public service effectiveness is cast in a solution of contract specification and quasi-market arrangements. In terms of the open system model, the New Zealand reforms have paid particular attention to the capacity of the centre to establish and alter organizational structures and to the allocation of resources. The two policy instruments which were left relatively unattended to have, hitherto, been the measurement and reward of performance, and the formulation of policy limits or 'rules of the game'. This is reflected in the inattention given to the measurement function and the lack of equity statements embedded in the legislation governing resource allocation. To some extent, such inattention is understandable given the major design premise of New Zealand's control framework, that is, the 'problem' of public service provision was firmly cast in the 'agency and capture' model and, hence, the 'solution' was identified as purchaser–provider split and contracts.

Such a framework, however, ignores (or does not concede any validity to) the social cohesion and interdependence objective of core public services provision. In a very real sense, the control framework does not admit of any interest other than self-interest.

We have already seen in chapters 2 and 3 that officials within New Zealand's ministries considered that the pace of reform and the direction of reforms allowed for no experimentation and that important institutional values were lost in the reform programme. The agency theory model is the cornerstone of much of New Zealand's legislation and administrative structures. Agency theory posits the argument that the closer the agents' decisions are to the preferences of the clients, the more efficient is the outcome. Hence, incentive structures should encourage the actions of agents so as to minimize costs of transactions (broadly the cost of delivery of services) and deliver more efficient services. I examine the practical effects of these changes in New Zealand's education system in the next chapter. This separation of provider and purchaser in service delivery is also applied at central government level to the ministries. Huhn (1994) in a review of performance measurement in New Zealand's ministries reports.

> Greater contestability in policy advice has undoubtedly reinforced various partisan positions. The separation of policy advice and implementation has engendered some fragmentation in the policy sphere, and perhaps a lack of overall co-ordination. Costing policy outputs has focused attention on costs but it remains unclear whether this process has improved the quality of policy advice. It is also difficult to gauge whether present day policy advice has dramatically improved compared to previously. *(1994, p. 33)*

I will examine the New Zealand performance framework structure in detail in chapter 7. Here it can be noted that greater specificity in legislation assists in the strategic control process.

Legislation is, however, only one of the 'means of influence' open to government and attention has to be focused on the professionals delivering the service. As chapter 2 argued, there has to be congruence and balance between the agendas of government and professional associations. Strategic control, to be effective, has to attend as much to the processes of control as it has to the formal framework of control.

The UK approach to health policy has shown that the State (as general headquarters) has been selective in its application and use of the means of influence open to it. Thus, there have been many initiatives in health care in the use of organizational structures, the measurement function and to some degree the use of resource allocation models (RAWP). What distinguishes the UK from most other European nations is the absence of any use of the means of influence central to strategic direction and control – the formulation of policy limits or 'rules of the game'.

The Chairman of the British Medical Association, speaking in 1994, stated:

> There is impotence in the face of the replacement of the hallowed ethic of care by the dictates of cash. Our professionalism is challenged, as never before in our time, by compromise of conscience as the price of survival, and even by temptation to self-interest over the best interests of patients. Evidence mounts daily of intimidation, of gagging clauses, of fear to put one's head above the parapet. *(Macara, 1994, p. 6)*

Clearly, the NHS reforms did not seek to align themselves with professional interests: as seen in chapter 3 neither did the reforms take active account of citizen 'voice'. The concentration on budgets, operational improvements and information technology are important initiatives, yet they do not, in strategic terms, constitute a clear mission or strategy. Wrigley (1989) stated in respect of health care control that:

In private enterprise the ultimate control of the working of any particular firm lies with the customers or competitors in the market place, more exactly, with the tastes and budgets of customers, and with the strategy and production costs of competitors. The legitimacy and effectiveness of the control system within each particular firm is derived from this; from the customer's budgets and competitors' costs. There is, today, no equivalent source for the legitimacy and effectiveness of the control system in public health care. *(1989, p. iv)*

The United Kingdom, therefore, needs to articulate a strategic framework for health policy if it is to have a control system on a par with other European countries. Failure to attend to this sovereign task will leave the system in thrall to the vagaries of politics and medical interests and the position of managers will be an unenviable one of trying to 'hold the line' in a system where control is dependent on the play of competing interest groups.

Budgets, Bureaucrats and Health Care

In large measure, administrative reforms and managerial initiatives in the public sector across many countries ignore one central element of the process of reform.

This omission can clearly be seen in the US best-seller *Reinventing Government* (Osborne and Gaebler 1992) where especial stress is laid on the policy level and in the design of organizational and regulatory frameworks that seek to engineer organizational responsiveness and citizen empowerment.

Little attention is given to enabling the providers to respond to the new environment, to skill or re-educate managers and professionals to cope with the new frameworks that embody quite complex and highly specified contracts for service delivery. It would seem that excitement is engendered amongst the top officials and politicians as to the broad sweep of reforms: the operational core (in Mintzberg's terminology) is presumed to have the capability and adaptability to alter significant working patterns of mutual adjustment, built up over, in some cases, many years. Concepts such as 'public service traditions' and 'professionalism' are viewed as, at best, special pleading and, at worst, cloaks of self-interest. In an organic environment such as is found in the core public services, where the act of service is often an intense process of personal interrelationships, this mechanistic approach is unlikely to be successful. Indeed, the 'failure' to broker reform or progress can lead, perversely, to the centre increasing its attempt to pursue a policy of reform thereby further reducing its effectiveness.

The purchaser–provider separation is intended to increase efficiency in health care delivery by stimulating competition between GP practices and institutional hospital care. The objective is that by allowing GPs to 'buy' the most cost-effective package of care for their patients from competing institutions, costs will be driven down and, hence, the overall system will be more efficient.

In parallel, the Patient's Charter is intended to promote quality of service delivery and the promotion of a responsive health care delivery system. A recent report of the Audit Commission (1997) in respect of GP fundholding practices found that fundholding lacks accountability and threatens to undermine the government's national strategy on health promotion. An additional characteristic of the new quasi-market system is the fragmentation of budgetary systems between District Health Authorities, NHS Trusts, GP fundholding practices and family health service authorities (FHSA): Districts spend some £25 billion a year in England and Wales, and family authorities some £7 billion.

Co-ordination of these budgets, together with those of NHS Trust hospitals cannot be easily achieved, especially when GP fundholding practices are allowed to retain operating 'surpluses' for their own non-medical use.

Attempts to simulate a health care market which provides monetary incentives is flawed as it operates within a centrally controlled system of fixed funding. It assumes that the doctor–patient relationship can be modelled onto a standard purchasing decision such as is found in a competitive private market. Conflicting incentive structures, together with fragmented budgetary systems do not provide strategic control in a non-market environment. Let us examine the nature of health care purchasing decisions in such an environment.

In health care, as in other areas of social expenditure such as education, there is a great disparity between the providers of the services and their clients/ patients in respect of knowledge as to the efficacy of the service. That is, in the language of chapter 2, there is information asymmetry in the system and the doctor is placed in a position of trust, or agent, in respect of the patient. The patient/client cannot increase their understanding of the service through repeated 'purchases' or through going elsewhere for service, as there is (usually) only one provider (the State) and because of the unusual nature of the services, that is purchase and supply are instantaneous, they cannot be separated or stored for future consumption. As a consequence, society usually provides such services through the State and places an important ethical responsibility on medical personnel to act in a professional manner. This concern is reflected in the development of performance measurement systems, sometimes in co-operation with the profession (Peer Review) yet more often 'imposed' by management (Performance Indicators) and seen as an expression of 'rule by bureaucrats'. If the earlier relationship between the doctors and patients could be described as professional-custodial, the new performance control systems might be seen as transforming that relationship into a manager-custodial one. Also, increasing emphasis on improved management is now placing quite demanding and conflicting priorities on health care workers.

If modern social democratic countries do not confront the pressing social conflicts of resource allocation to competing interest groups, then the passage of laws or the installation of administrative structures which embody vague and non-operational objectives only serve to place the manager in an untenable position. Confronted by limited resources, unaided by clear objectives, the manager has to ration available resources using whatever organizational or professional standards and norms are available. Such a process can lead to rigidity in the allocation system and give rise to administrative structures which have as their basis a defensive approach to citizen need: these issues are explored in depth in the next chapter.

▬▬▬ Summary and Conclusions ▬▬▬

The argument that legislation can provide a framework for strategic control is supported by the data from countries as diverse in their historical traditions as Sweden, The Netherlands and New Zealand. We should be cautious, however, of ascribing to legislation an overtly dominant role in strategic direction; it is an important but not a sufficient condition for achieving congruence between strategic objectives and operational control. I identified early in this chapter that control embraces both technical and human aspects as it seeks to balance the interests of staff with the legitimate needs and expectations of the citizen–client. Over-reliance on legislation especially when it is primarily administrative and technical in its orientation – as the UK 'reforms' – can result in a technical orientation that reduces good public management practices to the pursuit of cost savings and economy.

Management control in an organization, public or private, for profit or not-for-profit, has to do with the measurement of the organization's achievement and the assessment of information on performance relative to aims and object-ives. The challenge to management in core public services is a profound one when the incidence of uncertainty is so pervasive. This uncertainty takes many forms. In health care, for example, the most basic is the efficacy of the many modes of treatment that are available due to the rapid technological and therapeutic advances in medical science and practice.

Closely associated with this uncertainty is the cost of the medical care provi-sion and its allocation among the various parts of the system, that is, primary, community and hospital. The financing of medical care and its allocation relative to other areas of social or economic expenditure is also made more difficult if the control system is unable to effectively regulate the activities of the individuals delivering the service. The advocacy of public or private provi-sion of health care does not, however, remove the challenge of control and regulation. As Battistella and Eastaugh remark in the context of hospital cost containment in the United States: 'Among regulators, the service ethic is often derided as a synonym for softheartedness and weakmindedness. Such disdain contributes to the surprise of regulators over the felicity with which hospital administrators manage to avoid the intent of quantitative controls' (1980). Thus, it is important that the professionals within the system and those charged with its management agree as to the objectives of the enterprise. I examine the relationship between professionals and performance measure-ment in chapter 7.

The nature of measurement in the context of the research model presented in this chapter can be summarized as follows: measurement must relate to the objectives (mission) of the organization and complex organizations require multi-dimensional measures. The system of measurement must be understood by the people whose activities are being measured ('rules of the game').

A two-way flow of information is critical. The need to adapt organizational structures to suit the environment in which core public services operate is the subject of chapter 6. We have already seen that an incremental or emergent process of strategic change is suitable in core public services. In such change processes, the social interdependence that follows tends to endow prominance to the human and social value of both providers and citizens.

One way that organizations can effect improvements in their service standards is to structure their delivery systems to best meet the needs of their clients. Thus, for example, McDonald's is expert at delivering fast food to children and adults in a friendly, hygienic atmosphere. People's expectations are of a standard service and McDonald's achieves this through attention to operations, staff training and imbuing a culture of service in their organization. With public services, delivering sometimes complex services to clients who may be young, confused or illiterate, the service challenge is immense. The services and their clients are not always standardized and customized, nor are all services universal in their scope. Many public services are targeted at specific client groups – selective services – but they are delivered and controlled in a mechanistic way. It is here that critics of bureaucratic practices have a telling point; it is hardly feasible to expect large, rule-bound organizations to be responsive and alert to client needs. Yet public service organizations can innovate and deliver responsive and dignified service. They do so by adapting their organizational structures, by reaching out to clients rather than expecting clients to come to them. I turn to this issue in chapter 6.

In a review of the experience of a number of countries it can be seen that frameworks for strategic control are complex and, at times, unintentionally conflicting: the open-systems model allows us to see that the assumption of administrative and legislative coherence is naive and predicated on a rational order not found in the complex world of core public service management. The objectives of public service management can, however, be supported through legislation which embodies strategic objectives that allow for measurement of the investment decision.

In summarizing the research and field data examined in this chapter we can observe that:

- legislation provides a framework for strategic control in public service organizations;
- the UK model of administrative control lacks coherence as it is not embodied in a framework of legislative control;
- New Zealand's framework of control explicitly targets the behaviour of providers through formal statements of objectives linked to performance measurement.

CHAPTER

6

Organizational Structures for Effective Service Delivery

 **Introduction**

This chapter examines the internal structure of the SLPO and examines how organizations can manage their internal affairs to deliver effective services to the citizen–client. The structuring and design of organizations is an important part of the public manager's job: without effective organizational design, service delivery can become a provider-led phenomenon. Indeed, as we saw in chapter 5, one of the primary motivations for the New Zealand reforms was the conviction that providers were a key obstacle to effective service delivery – such suspicions of *providers* also lies behind much of the recent UK reforms in core public services. As chapter 5 argued effective strategic control requires use of all the 'means of influence' open to government; this chapter examines one of these means – the design of organizational structures. I examine evidence from a number of countries – Germany, New Zealand and England – and utilize two important models from the general management literature to critically appraise this evidence.

The chapter examines three areas:

1　the SLPO in its relationship with its environment;
2　the New Zealand and German model of school management;
3　the idea of decentralized authority and effective organizational structures.

Organizational design and academic commentary is as subject to fashion and trends as any other facet of critical activity. The current orthodoxy in the area of organizational structures can be summarized as follows:

1　bureaucracy is rigid and unresponsive;
2　decentralized structures ('close to the customer') are the most appropriate organizational form;
3　smaller units are preferable to larger units.

I will examine these arguments in this chapter, drawing on comparative data from New Zealand, Germany and England.

Metaphors and images are a powerful source of influence on our everyday thinking; so too are organizational structures influenced by wider movements in the intellectual and political community. Thus, for example, the German genius for organizational efficiency finds expression in the Prussian military efficiency of the nineteenth-century Franco-German wars or its twentieth-century effectiveness in absorbing the former German Democratic Republic into a unified federal Germany. A consideration of Germany must include recognition of its laws and regulations (its brewing regulation dates from 1640), codification of rules, and the preponderance of lawyers in the public service. There is a tendency to view the Anglo-Saxon tradition of enterprise, individualism and *laissez-faire* capitalism and to contrast it with the North European (including Scandinavia) tradition; British 'good sense' is compared with Germanic rules and regulations. The next chapter examines two quite distinct cultural and historical concepts of professionalism – the 'power' model of the professional drawing on the Anglo-American tradition and the 'custodial' model drawing on the Northern European tradition. Each of these traditions, supported by laws, regulation and organizational structures, give rise to quite distinct strategies in the management of professionals.

In evaluating reforms in the core public services across a range of countries, we need to be sensitive to these traditions – this sensitivity to collective values and traditions is, as we have seen, not something that all governments and reformers have attended to, and hence they have rendered their proposed reforms less effective. That is, reformers have relied on the use of one set of influences and ignored the need for coherence between these influences and professional or client interests.

Organizations, like individuals, are embedded in a social, cultural and historical context. Indeed, the thrust of many reform efforts seem to ignore this context. The politician emphasizes change, restructuring and administrative devolving of functions as if the organization were simply the sum of the parts of its administrative rules, office technology and full-time equivalent staff members. To perceive organizations in this fashion is, on the one hand, to reduce the chances of 'success' by seeking to ignore the social reality of professional and administrative life, and, on the other hand, to engender in the provider–client relationship a sense that costs and efficiency are the only coinage of social exchange. Public service managers and professional staff are not solely driven by self-interest, which is the conceptual underpinning of quasi-markets and purchaser–provider contracts. The interview data reported in this study clearly show that providers are concerned with standards and that they do perceive benefit in some of the reforms. They are sceptical or, indeed, embittered by the constant political denigration of their role. It is a strangely Manichean view of human relations that impels the reformer to attack the very values that support social cohesion and interdependence.

In examining the organizational structures devised by various countries we should remember that such structures are not easily transferable between countries and cultures. However, the challenges faced by public service managers who operate in a highly professional context are broadly similar. Every citizen with rights to a service expects to be supported by the organizational structures that deliver such services.

The marketing aspects of service delivery were examined in chapter 3, and it was seen that citizen voice was not actively encouraged in the United Kingdom reforms. The institutional framework of measurement which deals with resources and legitimacy was clearly dominant. The marketing of core public services clearly needs effective provision for citizen voice and their active involvement in structuring service provision.

The professional delivering a service requires sufficient autonomy to meet citizen needs – an autonomy that is subject to the political and economic constraints that govern national priorities. The middle manager is the linchpin of this service relationship and also requires training and development to accomplish this task. I am particularly focusing here on the needs of the middle manager for relevant and appropriate development. Indeed, the impetus for this book arose from the experience of designing education programmes for such managers. With constant environmental change (and persistent attempts at a political level to change the 'rules of the game'), the middle manager, both professional and administrative, needs to be alert to the skills, techniques and approaches that yield appropriate levels of service in the public service heartland. I will return to the management and development needs of middle managers in chapter 8.

These management skills can include the design of relevant consumer surveys, the implementation of robust investment appraisal systems, and the building up of effective performance measurement systems. I examine data on these approaches in this book. Moreover, a middle manager has to appreciate that effective service is the result of the sensitive and selective application of such techniques within the tolerance level of existing organizational custom and practice. The policy makers, too, need to be aware of the strategic tests of feasibility, suitability and acceptability of proposed innovations: the Dearing Report (1994) in England on implementation of the national school curriculum is a good example of how governments can be fettered by the challenge of inappropriate and untimely widescale change. If such changes had the active involvement and support of teachers then, perhaps, the controversy and disruption caused by their imposition may have been avoidable.

We need to remind ourselves of the range of environmental forces that influence the street-level public organization: figure 5.1 describes the conflicting environmental forces in this environment, and the recurring tension points in this relationship. It will be seen that the immediate source of recurring tension is point A, the relations between central government and the professions. The model enables us to see an essential fact – SLPOs are under a rival set of influences. From central government, there are four modes of influence, general legislation (see chapter 5), allocation of resources (see chapter 4), organizational structure and performance measurement. I will examine performance measurement and professional management in chapter 7.

▬▬ **Organization and Environment** ▬▬

The SLPO is subject to a range of environmental influences and a number of them have been examined in this book. We need now, though, to move inside the SLPO and to see how the external environment impacts on the internal structure of the organization. This is of primary importance because not all organizations or environments are similar and we need to know how the different states of the external environment can be reconciled with the tasks carried out within the organization. In looking at the tasks carried out within the SLPO, I draw upon private sector models of management, in particular the pioneering work of Burns and Stalker (1994), and the distinction between standardized production-type processes and those involving non-routine, knowledge-based decision making. The environment can be classified as stable or changing, and different organizational forms are appropriate given the relationship that exists between task and environment. Burns and Stalker (1994, pp. 119–22) label the two organizational systems they observed as mechanistic and organic. An important point to observe is that either form can be 'rationally created' and appropriate depending on the relationship between task and environment. That is, there is no 'one best way' of designing structures; what is relevant is that the chosen structure is appropriate to the needs of the organization and the demands of the external environment.

The management task is, therefore, to choose an appropriate organizational structure which is dependent on the type of work carried out in the organization and the type of environment that faces the organization. An important subsidiary consideration is the type of workers required to do the work of the organization. I examine later in this chapter a type of organization that dominates in the core public services – the professional bureaucracy.

Drawing on the work of Burns and Stalker (1994), it can be seen that the mechanistic organization is appropriate to stable external conditions and production type processes – that is, continuity – and is characterized by:

1　specialized differentiation of functional tasks into which the problems and tasks facing the organization as a whole are broken down;
2　the abstract nature of each individual task, which is pursued with techniques and purposes more or less distinct from those of the organization as a whole; that is, the functionaries tend to pursue the technical improvement of means, rather than the accomplishment of the ends of the organization;
3　the precise definition of rights and obligations and technical methods attached to each functional role;
4　hierarchic structure of control, authority and communication;
5　a tendency for operations and working behaviour to be governed by the instructions and decisions of the supervisors;
6　insistence on loyalty to the organization and obedience to superiors.

The characteristics of the organic organization, which is appropriate to chang-ing environmental conditions and non-routine tasks include:

1 the contributive nature of special knowledge and experience to the common task of the organization;
2 the adjustment and continual re-definition of individual tasks through interaction with others;
3 the spread of commitment to the organization beyond any technical definition;
4 a network structure of control, authority and communication;
5 omniscience not imputed to the head of the organization: knowledge about the technical or commercial nature of the 'here and now' task may be located anywhere in the network;
6 a content of communication which consists of information and advice rather than institutions and decisions.

Burns and Stalker went on to observe that whilst organic forms are not as hierarchic as mechanistic ones, they do remain stratified and that commitment to the goals and purposes of an organization is much more extensive in the organic type.

The organic type is also much more an institution than simply an organiza-tion, drawing as it does on rules, behaviours and procedures from outside the organization that are based on technical or specialized knowledge. I look at the nature of institutional environments and their effects on organizational structures later in this chapter. These institutional environments of the core public services are important as they contribute significantly to shaping the internal process of the SLPO; thus, for example, reforms such as those in New Zealand, which sought to radically restructure education provision, can suc-ceed only if they are supported by the values and standards of the teaching profession. Similarly, as we observed in respect of the UK curriculum reforms, changes which are resisted by the profession because of mechanistic methods of implementation (in an organic institution such as a school) can be rendered ineffective.

The purpose of the SLPO is to deliver non-marketable services to the citizen–client in a manner which is supportive of social cohesion and inter-dependence (see chapter 2). The SLPO is largely comprised of professional staff and dependent on mutual adjustment and co-operation rather than, as in mechanistic organizations, on hierarchical authority and control. An organiza-tional form, such as the SLPO, depends on appropriate internal structures and control being appropriate to its tasks and its environment.

When we examine recent structural reform in the core public services across a range of countries there is plenty of evidence to suggest that the reforms are driven by a mechanistic model. Why should this be so? To some extent it reflects a distrust of professions (see chapter 7) and it also, perhaps, reflects a reversion to simpler times, where hierarchy equalled authority, where knowledge was restricted to the few and where there seemed to be a 'one best way' to manage. I am here referring to the classical view of organizations (both public and private) described by Weber.

In his discussion of organizational types Weber presented bureaucracy as representative of rational order, stable decision making and the efficient processing of information required for the decisions. Bureaucracy was the exemplar for public service organizations and the bureaucrat the model for the professional administrator.

Weber's work is densely written and there is controversy surrounding its interpretation. Weber was in fact interested in formal rationality rather than drawing out the attributes of 'efficiency' but the characteristics he identified have often been interpreted in this way. The main elements of his summary depiction of bureaucracy were:

- rules and procedures to enable the organization to function in a predictable and routine manner with specialization and division of labour;
- a hierarchical chain of command;
- selection to posts on the basis of competence;
- separation of ownership and administration;
- written documentation of acts, decision and rules.

(1947)

Of course, the Weber formulation was descriptive of simpler, pre-democratic and information-poor conditions of the nineteenth century. Thus, while his descriptions are valid in certain contexts they cannot be seen as representative of the complex, unstable environments as set out in Figure 5.1. The disadvantages of the classical bureaucratic model can be summarized as follows:

- rigidity and defensiveness, inward looking orientation;
- emphasis on defining a minimum acceptable level of performance;
- sub-unit goals take precedence over central organization's objectives;
- over-departmentalization of functions.

Organizations are a social device for the handling of information, for the provision of stable social relations between professional and administrative staff, and the means by which services are delivered to the citizen–client. Not all citizens require the same type of service, and the public service organization has to cope with diversity of need and demand.

For example, a large acute hospital has to have 24 hours, 365 days availability of accident and emergency services while providing for specialized capital-intensive tertiary care. As in the private sector, public organizations have to design structures to deliver their strategic objectives, to devise ways to reconcile the need for overall direction and control with the requirement for flexibility to accommodate specialization of functions.

These tensions are expressed in a number of ways: for example, the headteacher has to decide, within the context of the school's overall budget, the amount of discretionary timetable hours and resources to devote to non-core curriculum activities. The school has to maintain standards through consultation, partnerships and leadership at the organizational level as well as being accountable to national standards and norms. This chapter examines how different countries seek to balance these tensions through the design of organizational structures. Similarly, in health care, hospital management has to maintain financial accountability whilst allowing appropriate discretion and autonomy to the physicians providing appropriate medical care. We will see that such operational control, while incorporating technical rules of accounting and costing, is the result of quite complex social relations which are clearly supported (or weakened) by wider societal values and priorities. Thus, for example, the techniques discussed in chapters 3 and 4 have to be sensitively applied in the wider organizational and social context of the SLPO. There is sufficient evidence in this study to show that the application of mechanistic measures of change, including organizational structures and performance measurement, to the SLPO creates further difficulties with both clients and service providers.

Professional Bureaucracy

I have already discussed the organic and mechanistic form of organization and how the former type is representative of professional or technical skills operating in a changing environment. It was seen that Weber's bureaucracy was characteristic of pre-democratic, information-poor, societies and that it also led to an over-concern with departmentalization of functions to the detriment of the overall organization. We need now to examine a particular type of bureaucratic organization – the professional bureaucracy as it represents, in one form or another, a dominant organizational type in the core public services. The professional bureaucracy is similar to the organic type identified by Burns and Stalker in that standardization of skills and decentralization are its two prominent features: schools, general hospitals, social work agencies are all examples of professional bureaucracies. Mintzberg (1979) has examined the professional bureaucracy in some depth and it is on his work that we now draw.

Mintzberg (1979) notes how the professional bureaucracy relies for co-ordination on standardization of skills, training and indoctrination. Professionals have a high degree of control over their work, but they work closely with the clients they serve, for example, teachers and students. We examined in chapter 2 the nature of a professional code of ethics and the associated social obligation that professionals owe their clients. Standardization of skills, of course, does not mean that all professionals will agree on how to perform a similar task; judgement and discretion is characteristic of the professional in his/her dealings with the client. The professional bureaucracy, unlike Weber's bureau, emphasizes the authority of the professional and the power of expertise. In Mintzberg's terms the 'operating core' is the heart of the professional bureaucracy – where clients are provided with professional services; a key characteristic of the organization that follows from that feature is that professional bureaucracies are highly decentralized in structure, both vertically and horizontally. Autonomy (power) is high within the professions and this is because their work is too complex to be supervised by managers or standardized (in terms of output) by analysis.

What is the role of the manager in this professional bureaucracy? One key role is that of handling internal allocation decisions on resources (for example, who will lead on curriculum reform in the school). Another key role for the manager is handling the relationships with the external environment, such as attraction of resources and legitimacy (remember our discussion in chapter 3 on Kanter and Summers institutional performance measures). Strategy formation is difficult in professional bureaucracies and Mintzberg (1979, p. 364) concludes that 'the strategies of the Professional Bureaucracies are largely ones of the individual professionals within the organization as well as of the professional associations on the outside'. We will see, however, that such an evaluation has to be modified in the light of the data discussed in this chapter and in chapter 7.

What are the associated problems with this form of organization – the professional bureaucracy? One of the most immediate problems is that there is no control of the work, outside of the profession, no way to correct deficiencies that the professionals choose themselves to overlook.

The professional bureaucracy cannot easily, therefore, deal well with the professional who is incompetent or not discharging their responsibilities. Because of the amount of discretion granted to the professional, she can ignore both the needs of the client and of the organization; that is the flip-side of autonomy. Mintzberg concludes that:

> Changes in the Professional Bureaucracy do not sweep in from new administrators taking office to announce major reforms, nor from government technostructures intent on bringing professionals under control. Rather, change seeps in, by the slow process of changing the professionals – changing who can enter the professions, what they learn in its Professional Schools (ideals as well as skills and knowledge), and thereafter how willing they are to upgrade their skills. *(1979, p. 379)*

I will return to the important topic of control of professionals, through performance frameworks, in chapter 7. Here it is relevant to note the importance of decentralized structures in the work of professionals and the emphasis in professional life of the standards and norms that are indoctrinated through education and training outside of the organization. As you will recall this external environmental influence is described in figure 5.1. Equally Mintzberg's stress on the professions and of changing them gradually is in agreement with two of the central messages of this book; the importance of time-frame in institutional changes and of not attempting to impose a mechanistic form of control in an organic organization like the SLPO.

The public service middle manager has to reconcile a number of potential difficulties in designing SLPOs for effective service delivery:

1   freedom for professionals to operate and make decisions within the organization's overall financial constraints;
2   maintenance of strategic control with the necessary flexibility of autonomy at the point of service delivery;
3   adequate performance measurement which satisfies both financial and professional standards;
4   adequate voice for the citizen/client in the monitoring of organizational effectiveness.

We examine here how a number of countries have sought to reconcile these difficulties, in particular the role of the centre versus local autonomy in service provision. As noted in chapter 3 some countries have sought to grant greater voice to the citizen–client in service relationships: New Zealand provides a good example of this strategy.

——— New Zealand: Educational Change ——— and Community Involvement

New Zealand's reform of its educational structures closely mirrors the ten-year programme of change in its wider public service. We have already examined the legislative framework of these reforms in chapter 5. This programme emphasized a clear separation of the purchaser–provider role in service delivery and has gained interest and praise from the Organization for Economic Cooperation and Development:

> The structural policy framework put in place in late 1990 has attempted to respond to identified major policy problems by promoting increased competition – in a wider sphere and better defining the role of government. (*OECD 1993, p. 35*)

The New Zealand reforms have, at their core, the redefinition of the role of central government ministries (who are statutorily 'paid' for their policy advice to government), the deregulation of the public service labour market (under the Employment Contracts Act 1990, collective agreements are largely abolished), and the establishment of the contract model as the primary arrangement for the provision of public services (for example, all general hospitals are now companies with limited liability). The influence of the New Zealand Treasury Ministry has been very significant in all areas of administrative reform; this, together with the lobbying and support of the Business Round Table has ensured that the public choice theory and agency capture model have dominated official thinking in proposals for organizational and administrative reform.

Indeed, so closely have changes in education paralleled wider public sector change that one respondent observed, in respect of Treasury and State Services Commission influence that:

Figure 6.1 Relationship between government agenda, differential information and professional ethics

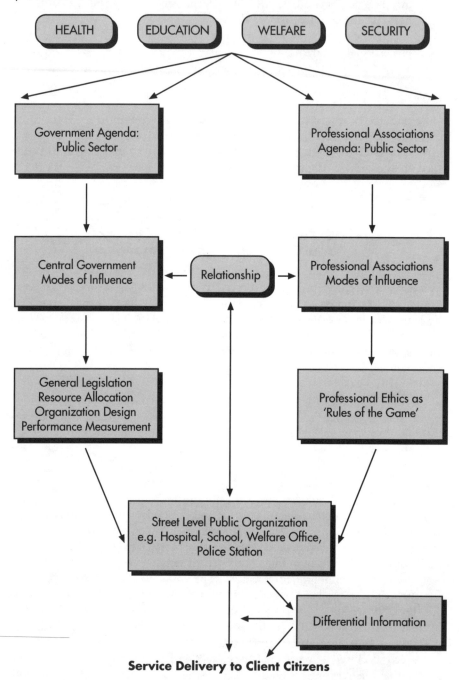

Source: Wrigley and McKevitt 1995

> To some extent, the Ministry [of Education] has been the 'whipping boy' because it didn't achieve changes that were the responsibility of other departments, e.g. 'break the power of the teacher unions'.

The legislative and administrative reforms in New Zealand's education system built on the earlier changes within that country's public sector (see chapter 5). At the heart of the reforms lay a distrust of the providers – teachers, doctors – and an insistence on the contract as the correct form of relationship between the state as the financier of services and the public servants as the providers of services. The more general move to distance central departments of State from any involvement in operational matters (to some extent the parallel of the Next Steps Agencies in the United Kingdom) also meant a substantial reduction in the number of central civil servants: indeed, New Zealand abolished its education inspectorate as an area of the Ministry of Education and set up an independent inspectorate, the Education Review Office. In terms of the model shown in figure 6.1 government sought to exert direct influence on the institutions through changes in general legislation, resource allocation (through direct funding of schools), organization structure (abolishing the regional tier of administration) and through more explicit performance measurement (discussed in chapter 7). Relations between government and the professions were, however, quite strained. Indeed, one active participant in that relationship observed:

> The Treasury has led a sustained assault on the educationalist stance (at times the attacks were quite vicious): for example, *Tomorrow's Schools* was barely in print, when the Picot Committee was set up which was their [the Treasury] way of trying to relitigate government decisions which from their point of view did not go far enough.

We will look at the effect of these tensions between professions and the State in chapter 7; and the government paper setting out the principles underlying reform of New Zealand's primary and secondary school system (Ministry of Education, *Tomorrow's Schools*, 1988) an extract from which is set out below:

New Zealand Education Reform

Institutions will be the basic 'building block' of education administration, with control over their educational resources – to use as they determine, within overall guidelines for education set by the state.

    The running of the institution will be a partnership between the professionals and the particular community in which it is located. The mechanism for such a partnership will be a board of trustees. Each institution will set its own objectives, within the overall national guidelines set by the state. These objectives will reflect the particular needs of the community in which the institution is located, and will be clearly set out in a 'charter' drawn up by the institution. This charter will act as a contract between the community and the institution, and the institution and the state. Institutions will be accountable, through a nationally established Review and Audit Agency, for the government funds spent on education and for meeting the objectives set out in their charters.

This agency will carry out regular reviews of every institution. Institutions will be free to purchase services from a range of suppliers.

Community education forums will be set up to act as a place of debate and a voice for all those who wish to air their concerns – whether students, parents, teachers, managers or education administrators.

A Ministry of Education will be established to provide policy advice to the Minister, to administer property, and to handle financial flows and operational activities.

An independent Parent Advocacy Council will be established. This council will promote the interests of parents generally and will, in particular, provide assistance and support to parents who are dissatisfied with existing arrangements to the extent that they wish to set up their own school. Groups of parents representing at least 21 children will be able to withdraw from existing arrangements and set up their own institution, provided that they meet the national guidelines for education. *(Ministry of Education, 1988)*

The model of reform as articulated in *Tomorrow's Schools* sees the individual school (the 'institution') as the primary focus of attention. The focus on the individual school, with its attendant control mechanism of the Boards of Trustees, displayed the mechanistic perspectives of the reformers: schools were like any other 'institution', a set of contract relationships, financial systems and employee relationships that could be managed through formal and specified contracts. Indeed, the New Zealand School Trustees Association (the representative body of boards of trustees) sought to give primary influence to the boards of trustees as managers of the schools. Education was too important to be left to the educational professionals and the Ministry of Education itself was restructured so that it would only concentrate on 'policy matters': the fracturing of the older institutions – the inspectorate and the regional structures – was seen as the best way to reform the system.

The tone of the political debate which surrounded education reform can be seen in the comments of Roger Douglas who helped pioneer many of the early New Zealand reforms in public management:

Our educational establishment has long contended that New Zealand has an education system that is one of the best in the world. Over the years there have been changes intended to make education more effective. But, by and large, concern from outside the profession, from parents, students, politicians and employers, has met with complacency and aggressive admonitions to leave education to those qualified to deal with it. *(Douglas, 1993, p. 88)*

In terms of this chapter's key issues, the New Zealand reforms focused on decreasing the size of the centre and to decentralizing authority down to the individual school. However, decentralization contains within it an administrative paradox: the only way in which the centre can be satisfied with such a strategy is if it so constrains institutional autonomy through rigid application of the 'rules of the game'. In some measure, the contracts for school principals sought to have a unified model of control between principals and boards of trustees.

The management of the system was deemed to be generically similar to any other management system; specify the administrative relationships, define contract specifications and measurements and then the system could operate independently of any other form of control. That is, it could operate without the commitment of the professionals delivering the service; hierarchy and authority was sufficient to achieve the proposed strategy.

The New Zealand reforms had a clearly defined strategy: to 'push down' responsibility to school level, to recognize the idea of partnership between the schools and the community, to install appropriate performance review measures, and to give adequate 'voice' to parents. Initially, at least, there was also the idea of a contract embodied in the School Charter which would embrace both the school, the community and the State. Reproduced below is the contract that was proposed by the education trade unions and the New Zealand School Trustees Association: it was never signed by the Ministry of Education. Clearly only some contracts were actionable! In New Zealand school governors have a much wider range of statutory responsibilities than their UK counterparts.

The Education Accord

The school sector endorses the national curriculum framework in its broad directions. In order to put such a framework in place there must be:

1. A five year plan to implement the national curriculum.
2. A five year plan to ensure certainty of policy direction and resourcing to improve standards of excellence.
3. A clear, explicit process of consultation and involvement in policy development, implementation and evaluation.

For this to occur:

4. The government must be responsible for fully and fairly funding the state school system.
5. The provision and delivery of education must be fair and just for all.
6. The particular needs of Maori education must be recognized and addressed through comprehensive planning processes that directly involve iwi/Maori organizations and education sector groups.

Given the above:
Appropriate areas and levels of self-management will be determined through consultation.

We are committed to deliver processes of accountability which will ensure that money is spent effectively so as to achieve educational excellence for young New Zealanders.

New Zealand School Trustees Association	New Zealand Post Primary Teachers Association
New Zealand Principals' Federation	Secondary Principals' Association of New Zealand

New Zealand Educational Institute	Principals' Council of New Zealand Post Primary Teacher's Association
New Zealand Intermediate Schools Principals' Association	

(NZEI, 1994)

Charters now have the status of an 'undertaking' laid on the school's board of trustees with compliance monitored by the Education Review Office. Building on the purchaser–provider model used to reconstruct central government relationships, the New Zealand reformers thought such a model applicable to education. The contract between the education partners was not subsequently implemented, albeit the devolution of financial responsibility to the institutional level was proceeded with together with the idea of all school principals having a contract with their School Councils.

The scale of reform in the education system was rapid, intensive and affected every one of some 2664 schools in New Zealand. New administrative structures were established (the old regional structures were abolished), the Department of Education's Inspectorate was abolished and replaced by a separate statutory agency (Education Review Office), Boards of Trustees were established with wider statutory authority, and the Ministry of Education became a policy department with little in-house research capability.

This rapid scale of reform (as in the case of the United Kingdom in respect of the national school curriculum) had its own structural and institutional problems. Indeed, so rapid was the restructuring – abolition of the regional tier, the 'contracting out' of educational research from the old Department of Education, the abolition of the inspectorate – that a senior official stated that 'institutional memory' had been erased at central level. That is, with large-scale restructuring and the setting-up of new institutional arrangements (the Education Review Office to replace the inspectorate, the School Trustees Association), there were few officials at the Ministry of Education who could provide a reference point with the previous system. Continuity with the past, the testing of the new against traditional ways was sundered. While continuity was, of course, partially provided by the schools themselves, it did seem as if, in its determination to apply new 'rules of the game', politicians and policy makers were insensitive to New Zealand's international reputation in educational achievement particularly at junior level.

One policy analyst in the Ministry of Education observed

> The legal framework governing education uses terms such as 'control, management and administration'. Stakeholders are now seeking to operationalize and agree as to the meaning of these terms. In some respects, intransigent attitudes have been conditioned by this legal framework. While principals would wish to see the law rewritten, the days when they could view schools as their personal fiefdom is past . . . It could be argued that there is something

wrong with existing structures if you need so many compliance agencies to ensure that equity objectives are being pursued.

The frontispiece of *Tomorrow's Schools* cited a reference from Thomas Jefferson:

> I know of no safe depository of the ultimate power of society but the people themselves and if we think them not enlightened enough to exercise their control with a wholesome discretion, the remedy is not to take it from them, but to inform their discretion.

A rather different interpretation of the reform proposals were presented by a senior member of the New Zealand State Services Commission who stated:

> comparatively speaking, the early reforms were easy and we ploughed into social policy because of our early success.

The same observer reported that:

> in proposed reforms in education, departments and politicians went through periods of change upon change, and politicians underestimated the value of existing institutional knowledge.

The comment is revealing as it demonstrates that New Zealand's reforms in education were effectively the application of a 'one best way' model in that all relationships – between pupils and staff, between hospitals and patients – could be structured around the notion of a contract. There was clearly a determination at the political level to dispense with past arrangements, the ways of working which had been built up over many decades in favour of a new way which envisioned that social and professional skills and traditions could be specified in a manner which broke the traditional in favour of the new contract.

We see in the evaluation of Germany's education reforms that continuity, incremental changes and co-operation with the education professionals was the dominant reform recipe. Traditions and continuity play an important part in social cohesion and New Zealand's reforms did not grant these traditions a valid place. A senior member of NZEI (the primary teachers' trade union) observed that:

> While *Tomorrow's Schools* contained elements of New Right ideology, it did contain elements of participative democracy which NZEI has encouraged . . . To some extent the primary system has gained through the reforms, especially due to increased parental support and involvement. The downside of change has been the attempt to 'atomize' the system; hitherto there was effective diffusion of good practice throughout the system; this, however, is much diminished. And [there is] growing evidence of growing [*sic*] inequalities.

This diminution in best practice was aptly described by a second-level school principal that, with the abolition of old structures (the 'former system was shoulder tapping'), the diffusion of best practice was 'gone'.

Power to the Parents: School Charters and Education Management

Central to the reforms in education was the idea that the school and its community would become a partnership, that parents and Boards of Trustees would be actively involved in school management and that Maori culture and identity would be respected and fostered. Harrison provides a summary of the legislative provisions in respect of the composition of Boards of Trustees:

New Zealand Schools: Boards of Trustees

(i) While the 'normal' number of parent representatives is five in the case of the lone Board of state school, such a Board may decide that it shall comprise not less than three but not more than seven parent representatives. The way in which parent representatives are elected is spelled out in detail.

(ii) Staff representatives must be members of the staff of the particular Board and elected by such members (excluding the Principal). Staff representatives are, like parent representatives, elected triennially.

(iii) Student representatives must be full-time students and must be elected by students (other than adult students) enrolled full-time in a class above form 3 at the school in question. By amendment introduced in 1991, Boards are now able to decide not to have a student representative.

(iv) Boards have a discretion whether or not to co-opt additional trustees. A Board may not co-opt a number of trustees in excess of one less than its number of parent representatives. In other words, if the Board has the 'normal' complement of five parent representatives, it may co-opt up to four additional trustees. An increase in the number of parent representatives up to a maximum of seven would enable a corresponding increase in the number of co-options. Boards when co-opting (or appointing) trustees must have regard to certain criteria aimed at making the Board reflect an appropriate gender, ethnic and socio-economic balance in relation to the character of the school and its community.

(v) While Boards now have increased powers to vary the way they are constituted – that is, to increase or decrease the number of parent representatives; to empower a body corporate to appoint a trustee or trustees to the Board; to set the number of co-opted trustees, and to dispense with having a student representative – it should be noted that Section 94B specifies a strict procedure for this.

In particular, Boards contemplating such decisions must take reasonable steps to ensure that parents of students have proper notice of, and the right to be present at, the Board meeting at which the decision is to be made. *(Harrison, 1993)*

The New Zealand School Charter discussed in chapter 3 was one of the primary innovations of the Education Act 1989. The Act stipulates certain mandatory content for the School Charter: that it should aim to meet national curriculum guidelines; that it should reflect New Zealand's cultural diversity and the position of Maori culture. The Act stipulates core Charter elements including the requirement that Boards enhance learning 'by establishing a partnership with the school's community' and to be 'responsive to the educational needs and wishes' of that community. In stipulating the powers and responsibilities of the Board, Section 75 of the Education Act 1989 states:

> Except to the extent that any enactment or general law of New Zealand provides otherwise, a school's board has complete discretion to control the management of the school as it thinks fit.

One School Trustee reported that Charters 'have tended to remain as a symbolic function rather than as a strategic guide to the School. It is the case, however, that Charters did give a sense of community ownership to the schools'.

In its view of the progress of reform, the Ministry of Education (1993) stated:

> The bureaucratic maze of the Department of Education, with its regional offices, and associated boards, councils and committees was demolished. In its place was established a simple and much less populated set of agencies. Day-to-day decision making on education, and the responsibility for the hundreds of millions of dollars necessary to make the decisions effective, were taken from the centre and moved to the institutions where education actually happens.

This is the official public view; get rid of bureaucracy, simplify the structures, empower the institutions and 'progress' is achieved. The New Zealand reforms viewed organizations and institutions as simply structural devices: in an ironic way the agency model reflected some of the character of Weber's bureau. That is, if effective services were to be purchased by the schools out of monies provided by the State, then new rules and regulations, new performance measures could be applied in a rational and technical way to provide impetus for the change.

This rational/technical vision is necessary but not sufficient. As chapters 2 and 5 have shown, the nature of core public services and their control require more than technical advances to ensure effectiveness. They require due recognition of the professionals and the duality of their provider–agent relationship with the citizen–client. They also require attendance to citizen voice. Indeed, the Ministry of Education-sponsored review of the reforms drew attention to the need for continuity with the past (see below). This is an alternative public view and a published record (University of Waikato, 1993) which is much less sanguine and which highlights the effect of reform on school principals.

Hear Our Voices

1. While respondents in this research project represented a broad spectrum of views on the balance of power that should be exercised at the centre, *vis-à-vis* individual schools, the weight of opinion suggests that the mix achieved in late-1991 to early 1992 was broadly acceptable.
2. For the most part, professionals and parents and other members of communities have accommodated to the sharing of responsibility for governing and managing their schools.

3. To the degree that the *Tomorrow's Schools* reforms have gained acceptance and have been successfully implemented, it may well be that their continuity with the past has placed an influential role.

4. After two and a half years of the *Tomorrow's Schools* reforms, the respondents provided little support for the [Picot Task Force's] prediction that the standard of educational outcomes would be improved under the new structure.

5. Respondents were generally quite critical of the way in which several aspects of the reforms were implemented. Their criticism centred on inadequacies of information flow, excessive demands on the participants, and poor resourcing of new developments. *(University of Waikato, 1993)*

The notion of professionalism, as outlined in chapter 2, can be a cloak for self-interest; if properly enforced and regulated it can be supportive of quality service. I return to the impact of professionals in chapter 7. If the public service in the UK is to be rendered more effective and responsive one key element of that reform is recognition of the value of professional codes of practice and values. Equally, professionals must, themselves, realize that the status awarded to them has duties and responsibilities attendant on such status. Client voice and effective public participation in service delivery mediates between the policies of political reformers and the defensive routines of professional self-interest. I examine this issue in chapter 7.

▬▬ Professional Bureaucracy and Germany's ▬▬ Education Reform

If the New Zealand education reforms are based on a decentralized model (originally the language was one of devolution) with clear attempts made to apply the purchaser–provider split as in other areas of social provision, then the German model allows one to evaluate quite a different approach.

The impetus behind the new School law (1992), which determined the scope and responsibilities of the School Councils was, in part, a financial one. It was thought that further delegation of autonomy to the schools could lead to new arrangements for managing their responsibilities and of possible co-sharing of financial responsibilities between the State and local communities. Another major source of impetus was to resolve the long running federal–state battle on comprehensive schools; the Catholic regions who fiercely opposed them could now, democratically, through their School Conferences, decide not to adopt a comprehensive model. The School Councils also simplified decision making within schools: hitherto, any teaching initiative required the separate agreement of three bodies, the teachers, parents and student conferences; now only the agreement of the unified School Council is required.

The general democratization movement in Germany since the end of the Second World War has resulted in a highly technical and administrative structure in education with clearly defined roles for the headteacher and subject teachers. Thus, for example, the headteacher is responsible for supervision of the implementation of civil service law in respect of teacher employment, whereas subject supervision (*Fach*) is the responsibility of the Inspectorate at regional level. In that respect one experienced observer of the system observed that 'a much less authoritarian school culture obtains in Germany than in the United Kingdom'.

The German model for the management of second level schools is, by and large, to accommodate the professional teachers and headteachers within a restrictive and detailed code of laws and regulations. While a federal structure allows for a great deal of independence to be devolved to the individual *Länder* (regions), the broad strategic controls are those of the education professionals rather than the more prescriptive national curriculum/testing and Ofsted model, as in England and Wales. In a very direct sense, the German experience confirms one of the research's main propositions: it is through a partnership between government and the professions that education services of a high quality are delivered.

Unlike the traditional bureaucratic model discussed earlier in the chapter, the German education system can be described in Mintzberg's terms as a professional bureaucracy. Mintzberg, in his work on organizational structures, defined a number of dominant processes which, depending on the organizational task, strongly influence the social and technical configuration of the organizations. The processes underlying education provision do include quite a number of issues identified in our model of the SLPO: allocation of resources and investment, legislation setting out strategic objectives, the articulation of 'rules of the game' and performance measurement. In large measure these functions and processes are technical devices which provide a framework for delivery and control. They do not, of themselves, constitute the core of service delivery and provision, which is the service relationship with the citizen–client.

Among the responsibilities delegated to the School Council is the school assessment strategy and the length of the school week, for example, a school could decide to have teaching on a Saturday. In respect of teacher motivation one school principal observed that 'at present much is owed to the idealism of the teachers; such a phenomenon can, over time, lead to a loss of motivation if it is not supported by the system'. Such an observation fits well with our earlier discussion of professional bureaucracy in that managers cannot assume professional commitment to change; such commitment has to be fostered and supported. The official job description of a headteacher is 'someone who has to implement the decisions of the School Board'. One principal described his management style as follows:

> to be successful, a principal has to 'grow' new teachers, to encourage their development of high standards, to seek more engagement from teachers and to encourage greater involvement with the local community.

As we saw in New Zealand, in Germany great attention has been focused on the role of the headteachers and their relationship with the School Board. While the New Zealand legislation does not formally embody the notion of a contract between the Board and the Ministry of Education, it did seek to clearly specify the management relationships at the school level.

In Germany the fact that, from the outset, the teachers and headteachers had, under legislation, a formal mechanism for collaborative management, helped to embed the partnership arrangements:

Observation of German Headteachers on School Reforms

An efficient school is one where the organization works well, where people enjoy coming to work on time: when teachers keep up with the literature in their subject area, where new ways are sought to teach more effectively and when there is openness to the parents.

It is permissible for a principal to 'interpret the law' provided she has the support of teachers, parents and students. There is room within the legal framework to encourage individual and group creativity.

The principal does not have the legal competence to force pedagogic change. It is good if the principal does not have to exercise his authority, but can do so. *(McKevitt, 1996)*

Decentralized Authority and Effective Organizational Structures

It has been noted earlier in this chapter that many SLPOs are organic professional bureaucracies, which are clearly influenced by values and norms in the wider society. For example, the democratic structures of German schools closely parallel the wider democratization of German institutions after the Second World War. The New Zealand reforms in education sought to impose technical and organizational changes which were common throughout the wider public service, including commercial public organizations. The thrust of these reforms was blunted by the values of the professionals themselves in alliance and co-operation with parents.

The tensions inherent in these public sector reforms can be clarified by identifying two distinct environments that operate on the SLPO, the technical and institutional. Scott and Meyer define these environments as follows:

> technical environments are those in which a product or service is produced or exchanged in a market such that organization are rewarded for effective and efficient control of their production systems . . . Institutional environments are, by definition, those characterized by the elaboration of rules and requirements to which individual organizations must conform if they are to receive support and legitimacy. The requirements may stem from regulatory agencies authorized by the nation state, from professional or trade associations, from generalized belief systems that define how specific types of organizations are to conduct themselves, and similar sources. Whatever the source, organizations are rewarded for conforming to these rules or beliefs. *(1991, p. 123)*

These environments, technical and institutional, are not mutually exclusive and figure 6.2 shows how the two environments can be cross-classified. In terms of

Figure 6.2 Combining technical and institutional environments

Pharmaceuticals

	Stronger	Utilities banks general hospitals	general manufacturing
Technical Environments	Weaker	mental health clinics schools, legal agencies churches	restaurants health clubs

Source: Scott and Meyer (1991)

this chapter's data it can be seen that schools operate in a strong institutional environment and in a weak technical environment.

Let us recall at this point Mintzberg's (1979) contention that changes in professional bureaucracies 'seep in' through gradual changes in professional recruitment, training and education. Yet we can observe in both New Zealand and England that large-scale and widespread changes were attempted in the education system, and attempts were made to sunder existing institutional values and practices.

The State, through the imposition of rational organizational structures, sought to minimize or curtail professional practice and autonomy and to impose technical measures of performance (such as school league tables in England). I referred earlier to the 'paradox of decentralization' whereby administrative discretion is curtailed though formal and detailed operating procedures.

To some extent, therefore, we can see how the State, through the imposition of new organizational structures and new control procedures, has tried to control an institutional environment that draws its legitimacy from outside of the state apparatus. In Germany, the laws and regulations (the technical environment) support the teaching profession and thereby a powerful coalition of interests is forged. In this instance, the German example supports Scott's assertion that:

> when beliefs are widely shared and categories and procedures taken for granted, it is less essential that they be formally encoded into the organizational structure. *(1991, p. 181)*

When examining the management of professionals in the next chapter further examples of how certain countries seek to impose control structures on professionals will be seen. The centralization of state control runs against the professional desire for decentralized discretion. In terms of the model outlined in figure 6.1, there is then a clear clash between the state and the professions.

The effectiveness of decentralization in SLPOs' operating practices thereby depends on partnership between the state and the professions. Effectiveness also depends on the relationship between professionals and the citizen–client: we have already seen how citizen 'voice' is not granted sufficient weight in the delivery of public services.

If the relationship between the State and the professions is not a harmonious one, then it is unlikely that effective organizational structures will be developed. The coercive power of the State is sufficient to impose new controls and procedures but these are unlikely to be effective as these data show. I return to this important topic in chapter 7.

■■■ Summary and Conclusions ■■■

The pursuit of organizational effectiveness is a relentless one as government and taxpayers seek greater economy and efficiency whilst maintaining service quality. The idea of bureaucracy gives rise to ideas of rigidity, inflexible rules and regulations and indifference to the voice of the citizen–client.

Such an argument (and there is no consistent empirical evidence that, at the micro level of the institution delivering a service, SLPOs are the more expensive) can be seen as relying on *a priori* values and ideologies that favour private provision of services. We are not concerned here with these arguments: the focus is, rather, on how public service organizations can be structured to deliver their existing services.

We may observe, for example, how organizational values can be an important source of structural effectiveness – the New Zealand reforms, predicated on the purchaser–provider model, succeeded in so far as teachers and parents saw them as consistent with the historical level of quality and professionalism in New Zealand's education system. That is, the professionals worked the 'new rules of the game' – in particular financial devolution to buttress and enhance what they perceived to be New Zealand's core competences in educational provision. In my fieldwork I was struck by how proud New Zealand teachers were in their system of education and how enthusiastically they sought to operate the new structures so as to further enhance their school's effectiveness. Another important feature of the New Zealand reform was the openness of debate and research, the very publicness of the arguments and the high level of enthusiasm and activity that the debate generated.

One example of such openness is the public availability of the effectiveness audit reports of schools carried out by the Education Review Office (ERO). Parents and the public thus have easy access to data on their schools which are not handled in the mechanistic fashion of league tables as in England. I examine the work of ERO in the next chapter.

Thus, the New Zealand reforms in education, while highly suffused with the language of devolution, parental involvement and purchaser–provider models of financial control, are in large degree a partnership between the State and the professionals.

In any event, the old dichotomy that professionals and State relations are, inherently, antagonistic (which is the basis of the 'capture model' of agency theory) is not as Powell and Di Maggio (1991, p. 71) observe very relevant today: 'professional power is as much assigned by the State as it is created by the activities of the professions'. That is, the State is in partnership with the professions in so far as they are either State employees or they are granted autonomy by the State.

In examining the role of organizational structures, and professional values, in delivering effective services we can observe that it is necessary to view organizations as institutions; that is, schools, hospitals and welfare offices are part of a wider societal framework from which the SLPO gains legitimacy and resources. The SLPO is an organic institution largely staffed by professional providers and it is located within a changing external environment. The application of technical and rational solutions to problems of organizational delivery is unlikely to be effective unless such solutions, as in New Zealand and Germany, are aligned with existing professional values and practices. Decentralized structures have to be consistent with the organic SLPO internal structures; hierarchy and authority may well reside at the centre but this is not where services are delivered.

I can summarize the data and argument in this chapter as follows:

- the SLPO is an organic professional bureaucracy and organizational change requires recognition of this institutional character;
- mechanistic controls and organizational structures that emphasize technical accountability are unsuitable to the SLPO;
- effective structures for service delivery require the commitment of professional providers.

CHAPTER

7

Managing Professionals

 **Introduction**

This chapter examines one of the most important relationships in the management of core public services – that is, the relationship between managers and service providers, the professionals delivering services to the citizen–client. I have already examined in chapter 3 the role of the citizen–client in service delivery and noted that, in general, citizen 'voice' is not a large part of delivery process, albeit that certain countries, notably New Zealand, have begun to give attention to this issue. In much of the debate on reform in core public services, the professionals delivering the services are seen as one of the main barriers to effectiveness; this is, at first sight, a paradox; why is it that the 'experts' should be identified as the main barrier to reform? I have examined in chapter 2 the role of differential information in structuring the relationship between the professional and the citizen–client. At the core of most relationships – education, health, welfare – there is an asymmetry of information between the provider and the client in respect of the outcomes for the client in the consumption of services. In this perspective, curriculum reform and surgical procedures are both similar in that, in each case, the client possesses far less information than the provider as to the outcome of their consumption. The impact of differential information, however, goes much further than the consequences for the individual citizen–client: there are important social consequences associated with those service transactions. There are, and have been developed over the last century, certain wider social values, for example, an educated citizenry, a healthy population, dignified care for the elderly, which governments have accepted as part of their agenda and which are not easily reducible to the micro-efficiency (value for money) framework of certain reform programmes.

There is a crucial distinction between the provider–client relationship in the public and private sector: in the public sector, the professional stands in a dual capacity to the client – both as provider of the service and as the client's agent, in that it is in the professional's interest to protect and defend the client. This duality of relationship has, historically and across many different countries, placed constraints and obligations on the professional: to place the client's interest above monetary gain; to treat each client in a similar manner regardless of social or economic differences; to defend the client's interest from sectoral or group self-interest. An important development, which is examined in this chapter, is the rise of the state-professional, as most professionals in the core public services have become salaried employees of the state. The development of the European welfare state has largely seen the incorporation of the professional within the structure of government employment. Yet the governance of the profession has, certainly in Anglo-Saxon countries, remained within the control of the profession itself.

In examining the management of professionals – teachers, doctors – I also examine the appraisal of managers themselves, in so far as they constitute an important part of the service delivery process. In many of the reforms examined in this text, a central impetus of reform has been the desire of governments to increase the efficiency and effectiveness of the SLPO.

Chapter 6 identified the key characteristics of the professional bureaucracy and the role that senior managers play in such organizations – internal resource allocation decisions, dealing with relationships with the external environment, the attraction of resources and institutional legitimacy. How well do managers perform these tasks and how can managers account for their responsibilities in this area? A number of countries have proposed performance measurement frameworks as conducive to the supervision of these accountabilities.

The appraisal of performance, both of the professional and the manager, has tended to concentrate at the individual level – that is, the focus has been on individuals delivering the service rather than on the actual outcome of the service relationship itself. This chapter examine instances of collective outcomes of service delivery (in so far as they can be found) because core public services are primarily directed at social cohesion and interdependence (see chapter 2). This perspective is important as collective or institutional services – the school, the hospital – is one of the primary functions of the core public service.

This chapter examines two issues:

1 the relationship between managers and state employed professionals;
2 the performance measurement frameworks that are applied to professional service providers.

Professionals, Citizens and Responsiveness

Given the importance of SLPOs in the workings of the public sector, and the conflicting pressures from the environment, we need to be aware that countries have evolved quite different institutional arrangements and organizational routines for the management of these organizations of professionals. Public organizations evolve complex arrangements for social control as they seek to accommodate competing and conflicting demands from their environment.

In this regard, we need to remember that the Anglo-Saxon tradition of public service by professional specialists is only some one hundred years old. Hitherto, in Anglo-Saxon countries, doctors, lawyers, teachers and engineers were self-employed or dependent on political patronage for their income. The present organizational and institutional arrangements for the provision of social welfare public services are quite recent phenomena. Their impetus lay in the sweeping away of poor law arrangements and their zenith lay in the period from 1946 through to 1970. Correspondingly, the Anglo-Saxon argument for market arrangements for public service provision is a most recent event. The arguments for the market are based on the assumption of information equality, which – as I argued in chapter 2 – are not valid.

This time frame has important implications. If society is not to be buffeted by changes which presage disruption of social cohesion, then it is the responsibility of professionals and managers to understand the character of the SLPO, including its environment and to attend to its purpose rather than to experiment wildly on some far out theory with its internal rules and ethical codes. Assuming that progress is best made one step at a time, then the first step is to develop the professional codes, in relation to the durable sentiments of society, and to do this as part of a strategy, of a 'timed series of conditional moves'.

This surely entails the government and the professions establishing good working relationships with each other. Here, there is a problem in countries that have no traditions in this matter.

The development and maintenance of a code of professional ethics is not separable from the general development of a society's norms and traditions. Thus, for example, the German tradition of a salaried and university educated professional civil servant paralleled the more general developments of the Bismarckian welfare state in the late nineteenth century. In large measure, the north European tradition of professional development and institutional cohesion was a reciprocal relationship that developed in the nineteenth century between the emerging professional class and the modern nation state. Hence, in the Nordic countries the professionals were instrumental in legitimizing the governance of the modern welfare state as they embodied the act of service to the citizenry. Such developments were reflected in the wider development of the socio-legal arrangement whereby citizen rights and not responsibilities and entitlements were embodied in the law.

By contrast, the Anglo-Saxon tradition of professional development was one whereby, in general, the professionals acquired or were granted great autonomy in their arrangements for self-regulation and control. Thus, doctors, lawyers and teachers, mostly state employees, were allowed to codify their own standards and guidelines, entry requirements and promotion criteria. It is only in the last decade that there has been sustained government attention given to the curtailment or abridgement of these professionals 'freedoms'. This process has largely been an adversarial one, reflected in the idea in the English-speaking countries that a competitive market ethic is now in the ascendant, with the professionals on the defensive, ethically, socially and economically.

Indeed, we would argue that much of the recent academic commentary in Anglo-Saxon countries on professionals is largely couched in terms of competitive analysis: its framework is driven by the notion that professionalism is, by and large, a cloak for self-interest, that its ethical base is a measure of social closure not a means for ensuring standards in service delivery. That notion itself seems based on the assumption that in this world, there is no such thing as society, there is no space for a sense of community, and there is no room for civic responsibility. Such assumptions may be useful for theoretical developments of a certain kind, but not we would argue, for operational purposes, even in very pessimistic eras.

At the same time, it would be unwise to view all UK government challenges since the mid-1980s of professional claims to autonomy and self-regulation as intrinsically a 'bad thing': one has to acknowledge that claims by professionals to act on an ethical basis in their relationships with citizens have to be balanced against the wide spread public disenchantment in the UK with a perceived poor standard of street level service delivery. Similarly, as the system of internal regulation by professional bodies has yielded little in the way of consistent debarment of its personnel, for bad behaviour, one can legitimately question whether self-regulation is working to the advantage of the client. Simply put, the professions seem not to give near enough attention to matters of discipline, including the disciplinary process itself, so in practice some professionals seem to be able to cheat and to get away with cheating. Yet for a government to refashion important relationships with the professionals through a series of laws and systems of crude performance measurement frameworks without a general consensus is not in the circumstances the best way to seek progress. Professionals play a complex role in the system.

In this regard, my research in this area has found that professionals are indeed attempting to 'hold the line' between pressures for cost containment and the threat of a decline in service quality. That is, professionals at street level with their conceptions of their work are a bulwark between the State's need to curtail expenditure and the necessity to maintain the minimum standards of services needed to promote and sustain social cohesion. Results vary. Countries as diverse in their historic and cultural traditions as Sweden and Germany have succeeded in mediating between government cost cutting and the maintenance of social cohesion and proper standards of service delivery. The relationship between professionals and clients, and between professionals and government in these countries tends to be one of mutual respect and trust, and of continuous evolution in line with evolution in traditions of behaviour. Backing that relationship are well-respected disciplinary processes.

In the UK, Ireland and the United States the situation is different; here, professional claims to autonomy are uneasily balanced against the legitimate sense of government to ensure efficiency and efficacy in service delivery and to control general public expenditure. However, the recent UK reforms of public service agencies have, in large measure, been revolutionary attempts to impose mechanistic controls in an environment where organic relationships are dominant.

It is not surprising, therefore, that there is evidence in the UK of public dissatisfaction with the reforms. These 'reforms' are inappropriate as a first step: the provision of social welfare public services is quite consistent with a need to seek 'value for money', as shown from my research in Sweden and Germany. But the first step in the Anglo-Saxon world is to develop good relationships between government and professions.

To do this, however, requires working with the grain of professional interest in quality, granting the professional specialists a voice in the formulation of general legislation, and attending to their historic role in civilizing state–citizen relationships. Replacing professional codes of ethics with market competition is not how modern democratic nations evolved, nor is it the way to resolve complex and important social problems. However, each country should undertake more research on the best practices of other countries to discover clues as to how to improve the management of professionals in their own public sector, bearing in mind that differences in national culture *per se* may lead to differences in the organization for the management of professionals.

To reform present day administrative or social arrangements one has to understand the past – the historical, economic and social influences that have shaped present-day arrangements. Any programme of reform in the public sector reflects assumptions as to the origins of the present 'problems', for example, in respect of the creation of quasi-markets in the NHS, the problem was perceived as the lack of competition between the various providers, that is, hospitals, general practitioners and District Health Authorities. By separating purchasing and providers, the assumption was that provider power would be lessened and, as a consequence, citizen responsiveness would be increased. Leaving aside, for the present, the fact that in a fixed cash limit environment the effect would be to rearrange the power relationships (GP fundholding practices would be now more influential than hospital consultants), the objectives of the reformers centred on the idea that managers required greater compliance and accountability from the professional providers.

A related issue is the idea, prominent in the Anglo-Saxon tradition, that organizations are merely instruments for the delivery of services, and hence once the 'rules of the game' (chapter 5) are altered, the organization will deliver the services under the new arrangements. An alternative view discussed in chapter 6 is that organizations are value systems, embedded in their institutional environments and reflect and defend the dominant values in their environments. When changes are made in the 'rules of the game', deemed inimical to the organization's values, then members of the organization will seek to deflect policies which they consider threaten the organization's mission or strategy. You can have, therefore, as we saw in the case of Sweden and New Zealand, examples of professionals seeking alliances with the citizen–clients to curtail or deflect government policy. Such alliances if they are successful may blunt the effects of government policy. A more salient question is why policy was evolved that did not take account of citizen 'voice' and professional interests.

It was pointed out in chapter 2 that one of the distinguishing characteristics of the public service environment is the pervasive nature of differential information between providers and clients of services. The agenda of modern government is, as a result, inextricably linked to the regulation of the relationship between the professionals and the citizen to ensure social cohesion and effective service delivery.

It is, perhaps, an irony that the United Kingdom, which pioneered the development of some modern State services in the core public service, has adopted a very mechanistic, rule-bound, strategy that runs directly counter to the interests of the citizen/client. Michael Oakshott, writing on the propensity of political and social reformers to have naive views on the rationality of their reform efforts neatly captures the dilemma of reformers who seek to reduce complex social relations to an economic calculus:

> To the Rationalist, nothing is of value merely because it exists (and certainly not because it has existed for generations), familiarity has no worth, and nothing is to be left standing for want of scrutiny. And his disposition makes both destruction and creation easier for him to understand and engage in, than acceptance or reform. To patch up, to repair (that is, to do anything that requires a patient knowledge of the material), he regards as a waste of time . . .
> *(Oakshott, 1994, p. 5)*

Belief in the rationality of an economic calculus as an organizational framework in the core public service management rests on the assumption that service relationships can be measured and regulated via such frameworks as value-for-money, league tables of performance and providing incentives for providers. All of these mechanisms are necessary but insufficient criteria for progress – the warp and weft of social relations require attention to the core relationship between the professional and the citizen. If we accept the dualism inherent in the professional relationship – that of provider and agent of the citizen in the service transaction (see chapter 2) – then reform needs to proceed on both these axes. The brunt of UK reform has focused on administrative arrangements – organizational restructuring, increasing centralization of central authority, and a weakening of the relationship between the local community and the citizen – designed to increase organizational efficiency.

It is fashionable to claim that the Thatcher years saw a diminution in the power of traditional networks, for example, trade unions, while laying stress on individuals as being in control of their own destiny. Yet the atomization of social relationships – 'we are all consumers and customers now' – fractures more than the influence of trade unions; it runs the risk of applying inappropriate yardsticks to the measurement of reform.

At this point it is appropriate to turn to the case study 'The Metropolitan Police plus programme' in the appendix. Please read it now and then answer the questions set out at the end. This examination of change in a professional bureaucracy highlights a number of key issues in this chapter – the measurement of professional performance, the influence of stakeholders in designing performance measures and the difficulty of implementing change in a professional environment, where professional values impact on the change process itself. There will be further examples of change in a professional context later in this chapter.

The Management of State Professionals

I posed the question at the beginning of this chapter 'why are professionals seen as one of the primary barriers to effectiveness'? As discussed above, in the Anglo-Saxon tradition, professionals are viewed as having undue power and influence and that their ethical base is seen as a means of social closure rather than as a support for standards in service delivery. The traditional arguments relating to professional power have some validity and, indeed, such arguments underpin much of the financial and organizational restructuring in the core public services.

The list below outlines the main characteristics of professionals – this commentary draws on the Anglo-Saxon tradition of professional critique.

- Professions are interest groups and as such they are engaged in competition with other interest groups up to, and including, the state.
- Such groups may pursue economic interests, but they will have other motives for their collective action. The drive for economic advantage is linked to the pursuit of social advantage. Professions, therefore, operate in both the economic and social order.
- Professions, who have opportunities for income based on their knowledge and qualifications, have a significance with those whose position derives from their capital or labour power.
- The collective action of professions can lead to 'social closure', that is, the closure of economic opportunities to non-professionals.
- The theories of professions can be grouped into the functionalist, structuralist, monopoly and cultural schools. *(Adapted from McDonald, 1995)*

The main parts of the tradition can be summarized as follows:

1 professionals give allegiance to their profession, in the first instance, rather than to the organization;
2 professionals control the performance criteria by which they are evaluated;
3 professionals are not competent (or trained) to manage resource allocation for collective provision;
4 professionals have authority for resource usage decisions but disclaim responsibility for the effect of these decisions.

Chapter 6 demonstrated how many SLPOs are characterized by an organic structure, reliant on mutual adjustment and knowledge for co-ordination and control rather than on the traditional hierarchy model. The nature of institutional environments and how a rationalized cultural environment is typical of a professional environment was also examined. There is, of course, a clear tension

Table 7.1 From bureaucracy to technocracy

Professionalism	Technocracy
Relatively autonomous work situation; collegiate control	System integration
Collegial control of training and gatekeeping	Institutional credentialism
Client orientation, ethic of service	Organization, system, orientation; ethos of efficiency
Broad mystique of competence	Specialization of skill: technical expertise as the basis of legitimation

Source: Adapted from Burris, 1991

as the state (or managers) seeks to impose structural devices and centralized forms of authority on such environments. This was seen in respect of UK reforms in health care and, in part, recent Swedish reforms in the same sector. Indeed, much recent organizational change in the public sector can be seen as a transition from professional status to one of technocratic control; table 7.1 outlines the argument in this area.

The emphasis in the technocratic model is on integration and control; the client orientation and ethic of service now shifts to an ethos of efficiency. The primary purpose of management is directed at organizational efficiency. Such an orientation reduces the likelihood of professional participation in the reform programme, as the data in this study demonstrates.

To be efficient, to demonstrate value-for-money, to be 'lean and fit' are all qualities deemed relevant and necessary in modern public management – recall here the discussion in chapter 4 of Hood's values. The 1980s witnessed a plethora of reform proposals broadly based on the crises in the welfare state (indeed, in 1981 the OECD published a series of papers entitled 'The Welfare State in Crisis'). Trends such as the ageing of the population, rising public indebtedness of governments, slow economic growth and high unemployment all brought pressure to bear on core public service programmes. Public expenditure was seen as inefficient and wasteful, public servants (including professionals) as sheltered from the 'discipline' of the market which was seen as beneficial to competitiveness and efficiency.

The reform programme in the UK was driven by the belief that the public sector manager needed to apply the same skills and techniques as those obtaining in the private sector – chapters 2 and 3 have discussed these frameworks and their relevance to management in the public domain. Governments sought to alter the 'rules of the game', to amend institutional relationships with the SLPO so as to encourage the creation of quasi-markets in large areas of social provision – health, community care and education. Let us examine more closely this concept of efficiency in the provision of public services: table 7.2 sets out the main economic definitions associated with this term.

Herbert Simon coined the term 'ruthless efficiency' in respect of the application of inappropriate efficiency frameworks to public service decisions:

Table 7.2 Definitions of efficiency

Technical efficiency:	measures the physical use of resource inputs in relation to resource outputs.
Economic efficiency:	measures the cost of using inputs in relation to the value of outputs.
Allocative efficiency:	the optimal distribution of resources, guided by prices whenever possible to ensure that resources are distributed among producing units to serve consumers wants in ways that reflect the costs of provision.
X – efficiency:	is concerned with productivity in the use of resources, producing at minimum cost.

> Efficiency, whether it be in the democratic state or the totalitarian, is the proper criterion to be applied to the factual element in the decisional problem. Other ethical criteria must be applied to the problem of evaluation . . . Yet in the actual application of the efficiency criterion to administrative solutions, there is often a tendency to substitute the former distinction for the latter, and that such a substitution inevitably results in the narrow, 'mechanical' efficiency which has been the subject of criticism. *(1994, p. 44)*

Simon goes on to argue that a proper weight be given to 'all community values' in reaching an administrative decision; administrators cannot (or should not) choose to give weight to only those values which lie within their own area of competence. Thus, for example, the indirect consequences of care in the community on the quality of life of former psychiatric patients would have to form part of the overall evaluation of such a policy – recall here the discussion of this policy in chapter 4.

The 'one-best way' to reform – examined in chapters 5 and 6 – of contract models, the design of organizational structures that promote efficiency, the installation of performance measurement frameworks that track resource usage rather than programme outcomes are characteristic of many efforts to change core public service delivery. It has been seen that there are advantages to be had from some of these reforms; that providers, including in some instances trade unions, have co-operated with them in so far as they are perceived to be in the interests of the citizen–client. It should also be recalled that the development and promotion of social cohesion and interdependence is a key characteristic of core public services. Performance measurement systems which do not take account of this collective purpose run counter to the collective character of core public services – this component of performance appraisal is examined later in this chapter.

Let us now turn to the case study 'Wellcare Hospital Trust' in the appendix. Please read the study and answer the questions set out at the end. You will see that the case illustrates some key themes of this chapter – the management of professionals and the design of performance measurement systems. The case also highlights another central issue in this text – the engagement of citizen–client voice in the management process. In the case study, patients do not have a high profile, something we also saw in chapter 4 when examining the Health Commissioner's report. In the next section I report on recent research on performance measurement in some one hundred UK public sector organizations. At this stage of the discussion we can reflect that the traditional view of professional 'power' is now under threat from recent changes that represent a technocratic 'solution' to problems of organizational efficiency. The New Zealand contract model (chapter 5) is now in the ascendant in many countries; the older tradition of trust and professionalism is now replaced by the idea of contract or performance measurement.

The organic institution reflecting the norms and values of society, staffed by professionals whose code of ethics values service to the client, is now replaced by the profit centre where values of efficiency and value-for-money are the norm. March and Olsen describe this change in institutional character in the public sector as follows:

> Contemporary welfare states appear to be in the process of redefining the appropriateness of different institutions, for instance the boundary between a sphere of solidarity based on universal citizen rights implemented through state bureaucracies, a sphere of self-interest and competition implemented through the price system . . . They appear to be developing an interpretation of history by which to explain the expanded agenda of the welfare state. But whether that interpretation will picture the welfare state as resulting from a coalition of self-interested beneficiaries, or as resulting from acceptance of ideal of justice is not clear . . . The outcome of that process of interpretation may affect the extent to which the next historical period will see co-operation as based on communities or as based on contracts. *(1989, p. 167)*

It is clear from the data reported in this text that the emphasis in many countries is towards the idea of contracts. Whilst strictly speaking many service contracts are not actionable in law, the notion of community is certainly not one on which many core reforms are based. We have seen, however, that professionals and citizen–clients in collaboration, such as in Sweden, Germany and New Zealand (in education) can exert a countervailing influence on reforms based solely on efficiency criteria.

Middle Managers, Professionals and Performance Measurement

In this section recent research (McKevitt and Lawton, 1996) on the installation of performance measurement in over one hundred UK organizations is examined; part of this research has already been discussed in chapter 3 where the role of citizen voice in the design of service delivery systems was examined. One of the guiding questions in this study was if middle managers were not directly involved in the process, then it is difficult to envisage that the performance measures would satisfy one key stakeholder, that is, those staff whose job it is to mediate between the professionals and the needs and expectations of clients. Inattention to the needs of middle managers has led to criticism by politicians of the success or otherwise of performance measurement systems. This may be partially explained by the command-control model of organizational life that politicians may hold – instigate the reform and 'let the managers manage'!

As seen in chapter 3 the primary impetus for performance measurement came from legislation and senior politicians and its over-riding purpose was on institutional measurement, that is, the attraction and justification of resources based on a control framework which paid little account to other stakeholder interests. The form and process of installation is also noteworthy; it was primarily a top–down, non-consultative one and a single model was adopted in most organizations. There was little evidence of piloting the change, review or adaptation in the light of experiments; the process was deliberate and mechanistic – characteristics that are unsuitable to the organic environment of the SLPO.

Institutional Functions

There was evidence to support the view that performance measurement has been used as a top–down instrument of senior management control in both central and local government. In one government department, performance measurement arrangements were described as reflecting the historic fiscal relationship between the executive and the government. Objectives were set to achieve a planned service output given an approved resource input. In a second government department, stakeholder issues were seen as secondary to servicing the requirements of legislation and the pressures of efficiency. Systems had been designed to provide information about the flows of cash, rather than to identify costs. And the political accountability process emphasized procedural considerations, rather than performance or quality of delivered services. The function of performance indicators in one central government agency was described as 'to assure the Permanent Secretary, who represents the Secretary of State and Ministers, that [the agency] is effective, efficient and provides value for money'.

Reflecting upon the various citizen and customer charters, a manager working in a central government department reported that:

> On the one hand such published assessment criteria will invite public scrutiny of the Executive's performance but on the other hand it may serve to publicize the shortfall in government funding which the Executive is suffering and which constrains its ability to tackle the demand for [its] services.

Similar views were expressed by a local authority manager:

> Stakeholders should be included in the debate on measuring performance; this may overcome suspicion, create a realistic appreciation of the issues and enhance quality of debate. It may, however, cause expectations, that resource

restrictions are unable to satisfy, and this issue should be clearly exposed in the debate.

One central government manager put it:

> Disbelief in the achievability of policy aims affects the creation of feasible objectives for middle and lower management and staff. In a situation where the demands of stakeholders cannot be fully met – because of resource pressure – it is more important than ever to be clear about the purpose that objectives serve.

That customer charters and nationally-designed measurement criteria may raise customer or client expectations is an additional burden on middle managers and front-line staff who may not be allocated additional resources for training or increased investment in facilities. A manager reported that:

> Genuine concerns are expressed that the changes are disadvantaging the underprivileged, homeless and poorer members of the community. The caring public sector orientation which many staff have is being seriously challenged and questioned. This has unforeseen consequences at all levels as we adopt and develop new 'bottom lines' including that of profit.

As Baier, March and Saetern reported (1994, p. 161), one explanation for difficulties in implementation can be attributed to conflicts of interest between policy-makers and officials and 'An interest in the support of constituents, whether voters or stockholders or clients, leads policy-makers to be vigorous in enacting policies and lax in enforcing them'.

The overwhelming evidence from the study is that performance measurement was implemented to satisfy the demands of the institutional environment of public service organizations (Meyer and Rowan, 1992). That is, if politicians and Treasury demand that public service organizations are required to show that they are visibly responding to the needs of external accountability, then the installation of performance measurement systems are largely a routine device to demonstrate compliance with external stakeholders. The unintended consequences of such a strategy are, however, considerable. Middle managers now find themselves uncomfortably 'close to the customers' to the extent that they now have to take responsibility for what they perceive to be inadequate levels of resources. This shifting of responsibility, from the political to the organizational, has given rise to significant pressure on middle level managers which is explored later in this section.

Managerial Functions

Professionals

My findings indicate that professional concerns feature prominently in NHS performance measurement. As one health board manager expressed it:

The service delivered is based on normative need, as perceived by the professional service deliverer, rather than on need felt or expressed by the client . . . finding a suitable, feasible and acceptable way of introducing client-based performance assessment is not easy. In particular those who have strong professional allegiances will inevitably feel that these may be compromised by being influenced by customers.

Professionals may also seek to resist what are perceived to be managerial initiatives particularly where:

The acceptability of PIs to staff will depend not just on the technical design of the system but also on the broader implications it has for the distribution of power within the organization. *(Carter, 1991, p. 97)*

This argument is well-supported by one NHS manager:

The professions have efficient networks in place, and have a strong sense of solidarity when in disagreement with generalist management. They view management as only being interested in resource-use assessments, and they will resist any indicators which threaten professional autonomy or interests.

The obvious place where professional interests may be paramount is in the NHS. However, I found similar concerns with professional power in higher education where performance measurement was seen by academics as 'state interference in professional autonomy'; in information technology where services are defined by professional needs rather than customer requirements; and in a government agency employing scientists whose 'concern for scientific excellence may be undermined by customer-focused assessment'.

The pursuit of professional goals may lead to goal conflict with the organization. However, it seems that to assume professional autonomy is necessarily dysfunctional for an organization is too simplistic. Further work needs to be done concerning the extent to which professionals may further and protect the interests of another group of stakeholders, for example, patients or clients, against the wishes of a further group of stakeholders, for example, senior managers. Under pressure from external sources, the possibility is that there can be a coalition of stakeholder interests between producers and clients facing conditions of resource constraints. Evidence for such emerging conclusions can be found in education alliances between parents and trade unions in New Zealand and trade unions in Sweden facing expenditure cuts in local authority budgets.

Middle management and ownership of performance measures

The central finding of the research is the lack of attention paid to middle and junior management in the development and implementation of performance measurement systems and hence the lack of embeddedness of systems throughout the organization. Guth and Macmillan describe the role of implementation as follows:

General management is not omnipotent. It is, in varying degrees, dependent on middle management for technical knowledge and functional skills . . . There is an imperative to seek strategies that are both competitively effective and capable of gaining organizational commitment. If general management decides to go ahead and impose its decisions in spite of lack of commitment, resistance by middle management can drastically lower the efficiency with which the decisions are implemented, if it does not completely stop them from being implemented. *(1989, p. 315)*

In a county council social services department:

The major problem with the charter and guarantee systems will be in terms of 'ownership' by middle managers and staff alike. Unless the targets are seen (or perhaps 'sold') as realistic and likely to be of benefit to users the scheme will not achieve its stated aims of improving the organization's responsiveness. This is a worrying scene currently as all the work has come from the top down (much of it member driven) with virtually no consultation with users or staff.

A similar lack of congruence and lack of ownership was reported in a NHS health board:

The goals in the Framework for Action and Patients Charter were developed internally, and reflect the views of politicians, civil servants, senior managers and professionals. There is evidence that the upper echelons of the organization are beginning to work together to improve the performance of the Health Service, particularly through the introduction of Clinical Directorates. Goal congruence with junior staff, patients and the public has still to be achieved.

The lack of communication with middle managers including poor feedback, and inadequate information on user needs was a persistent theme of the management reports. One authority, with the best of intentions, sought to increase its responsiveness to the public through flattening its structure. This was put in place from above with no explanation or training in what this was intended to achieve. Tiers of management were stripped out and the number of staff was reduced. Those who remain are in no frame of mind to deliver very much'.

In another local authority case, there was clear goal incongruence between the systems designed for performance pay of chief officers and the actual operational component of middle-managers' jobs:

Therefore, the performance indicators do not necessarily reflect what operational managers are actually doing and are not an integral part of the operational management process. There should be greater involvement of managers and staff and users in developing performance indicators. This would ensure ownership of the indicators and motivate people to achieve targets. It would also ensure goal congruence.

Implementation of strategic change has to address the internal context of the organization. Kotter and Schlesinger (1989) argued that successful change needs to fit with organizational variables which include the kind and amount of resistance to change that can be anticipated; the relative power of those who wish to introduce change and those who might resist it; the locus of relevant data for designing the change (in the case of performance measurement it is likely that those charged with delivering the performance will be aware of the impact on the users, customers or clients). In reviewing implementation in a local authority context, one manager's perception of the implementation process captures quite well the narrow definition of stakeholder involvement:

> The performance assessment activity tends to be dominated by the demands of more powerful stakeholders, leaving weaker groups of users and providers under-represented when decisions are taken in the light of such assessments.

The lack of attention paid to the need to gain commitment from middle management is symptomatic of a 'command and control' view of organization dynamics. Senior managers and politicians decide on the desired direction of change and then proceed to implement a top–down process of change. Such a strategy – which Kotter and Schlesinger remind us is appropriate if there is an overwhelming need to produce fast results – does not reflect the organizational or cultural character of many public services. The provision of services such as health care, education or social services is highly dependent on the quality and motivation of the service providers – a mechanistic approach to change implementation in this highly organic environment is not appropriate. Evidence of such motivation and commitment is available, despite the problems identified above. In a district general hospital it was one manager's individual commitment that ensured the support of her team 'but there is no resourcing from outside the department itself and the system runs entirely on goodwill and voluntary effort'.

However, the fact that individual initiative was successful in this case only serves to confirm the more general finding that emphasis on institutional measures of performance combined with a top–down implementation strategy fails to engage middle manager commitment. It is also clear that essential supports – training, participation in design, additional resources to monitor the system – were not provided in the great majority of the 100 organizations studied.

In this study, we see the unintended consequences of a change of strategy that does not have regard for the values and beliefs of the middle managers – 'the caring public sector orientation which many staff have is being seriously challenged' – such a strategy runs quite serious risks. In reflecting on the plethora of organizational change that many national public administration systems have been subjected to over the last twenty years, Brunnson states:

> Forgetfulness is also easily achieved: most organizations thrive happily on the fact that almost all reforms look better *ex ante* rather than *ex post*. Reforms are often launched as simple slogans which attract and inspire, while the actual work of reform tends to reveal the complications and the drawbacks. So it is

easy to argue that the new reform now being proposed is better than the old one already tried, and a new attempt is always worthwhile. *(1989, p. 226)*

However, in recognizing that public sector organizations are influenced by a multiplicity of stakeholders, it may then be unrealistic to expect any system of performance measurement to satisfy the interests of all stakeholders. Organizations are political in nature, made up of different individuals, groups and coalitions all competing for power. It is likely that some stakeholders will resist change, others will be unwilling to give up power. As one manager put it: 'invariably very few performance management systems can reflect the needs of multiple stakeholders and the more powerful stakeholder interests are likely to dominate. Performance management is therefore a political and value laden process'.

However, the data from 100 public sector organizations, in a diverse range of service areas, clearly show that there are problems in the implementation of performance measurement systems that have as their ostensible purpose the design of responsive delivery systems for citizens.

The data reported above, which are drawn from a large and diverse range of public sector organizations in the UK over the last five years, clearly suggests that the performance measurement frameworks that are being applied are largely directed towards the interests of senior management and politicians. The middle managers, the citizen–client and the professional service deliverer are not central players in the process. The frameworks are seen as threatening to the caring public service ethos of providers and placing middle management in a position whereby they have to take responsibility for resource constraints which they regard as the domain of the politician. There is little evidence to suggest that performance measures are acceptable, in their present form, to professionals or that the citizen has been consulted in their design. The majority of the performance indicators are concerned with accountability for resource usage, as opposed to accountability for effectiveness of use. That is, the performance frameworks are mechanical and audit-oriented rather than outcome and process-oriented. Let us now examine the experience of New Zealand in education reform and the emphasis on a community or collective focus on performance and accountability.

New Zealand: Partnerships and Community

In New Zealand's education reform programme many of the instruments of reform (e.g., decentralization, performance review) are common to the UK experience and were applied. In New Zealand's case there was much greater involvement of the trade unions and other stakeholders in the reform project.

On fieldwork in New Zealand I was struck by the energy, enthusiasm and thought with which the trade unions engaged in the reform process. Whilst not accepting the political agenda of reform, the trade unions representing the teacher unions sought to shape the process of change in defence of what they saw as the high professional base of New Zealand's education system. One senior trade union officer reported that:

> The NZEI [primary teachers] sought to maximize those parts of the reform which they believed to be positive for education. While *Tomorrow's Schools* [see chapter 6] contained elements of New Right ideology, it did contain elements of participative democracy which NZEI has encouraged . . . It now considers that it could mobilize some 70 per cent of parents and school trustees to support its stance on educational issues. To some extent, the primary system has gained through the reforms especially due to increased parental support and involvement.

The education reforms placed the Board of Trustees of schools as a centre piece of their change process. Chapter 6 discussed the legal responsibilities of Boards: the legislative framework for New Zealand's education reforms placed special emphasis on the idea of the community in partnership with the headteacher and education professionals in the schools. The New Zealand School Trustees Association, representative of all New Zealand schools, saw as one of its central objectives that the school charters be renegotiated and to have them as a contract document.

The reform process laid special emphasis on the issue of contracts for headteachers who were charged with the professional leadership within their schools. Headteachers are legally obliged to carry out the duties as specified in the contract, which was a new contract consequent to the passage of the education reform legislation. With the abolition of old legislative frameworks in the civil and public services, the position of headteacher is now subject to contract between the Boards of Trustees and the headteacher. The model contract for primary teachers runs to some 48 pages and a summary of its provision is set out below.

Responsibilities of the Principal

The Principal accepts appointment with the Board on the terms and conditions contained in this Contract.

(a) During the currency of this Contract the Principal shall honestly and diligently carry out the duties and responsibilities of the Principal as set out in the job description attached as Schedule A to this Contract.

(b) The parties agree that in order to carry out the duties and responsibilities of this Contract it may be necessary for the Principal to work more than 40 hours a week.

The Principal shall not, during the term of this Contract or at any time thereafter, except so far as may be necessary for the proper performance of the Principal's duties and responsibilities, or as may be required by law:

(a) Disclose to any person, other than to a member of the Board, any official information which has come to the Principal's knowledge in the course of the performance of this Contract;

(b) Use or attempt to use any such official information for the Principal's own personal benefit, or for the benefit of any other person or organization, or in any manner whatsoever, other than in accordance with the Principal's duties and consistent with the obligation of honesty expected of a person in the Principal's position.

Upon the termination or expiry of this Contract, the Principal shall deliver to the Board any official information, and any other property of the School, the Board, or the Crown which may be in the Principal's possession or under the Principal's control.

Performance Review

The Board will review, either generally or in respect of any particular matter, the performance of the Principal in carrying out the duties and responsibilities of the position.

The Board shall, as soon as reasonably practicable, consult the Principal on the process and the criteria to be used to review the Principal's general performance.

The process and criteria to be used to review the Principal's general performance shall be recorded in writing and shall be called the Performance Agreement. A copy of the Performance Agreement shall be given to the Principal.

The process that is used to review the Principal's general performance shall take into account the duties and responsibilities of the Principal under this Contract, any particular objectives set by the Principal and the Board, the nature and priority of such objectives, and any other quantitative and qualitative performance indicators applying to the Principal's work.

The decision of the Board on the contents of any Performance Agreement for any year will be final, but the Principal shall have the right to attach written comments to the Performance Agreement if the Principal considers the Performance Agreement to be unreasonable.

The Principal will assist the Board to conduct any review under this clause and in particular will give to the Board such information as the Board requires to carry out the review. *(State Services Commission, 1992)*

Alcorn (1992) in a review of education reforms noted the following dilemmas for headteachers:

> Other dilemmas, however, are rooted in the disjuncture between the managerial efficiency model being officially propounded and the professional service model to which many educators subscribe. Whereas educational leadership theories have moved towards a goal of schools as communities of reflective practitioners, working collaboratively and in partnership with parents where appropriate, official policies increasingly appear to regard teachers as human resources to be managed and controlled. Boards are elected to exercise this control and principals appointed to implement their policies. The logic of this position is that self-managing schools could exclude teachers from participating in policy formation.

Here we see the growing encroachment of managerial notions of efficiency or accountability into an organic professional institution such as the school. The countervailing influence and authority of NZEI and the parents helped to blunt this mechanistic model of reform.

The New Zealand education reforms are monitored by the Education Review Office (ERO) which replaced the inspectorate of the Department of Education. One of the functions of ERO is to carry out Assurance Audits, available to the public, to measure schools' compliance with legislation, school charters and licences. The Audit is described as 'an information resource for governing bodies' and is made up of:

- background information about the school or centre and the scope of the assurance audit;
- a summary of findings confirming the areas in which the governing body is meeting requirements and identifying any areas which need action;
- details of the findings based on the requirements;
- the actions that the governing body needs to take to meet the requirements;
- suggested developments for improving performance over and above the standard requirements.

The ERO review looks at Board administration, curriculum management, student support, management of Maori education, personnel management, financial management and asset management. The scope of the ERO review combines elements which in the UK would be shared between Ofsted and the Audit Commission. Particular stress is laid on consultation with the local community of schools, as is shown from the extract of an ERO report set out below:

ERO Assurance Audit

The Board has sound policies and procedures for governing the school.

While responsibility for the implementation of the curriculum is delegated to the principal, the Board is able to monitor curriculum through the school's policy statements in subject areas and through background training before each monthly Board meeting. This usually takes the form of a presentation by a teacher or group of teachers.

The Board works closely with the community and has consulted regularly regarding such things as the charter development and local goals. The consultation process in relation to the school's health programme is conducted as required. The Board's handbook states the commitment to consultation and recognition that a wide variety of consultation modes will be necessary to make purposeful contact with the community. Policies have been referred to meetings of parents.

Meetings of the Board are open to the public and parents do attend. The agenda of each meeting is available through the school or from Board members. These meetings are advertised through the newsletter and minutes of the Board's meetings are available at the school. The Board has not formally adopted a set of procedures for meetings and the review team recommends that this be done in the interests of continuity so that new members or new Boards will have guidelines to follow on agreed style and standards.

Consultation with the Maori community has been appropriately carried out by co-option to the Board and by taking the school's Treaty of Waitangi policy to the local Kaumatua Council for its approval.

The Board attempts to reflect the school's community in its composition. A system of subcommittees is operated to cover important aspects of its operations. Members attend training and development workshops when opportunities arise. The Board regularly has a full day (Sunday) meeting to consider big issues or when there is a need for some training.

There is a system operating for the self review of policies. The school's handbook includes all the school's policies, the teacher's handbook and the Board of Trustees handbook. This latter section indicates the considerable efforts which have been made to formalize in writing the procedures and practices expected of and by the Board as it manages its responsibilities. It is a very valuable resource and would be excellent support to a new member and for continuity of style when a new Board is elected.

The Board is taking all reasonable steps to comply with the requirements of the National Administration Guidelines and there are no actions required as a result of the audit. *(ERO, 1993)*

This emphasis on partnership with the community is also reflected in the code of Ethics of the New Zealand Educational Institute (for primary teachers) which includes the following provision for teachers:

- that individuals can make a significant contribution to the community in many varied ways;
- that they should work with parents to promote the welfare of children, particularly by consulting and involving parents whenever this is desirable;
- an obligation to enhance in every possible way the standing of their profession in the community.

In evaluating the effect of reform in New Zealand education, Rae observed that:

> devolution is marked by increasing accountabilities placed upon school managers, by a Centre which is finding co-ordination structurally difficult to achieve. It has been suggested that the distinctive device of an Education Review Office as a separate department of state is set in a paradigm of Quality Assurance – possibly even Quality Control – rather than Total Quality Management. *(1993, p. 130)*

The impetus for reform in New Zealand education was, as noted in chapters 5 and 6, part of an overall programme which laid emphasis on accountability, performance and effectiveness. The devolution of responsibility to local communities, the strengthening of Board powers and new contracts for principals were all part of this reform process. To put these reforms in an international perspective, table 7.3 sets out the empirical basis for associating educational

Table 7.3 Degree of empirical support for educational process variables associated with achievement

Characteristic	Strong empirical basis	Moderate empirical basis	An as yet weak empirical basis	Mostly conjecture
Environmental incentives				*
Consumerism/parent involvement		*	*	*
Teacher experience		*	*	
Per-pupil expenditure		*	*	
Achievement-oriented policy, high expectations		*	*	
Educational leadership		*		
Consensus, co-operative planning		*		
Quality of curricula		*		
Evaluative potential		*		
Orderly climate				
Structured teaching				
Time on task				
Opportunity to learn				
Reinforcement				

Source: The OECD International Education Indicators: A Framework for Analysis, OECD, 1992, p. 67.

process variables with school achievement. As can be seen there is a weak empirical case for associating certain measures, such as co-operative planning and quality of curriculum, with school effectiveness.

It was shown in chapter 6 that Mintzberg (1979) identified a key lever for change in the working of professional bureaucracies such as schools in that 'change seeps in, by the slow process of changing the professionals'. In New Zealand and Germany, the professional base of teachers was broadly recognized, the major changes put in place were administrative and structural unlike the UK reform (discussed below). Terhart identifies this dual process – professional and administrative – and the inherent strain it can put on professional practice:

> The individual professional competence of a teacher – including his professional ethic as one dimension – can only unfold its positive educational effects in an organizational setting which provides autonomy and possibilities for (further) strengthening professional development. Professional expertise presupposes autonomy from too narrow or strict organizational/administrative guidelines. So it would be wrong to consider organizational reforms of schools as an alternative to strategies for raising professional competence of teachers . . . teacher competence can only develop under adequate conditions; it cannot grow against restrictive or even hostile circumstances. *(1994, p. 12)*

▬▬ Technical Rationality and England's ▬▬
Education Reform

Standaert (1993) in a review of education change in England, France and Germany noted the increase in external control mechanisms which can result in a growing distrust of professionals. He cites the following as examples of such external control:

- central curricula, central or external examinations; periodic external testing;
- increase of the inspection function; financial support of schools, taking account of their results;
- appraisal of teaching staff and school managers, possibly with a view to salary increase or business;
- publication of school results in external examinations;
- promotion of market mechanisms when recruiting pupils;
- recognition of subsidies and sponsorship from industry;
- introduction of a 'voucher system';
- strengthening of industry – geared school management;
- obligatory policies and school work plan;
- increase of parental rights;
- unrestricted free choice of schools *(1993, p. 162)*

Standaert identifies a trend towards central government to move control, often unpopular and condemned as bureaucratic, to the local level. We have already seen in chapter 6 the high degree of professional and school autonomy in Germany and the emphasis of headteachers on school leadership and development. The abolition of Her Majesty's Inspectorate in England, and the establishment of the Office for Standards in Education (Ofsted) was intended as a primary government instrument for raising standards and ensuring compliance with the objectives of the national curriculum and its assessment. One school principal described the Ofsted process as:

> It is a 'tick' system; it is not done professionally. It produces a snap-shot of the school. Perhaps after three to four inspections (12 years) it will be adequate. If Ofsted had issued their booklet and said 'let's help you, it would be great'. They collect mountains of information ('god knows what they do with it'). They are not obliged to give feedback to the teacher nor to give prior notice of inspection to the classroom teacher.

This relationship between the teacher and the requirements of the national curriculum was examined by Ofsted in 1992 in a survey of new teachers. Ofsted (1993) found that:

- New teachers considered that their training had not prepared them well to assess pupils' work.
- Assessment of their performance was largely impressionistic and provided an inadequate basis for identifying their professional needs.

■ Headteachers and governors take relatively little account of the new teachers' specialist expertise when making initial appointments and subsequently in their deployment, which is a matter schools need to address.

Perhaps the single most notable example of technical rationality was the introduction of the national curriculum in England and Wales for first level schools. The curricula and assessment strategies and content were decided, without wide-scale consultation with teachers, by government and made mandatory for all state supported schools. Such was the scale of protest from teachers that the government appointed Sir Ron Dearing in 1993 to review the operation of the curriculum and to make proposals for slimmed down national texts in core subjects, English, Mathematics and Science. The national curriculum is structured in four key stages:

Key Stage 1 – pupils aged 5 to 7
Key Stage 2 – pupils aged 7 to 11
Key Stage 3 – pupils aged 11 to 14
Key Stage 4 – pupils aged 14 to 16

The curriculum for each subject is set out in statutory subject orders which specify programmes of study (the matter, skills and processes to be taught) and attainment targets (the knowledge, skills and undertaking to be acquired).

A key part of the Dearing review was consultation with teachers; consultation sessions were held at eight regional meetings, some 1400 written reports were received from teachers and schools. Central to the review was the concern that the aims of the national curriculum were being undermined by complexity, over-elaboration, over-prescription and excessive content. The Dearing review clearly saw its purpose as 'helping teachers do a better job for their pupils', and its central recommendations were:

1   reduce the volume of material required by law to be taught;
2   simplifying and clarifying the programmes of study;
3   reducing prescription so as to give more scope for professional judgement;
4   ensuring that the Orders are written in such a way which offers maximum support to the classroom teacher.

It is clear that the latter two recommendations were directed at the teaching profession qua profession and a recognition that over-prescription was inappropriate in a classroom context. That is, the government accepted a legitimate role for teachers in deciding how subjects might be taught. In its response to the Dearing review the government accepted that schools be allowed a margin of roughly 20 per cent of time to use at their own discretion. The Dearing Report (1994, p. 25) specifically stated that 'more be left to the professional judgement of teachers . . . this increased trust in teachers, which I believe is very much in the interests of education, should, however, be matched by accountability to parents and society'.

The Dearing Report and its subsequent adoption by the government represented, in part, a turning point in the UK governments' attitude to the profession. Hitherto, the teachers were seen as an interested pressure group, another interest group which had to be restricted. No allowance was made for any interest other than self-interest. In terms of the comparative data we have seen from Germany and New Zealand, the UK teachers were not allowed expression of their professional judgement. The mechanistic nationwide implementation of the national curriculum in an organic environment such as schools clearly gave rise to difficulties, some of which should have been foreseen. The teacher's attitudes were also conditioned by the activities of Ofsted: in 1996 Ofsted's head claimed that some 15,000 teachers should be sacked; in 1997, in his third annual report, he targeted the 3000 headteachers who, he said, pull down performance in a minority of schools. Clearly in such an adversarial climate, it is difficult to talk of a partnership between the teachers and government.

The debate and controversy surrounding the introduction of the national curriculum, its subsequent scaling back under pressure from teachers, highlights a key research theme of this book. It is clear that the relations between the professions (including teachers) and the government in the UK were adversarial, that the professions were seen as a special interest group and that the role of government was to curtail professional freedoms. Yet it is equally clear that schools, hospitals, social welfare centres cannot be operated without the compliance (if not the commitment) of the professions. Clearly, the government needed to look to a relationship that was based on more mutual respect, a relationship that gave legitimacy to professional 'voice', and a relationship based on collaboration rather than conflict. The evidence from New Zealand, Germany and Sweden shows that such collaboration can take place without sacrificing quality or client interests. Indeed, the evidence suggests quite strongly that client interests will not be satisfied through conflict at all.

▰▰▰ Conclusion ▰▰▰

The management of professionals is a demanding and challenging activity for public service managers. Much of the operations of the SLPO are effected through professionals and their values, training and skills are largely outside the domain of the organization. In some countries, notably those of Northern Europe and Scandinavia the relationship between the state and professional is a harmonious one, and the idea of the state-professional is part of the historical tradition of these countries. In contrast, the Anglo-Saxon tradition has, historically, granted a large measure of autonomy to the professional, albeit that such autonomy is now under threat through the imposition of contract management devices that seek efficiency gains. The reforms in New Zealand and in the UK have largely been based on the premise of 'provider capture', that is, that the services are dominated by professionals and that the remedy for reform must be based on curtailment of professional freedoms. It can be seen from this chapter, and through the case studies and data reported throughout the

text, that to view professionals as the main barrier to reform is to misunder-
stand their role in the service transaction. They stand in a dual role to the
citizen–client, as provider of the service and as the client's agent; the brunt of
the reforms in the UK have been on the professionals as provider, yet the
client will, understandably, still view the professional as his agent in the service
transactions.

The evidence from Sweden, Germany and, in part, New Zealand, offers a
different way of viewing the reform programme. There is partnership between
the state, professional and the citizen: there is no recurring tension point in the
relationship which cannot be addressed through mechanisms such as consensus
statements, collaboration and reliance on professional codes of ethics. Legislation which provides a strategic framework of control can also assist in this
partnership. The 'seeping in' of change in professional-state relations requires
time – to adjust professional curricula, to align service protocols with citizen
voice and participation and to promote more management training in professional self-development. All of these changes, further discussed in the next
chapter, also require that public service managers accord to the professional a
value based on their role as agent of the citizen–client. To persist in simply
viewing professionals as providers of service will result in a further dislocation
of the state-professional relationship.

The data in this chapter and in the case studies presented throughout the
text support the conclusion that:

- state-professional relationships should be managed as custodial rather
  than adversarial;
- the management of professionals should accord status to their role as
  agents of the citizen–client;
- contract management and performance measurement has to include
  recognition of the professionals role in contributing to institutional
  and social development.

CHAPTER
8

Review of Reform Programmes

This study has examined reform programmes in a large and diverse range of countries: it is now appropriate to review these programmes and consider the lessons that can be drawn so as to form the basis for the better management of core public services. I stated at the outset of this study that I was concerned with three particular concepts:

1 differential information between providers and clients in service delivery;
2 core public organizations providing socially important, interdependent, non-marketable services for social optimality; and
3 professionalism as a relation of trust and agency between providers and clients.

These three concepts are taken to be interrelated and, as a consequence, are taken to call together for the development of a kind of management that is different from that appropriate for private enterprise, or even for public organizations in non-core areas. In dealing with our three key concepts, I proposed a model of core public management (figure 8.1) to show the relationship between government agenda, differential information and professional ethics.

I looked at reform programmes in the UK, New Zealand, Sweden, Germany and Ireland in terms of this model and considered whether the reforms displayed coherence and consistency – that is, were the reforms consistent with the beliefs and values of the providers, appropriate to the organizational context of the SLPO, inclusive of citizen voice, and demonstrating appropriate appellate channels for citizen-redress?

Some countries, notably New Zealand, have developed a very consistent and deliberate policy of reform based on the contract model, purchaser–provider separation and a distrust of the professional provider. However, in New Zealand the policy makers themselves were unsure of the appropriateness of a

Figure 8.1 Relationship between government agenda, differential information and professional ethics

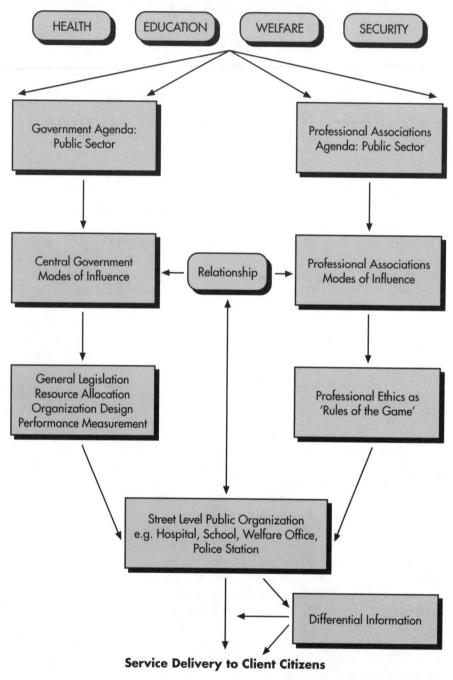

Source: Wrigley and McKevitt 1995

'one-best way' to undertake reform: 'we ploughed into areas of social policy because of our earlier success in financial changes'. The education reforms in New Zealand succeeded in so far as professionals and parents collaborated to get changes they considered appropriate to an organic environment such as schools. In Sweden, trade unions sought new ways of organizing and delivering services to enhance community services rather than adopt traditional ways of resisting changes. In Germany, the education reforms supported the professional ethos and values of the teachers and they were built on a community focus with the local population. Though German public management is highly regulated, the German reforms sought a balance between the economic demands of government and the legitimate professional base of the providers. In the UK, the education and health reform programmes were largely a top–down, mechanistic process, whereby the contract relationship and associated performance framework stressed efficiency rather than effectiveness, and where citizen voice was largely ignored.

The reforms placed middle management and professionals on the defensive; the values and ethics of professional providers were viewed as the special pleading of interest groups. There was also no strategic control mechanism, such as appropriate legislation, to guide the reforms. Indeed, as we saw in respect of health care strategies, the UK does not have appropriate strategic legislation and, hence, the reform programmes sought to impose efficiency-type solutions in an environment where organic relationships, provider–client partnerships, and wider societal values operate. The reforms do not allow for any interest, except self-interest; the measure of success is financial rather than community-based, and the reforms have begun to forge an alliance between provider and clients in opposition to the traditional model of professional power that has driven many of the reforms. That is, the model of reform is not appropriate to the environment nor is it consistent with the values of the providers. The reform programme does not take adequate account of citizen voice.

Clearly, there is no 'one-best way' to reform core public services that will satisfy the needs of government, citizens and providers. Yet some countries have proceeded on a path of reform which treats all service delivery, provider–client relationships and performance measures as similar. This is due, in part at least, to the belief that public organizations are similar in kind to private sector organizations; where the resources (inputs) are converted into services (output) in a manner specified by the purchaser. The SLPO is a complex institution, drawing legitimacy and acceptability from the wider institutional environment, and subject to pressures and demands that require an organic mode of management that supports collaboration, trust and openness.

This type of organization – SLPO – cannot be organized like a production-line process; it requires, as the data from New Zealand, Germany and Sweden show, consistent and long-term partnership between provider, client and purchaser. The development of core skills, or, indeed, their depletion, requires a long-term strategy that meets the needs of the SLPO for consistency and coherence. Short-term radical change is not appropriate to the institutional environment of core public services.

To achieve more responsive service, the SLPO also requires changes to the professional education of the provider and a more supportive and relevant performance measurement framework that provides for and supports citizen voice. As the data reported in the text and in the case studies has shown, citizen voice is still largely unattended to in many SLPOs. The SLPO, situated in a complex and turbulent environment, is not offered as some 'ideal type' of organization – it reflects the operational life of many core public service managers across a large and diverse range of countries.

For managers, the SLPO is a recognizable place and location: many of the people interviewed for this study helped to clarify the pressures and demands faced in the SLPO. The citizen–client requires an efficient and effective SLPO: yet the bulk of reforms have placed a high priority on efficiency yet neglected effectiveness. The professional provider helps to create an effective SLPO, albeit that the traditional stance of the provider – 'we know best' – has led to the diminution of their authority through performance frameworks that lay stress on efficiency and resource usage. Professionals need to rediscover their ethic of service, their obligation to the citizen–client if they are to be successful in having their voice heard in the reform programme.

Examples of effective professional voice, in partnership with the citizen–client, can be found in Sweden, Germany and New Zealand.

Drawing Lessons from the Reform Programmes

In seeking to draw lessons from the diverse range of programmes observed in this text, a frame of analysis to appraise the strategies pursued by governments, and a set of criteria for evaluating the coherence of these strategies are required. Again, it is worth remembering the purposes and objectives of core public services; those services which are important for the protection and promotion of citizen well-being, but are in areas where the market is incapable of reaching or even approaching a socially optimal state. I am concerned here with helping to improve the management of these services – health, education, welfare and security – through an analysis of best practice in a number of countries. The text has drawn on the direct experience, where possible, of managers, providers and clients so as to give insight into the management of the SLPO. It has been shown how the features of non-marketability, differential information and interdependence require an approach to management that is different from that in the private sector. These differences arise from the characteristics of the services themselves, the requirements of the external institutional environment and the needs of the citizen–clients. Examples have also been given of appropriate and inappropriate management in SLPOs across a range of countries where inconsistent or inadequate performance frameworks were applied.

How then can we appraise the strategies pursued by governments in core public services? One way is to apply the 'tests' of *suitability*, *feasibility* and *acceptability* (Johnson and Scholes, 1997) and examine the reform strategies using these criteria. While this framework of analysis is usually applied to private sector strategies, it can be adapted to suit our present purposes. It is particularly appropriate in that the criteria apply to the organization itself (i.e. SLPO), rather than to the wider institutional environment. Many commentators seek to evaluate reform at the system level and ignore the day-to-day management world of the SLPO. It is important to keep focused on the SLPO and its environment, at the street level, where services are delivered and rationed, where citizen voice is heard (or ignored) and where the manager and professional seek solutions to citizen demands in a context of limited resources.

Contextualize manag~

▬▬ **Suitability** ▬▬

The focus here is on the suitability of reforms to the environment of the SLPO; suitability as a criterion for judging strategy helps to screen for the appropriateness of the proposed strategy in the environment of the SLPO. Given the threats and opportunities in the external environment, the strategy should be designed to overcome the weaknesses of the organization and build on its strengths. The strategy should also help achieve the organization's purpose, namely, to help sustain and strengthen social interdependence and cohesion.

The SLPO is an organic professional bureaucracy, which is heavily influenced by its institutional and technical environment. In the UK, New Zealand and latterly Sweden recent reform has stressed the technical side – that is, performance measurement which gave prominence to issues of efficiency and resource management. One of the weaknesses of the SLPO is the dominant role exercised by professional providers and wherein they may unduly influence the measurement of organizational success. In seeking to introduce a countervailing influence, many governments have sought to increase the institutional measures of performance which lay emphasis on legitimacy and resource attraction. A more suitable strategy, seen in the New Zealand education reforms, might be to increase access for citizen voice, as this would fit more easily with the purposes of the SLPO and provide a focus for improving social cohesion.

One of the major threats to the SLPO is the continued restraint on public expenditure and effects of the related mechanisms of value-for-money audits and efficiency programmes. The threat here is not resource constraints *per se* but rather the suitability of the performance measurement framework itself. If the SLPO is measured solely on criteria of efficiency and resource management, the original mission of the SLPO (social cohesion and interdependence) may be lost sight of: we have seen such mission drift in chapters 3 and 7 when we examined the effect of performance measurement in over one hundred UK public organizations. An emphasis on citizen voice will also help redress one of the existing weaknesses of the SLPO – its provider orientation. While we have seen some relevant examples of citizen voice, it is clear that increased emphasis needs to be given to this important feature of core public services management.

Such an orientation would also help redress the institutional bias in existing performance measurement systems; effective service delivery, as seen in chapter 3, demands consistent and long-term relationships with the citizen.

Feasibility

My interest here is whether the proposed strategy can be successfully implemented, albeit that there is some difficulty in measuring what 'success' actually means in core public services. Feasibility also brings into sharp focus the SLPO's capability to build and sustain relevant and appropriate management skills to implement the strategy. Of importance too is whether sufficient resources are available to fund the strategy; this is particularly relevant given that the impetus behind many reforms has been the constraining of expenditure. In appraising the feasibility of strategy we need to be aware of the timeframe of change; many reforms were a rushed affair with little prior consultation among important stakeholders.

The success of strategic change in the core public services should relate to their chief purposes – the sustaining and development of social cohesion and interdependence. No evidence has been seen in the UK health care reforms of giving attention to citizen voice, nor did they reduce existing inequalities in health care provision or health outcomes. In education, the reformers were disdainful of the professional legitimacy of the teachers, although the Dearing proposals did include a recognition of a neglect of their professional voice. In New Zealand and Sweden it was the actions of trade unions that tempered the effects of reforms through collaboration with citizen–clients.

The reforms promoted managerial efficiency as the primary criterion of success; however, the wider consultation with stakeholders apparent in New Zealand and Sweden provide one mechanism for increasing the feasibility of strategic options. If citizen–client voice is canvassed and assessed it is likely that the feasibility of proposed strategic change will be strengthened.

Chapter 2 illustrated how the SLPO contains 'core skills', a mixture of technical and professional competencies that allow the organization, over time, to respond to its stakeholders and to accommodate itself to the demands of its institutional and technical environment. It was noted how in Sweden in the 1990s reforms ignored the traditional consensus route of consultation, pilot and review and how strategic drift had occurred between the original organization mission and the new reforms. In New Zealand it was seen that 'institutional memory' had been erased in the Ministry of Education; how in health care it was acknowledged that there was no 'community of interests', and how officials admitted that the unrelenting pace of reform was eroding traditional values of service. In the UK, in many organizations, performance measurement was oriented towards legitimacy and resource renewal rather than citizen–client voice. The case studies examining Community Care and the NHS Trust show how organization mission can be derailed due to inconsistent demands on providers. Many of the reforms studied in this text are quite feasible to introduce in terms of mechanical implementation; that is, there is in the public sector no barrier to implementation of government policy.

However, changing the organizational structure or the 'rules of the game' does not guarantee successful change. Clearly, there is ample evidence to suggest that to attempt widescale change in a short time period within core public services will result in the diminishing of core skills and the likelihood of provider distrust of the changes. The piloting of change programmes, including appropriate evaluation studies, will increase the feasibility of successful strategic change.

▬▬ Acceptability ▬▬

In discussing acceptability as a criterion for strategic success we need to ask 'acceptable to whom'? Clearly, in the provision of core public services there are many stakeholders: the major ones being government, providers, managers and citizen–clients. The demands and interests of these stakeholders are difficult to resolve, and it will not always be possible to reconcile these interests.

In the data and case studies presented in this text, it is evident that the dominant stakeholder is the government, albeit that the 'New Right' movement discussed in chapter 2 may well have reached its zenith in the late-1990s. The assault on professional privilege, at least in the Anglo Saxon countries, has not resulted in any clear improvement in service provision. Indeed, in the case of the NHS it has added hundreds of millions of expenditure in non-medical areas to support the measurement and appraisal system. In northern European countries, where a more consensual tradition of state–professional relations operate, there is evidence that collaboration still provides a mechanism to support necessary strategic change.

The reform strategy also requires support from the external environment of the SLPO, the institutional environment that gives legitimacy and support to the organization. It is here that many of the reforms are most problematic; citizen voice is, up to now, largely unattended to and we have seen instances of professional–citizen collaboration to mitigate the effects of some of the reforms. The professional provider, and indeed middle level managers, are also on the defensive and being asked to take responsibility for resource decisions that are not their responsibility. Does it make sense to pursue strategies of reform that are becoming less acceptable to providers and to the citizen–client? Governments possess the coercive power to impose organizational solutions on the SLPO; yet we have clearly seen that such power runs up against the professional ethic of client service and the related, if unmobilized, influence of citizen voice. The power paradigm of the professional, which underlies much of the recent reform, may need to be replaced by a paradigm that acknowledges consensus, collaboration and consultation.

So, managing in an SLPO requires, as we have seen across many countries, these attributes of consensus and collaboration. Clearly, changes in the education and training of professionals and managers are required to enhance and improve core skills within the SLPO. The professionals will need to incorporate in their training a greater awareness and sensitivity to citizen voice; such a programme of change needs to begin in the professional schools and continue with in-service training. Managers need also to acknowledge the legitimate needs of professionals to represent client voice and to provide appropriate mechanisms for professional client collaboration. The power paradigm behind many of the reforms needs to be replaced by consensus and dialogue. We have seen the beneficial effects of such change in this study.

Conclusion

The reform programmes examined in this text share a number of common features, not least their concern with resource management and efficiency frameworks. The programmes also display a trend, especially evident in the UK and New Zealand, towards the downplaying of professional voice in the delivery of services. The core public services are seen as similar to private sector enterprises, with their ethos and orientation being amenable to generic solutions that are based on contracts and performance measurement systems. The data and evidence examined here would strongly suggest a different paradigm, an alternative way of looking at and managing core public services. This alternative view has been developed based on best practices in a large number of countries, and it has drawn for its conceptual underpinning on the robust models of private sector management. The study has also drawn on the direct experience of managers and providers as they sought to accommodate themselves to the new reform programmes. It has been shown that a reliance on hierarchy and authority are not sufficient for effective change: partnership between the state and the profession is also required. It is also evident that the custodial relationship between the professional and the client has to be acknowledged: the older 'we know best' mentality is, and should be, redundant. It is damaging in core public service provision.

The management profession also needs to take a wider perspective on change in the public sector and to widen its own focus to include consensual and partnership models of management (e.g. Sweden, Germany) rather than to continue to rely on power frameworks which ignore citizen voice. It is only through acknowledging our own professional limitations and bias that we can contribute to the effective management of social cohesion and interdependence.

The reforms studied here demonstrate that consensus and collaboration can result in effective strategic change in the core public services. The management of strategic change in the SLPO requires close attention to citizen voice, professional ethics and the organic environment of the core public service.

APPENDIX

Case Studies

CASE STUDY

1

The Vision and Reality of an Executive Agency

Charles Ferguson and Deirdre McGill

In his opening remarks at the launch of the Social Security Agency (NI) in July 1991, the Chief Executive set out his vision for its future:

> My aim is for the Agency to become renowned for the quality of its products and its service; and to be a by-word for efficiency and value for money. I want its staff to be committed to the principles and aims of the Agency; and to be acclaimed experts in their field. I want them to be excited by the prospect of taking on new responsibilities; to be enthusiastic about their job; and to be proud to tell their friends, as I am, that they work in the Social Security Agency.

These sentiments reflect more than a personal vision by the Chief Executive. He is echoing the principles laid down in the *Treasury and Civil Service Committee 7th Report, The Next Steps Initiative*, 1991 which – building on the Financial Management Initiative (FMI) – aimed to introduce far-reaching reforms within the Civil Service that would bring about a sustained pressure for improving the delivery of services to the public and to Ministers and for achieving better value for money (see section A1.1, 'The Vision for Agencies').

This case examines three major issues arising from the introduction of Next Steps agencies:

1. The tension between the agency and its parent department over the location of accountability.
2. The requirement to move to a performance-based culture.
3. The implications for human resource strategies.

The Social Security Agency (Northern Ireland)

The Social Security Agency (SSA) was launched in Northern Ireland in July 1991. Previously all policy and operational matters relating to social security in Northern Ireland were dealt with under the umbrella of the Department of Health and Social Services (DHSS). The SSA is the largest executive agency in the Northern Ireland Civil Service (NICS) and the seventh largest in the UK. Employing over 5500 staff in a network of offices throughout the Province, the SSA is responsible for the administration of benefits worth £2000 million annually.

The context within which the SSA operates is unique in a number of respects. The SSA has to deal with particularly high levels of unemployment and associated requests for help arising from the social deprivation which has been emphasized by the spiralling poverty and violence of the last quarter of a century. It had to respond to damage to its buildings through the terrorist bombing campaign, intimidation threats from paramilitaries on its members and individual personal attacks on its staff. As one senior member of the Agency put it:

> Our business can be described as 'peddling poverty' and staff can as a result be the recipients of frustrated members of the public who associate the disallowance of their payment of benefit with the individual concerned, without a real understanding that they can only act within the legislation.

Although a demand-led business, the SSA has to bid for its resources within the 'block allocation system', which is the unique format for resource allocation of central government funds to Northern Ireland. This means that the Secretary of State for Northern Ireland has discretion to allocate resources between all Northern Ireland departments and agencies, and therefore the Northern Ireland block resources are subject to the pressures arising from all departments and agencies. Due to competing social factors there are often conflicting pressures arising within this block system, for instance whether to place priority on employment, training, security and so on. The SSA has to be responsive to fluctuating demands in claims for benefit and to changes in policy and legislation, yet must compete equally with other priority policy and security issues.

In practice this means the SSA can bid for more money in-year to meet unforseen demand or, alternatively, it may have to surrender money to meet the priority needs of other government departments within the block allocation system. Consequently the SSA, through the DHSS, has less management flexibility than its Whitehall counterparts. For instance, its sister agency, the Benefits Agency, deals direct with Treasury. The reality of working within the block allocation system has been neatly summarized by a senior member of the Agency: 'Working within the "block system" is a very uncertain and imprecise business. This lack of certainty about budgets can sometimes affect planning, and ultimately the quality of the service offered by the SSA.'

The SSA is involved exclusively in the administration of social security. Social security is a very unified business which has only two real activities: the administration of benefits and contributions. There is, therefore, virtually no opportunity to generate income and the SSA currently operates as a 'gross running cost' regime with all monies required to administer its business being voted through Parliament.

The limitations within which the SSA operates are well articulated by its Chief Executive:

> Running an Agency as far as possible on business lines is, of course, an important tenet of Next Steps theology. I say 'as far as possible', because there are limitations to how far we, in particular, can model ourselves on the commercial world. We cannot, for example, diversify into new product lines of our own choosing or decide to stop paying certain benefits or leave parts of Northern Ireland unserviced, just because the administration cost is too high. Nor can we pull down the shutters and serve only a certain number of customers if we're short of money. Instead we are obligated to run whatever benefit schemes the Government decides to introduce, deal with every single demand no matter how complex or how long it may take to clear and we must cover all areas of the Province whatever the cost.

The SSA took an early decision to put in place a new organizational structure. A six-member board comprising the Chief Executive and five directors was established to manage the Agency and to enhance the effective delivery of services. Two of the directors maintain responsibility for all operational matters, while the remainder are charged with specialist responsibilities in the areas of strategic and business planning, human resource management and financial management. The main managerial elements of this new structure are outlined in section A1.2.

In keeping with all agencies, the SSA's terms of reference are set down in the Social Security Agency's internal Framework Document published in 1991. The purpose of the Framework Document is to set out clearly the customer–contractor relationship, with the Minister contracting with the Agency to deliver particular services. The Chief Executive is given a specific and, where possible, specified set of objectives together with specified overall resources. By means of the Framework Document, and the attendant strategic and business planning process which follow from it, the Chief Executive's responsibilities and accountability for the delivery of services are determined. The respective roles of the Minister, the Permanent Secretary of the Department of Health and Social Services and the Chief Executive of the SSA are illustrated in section A1.3.

▰▰▰ Agency Objectives ▰▰▰

The SSA's overall objective, goals and key principles as reflected in its first strategic and business plan are set out in the box overleaf. The vision outlined reflects the important fact that the SSA serves multiple objectives, has a diversity of stakeholders and exists within a complex and uncertain environment.

That potential tensions might exist in delivering the visionary element of the strategic and business plan is well recognized by the Chief Executive:

> The Plan is the result of hard bargaining between those who allocate the resources and us, the providers of the services. And, of course, there will be a debate each year as to whether the resources are adequate to deal with the level of demand and the standards set. In the end it is for Government to decide what level of service it is prepared to fund and for the Agency to get the best possible value it can from those funds.

▰▰▰ Contracts – the Framework Document ▰▰▰

One of the key directives of the *Next Steps Initiative* is that chief executives are directly accountable to a minister in a quasi-contractual relationship and the foundation on which all executive agencies are built is therefore the Framework Document. Together with the strategic and business planning process, the Framework Document is designed to ensure that the responsibilities of the Chief Executive and the Minister are clearly defined.

As more and more agencies develop it is recognized that a number of conflicting interests need to be reconciled in a Framework Document. However, there lies in every Framework Document a paradox: how to give the Chief Executive the necessary flexibilities to run the business of an agency yet maintain accountability to the Department. The nature of this paradox found in the accountability interrelationships specified in a Framework Document is that:

- ministers, supported by their departments, must set clear policy objectives and robust performance targets and monitoring arrangements for their agencies;
- Treasury must retain a central responsibility for trends in public service costs and maintain the containing of expenditure as a key objective; and
- chief executives are entitled to expect that they will have power to act in accordance with their judgement without unwarranted interference.

Resolving the inherent paradox within framework documents can best be achieved, according to the Efficiency Unit, by developing and maintaining a clear and shared vision of what the Agency is there to do through the establishment of agreed roles and objectives for all parties. In particular, this

---

■■■■ Components of the Agency's Vision ■■■■

Our overall objective

Our overall objective is to meet the targets set by the Minister within the resources allocated and to do so efficiently, effectively and economically and with full regard for the varying needs and circumstances of its actual and potential customers, its staff and the interests of the taxpayer.

Our goals

To achieve our overall objective we have set the following goals for achievement over the next five years:

- The Agency will have established a reputation for efficiency and quality of service.
- Information and advice about benefits and services will be easily accessible to the public who will receive a speedy and accurate response to their enquiries.
- The Agency will continue to promote the take-up of benefits.
- Agency offices will be pleasant places for customers to visit and staff to work in.
- Managers will be organizing and delivering services in the way which best suits local community needs and will be held account- able for the results.
- Staff will have improved support through the increased use of information technology; they will be proficient, committed and proud to work in the Agency.
- Authority and responsibility will have been devolved to the optimum level.
- The Agency will provide an efficient service to Ministers in im- plementing legislative changes and providing information and advice on operational issues.
- The Agency will be providing an efficient and effective service to those Departments and Agencies with whom it has contracts.

Our key principles

We believe our goals will best be achieved by the adoption of a number of key principles. The four key principles which will underpin all Agency activity are: good quality services, efficient services, proficient and valued staff and delegated personal responsibility.

Source: Social Security Agency (NI), *The Business Plan*, 1991–92, Lon- don: HMSO.

---

involves clarifying responsibility for specifying service standards and for monitoring their achievement. The Efficiency Unit's view is that 'It is the identification of the right targets and confidence in the systems which underpin them which are at the heart of a healthy arm's length relationship between Departments and Agencies.' Thus the Efficiency Unit envisage that the Minister's role is essentially a strategic one and that there is little need for intervention in the matters of day-to-day management of an agency. It is for the Minister to determine the difficult question of what service standards, within resource constraints, are acceptable. This can be achieved by setting a handful of robust and high-level targets to measure financial performance, efficiency and quality of customer service. Departments can assist Ministers in this process and can also challenge the performance of the Chief Executive in meeting targets. Chief Executives, on the other hand, are responsible for addressing how these demands should be met and need to be given assistance in this process by the Department through the timely provision of any new policy initiatives and forecasted workloads.

▬▬ Major Issues for the Agency ▬▬

There is an in-built impetus created by agency status to engage in more rigorous strategic and business planning. A major difficulty for the Agency has been the mismatch of the strategic and business planning cycle and the Public Expenditure Survey PES cycle, although these have been reconciled and 1994 was the first year where both cycles were synchronized.

The environment within which the Agency operates is increasingly turbulent and numerous threats confront it. For instance, it is anticipated that there will be continued constraints on public expenditure and tight budget management. The continued introduction of new policies and schemes at short notice, plus the Agency's overriding legal obligation to process all claims, can be expected to create pressures on the Agency. Similarly, the increased introduction of market testing (where an agency's activities are scrutinized to consider whether the private sector could do the job better) poses particular problems for the Agency given that it is not entirely geared to withstand competition.

If the SSA's core business is defined as 'money transmission' there are interesting dimensions to what could lie in the future, especially in light of such technological developments as smart cards and electronic funds transfer schemes. Thinking in these terms invites the Agency to use banks and building societies as the evaluation basis for the comparative cost efficiency of service delivery.

Efficiency is a key strategic issue for the SSA and achieving 'more with less' is a touchstone within all the Agency's policies. Every aspect of service delivery is therefore kept under constant scrutiny. This pursuit of cost efficiency could mean future staff reductions; the move to 'one-stop shops' with a consequent rationalization of the network of benefit offices; the application of business process redesign to streamline administrative procedures and processes; more intensive use of information technology and further moves towards a more rigorous cost management financial regime.

▬▬ Measuring Performance ▬▬

The SSA's service targets are set out in section A1.4. Senior managers in the SSA believe that the current arrangements for setting targets might be improved. The approach taken by the DHSS in deciding what service standards should be applied in the SSA is simply to mirror, where appropriate, the targets set for the Benefits Agency. While these targets are extensive, the appropriateness of many of them is the subject of much debate within the Agency. This debate revolves around the balance to be struck between quality of service, financial and efficiency targets. In the words of the Chief Executive, 'there is a need to put much more emphasis on measuring quality'. Operational managers and staff in the SSA share this concern, particularly where meeting the targets set by the Minister means that 'staff can often only achieve the current clearance times targets set at the expense of the quality of service'.

Performance measurement is central to the ethos of an agency. According to one senior manager: 'Performance indicators are not value-free technical instruments of measurement. Rather, they reflect the various interest positions of different stakeholders, where each has a legitimate concern for meaningful information about the Agency's performance.' What performance criteria are used, who sets these and whose interests are being served by the evaluation of performance are therefore important issues for management accountability by the Agency to various stakeholders. To date, the stakeholder having least impact on the development of performance indicators is the client/customer. This is not to deny that 'customer service' is an important concern within the Agency. In keeping with other public service organizations, and influenced by the Citizen's Charter, the Agency has spawned its own variant of the ubiquitous 'customer charter'.

The performance indicators for the Agency, given that they basically replicate those for the Benefits Agency, provide a benchmark with the performance of this sister organization.

▬▬ Workload Forecasting ▬▬

Related to the issue of targets is the question of workload forecasting. Forecasting is a critical activity for any service organization as it determines resource requirements based on projected demand. This is a particularly important issue when it comes to social security provision where accurate predictions of the future demand for benefits can be difficult. Unlike Trading Fund Agencies, which have a measure of control over their own demand forecasting, the SSA is entirely dependent on another party, namely the Department of Health and Social Services. Such an arrangement creates in-built tensions, especially when demand projections prove to be incorrect, as happened, for instance, with the introduction of the new benefits for the disabled in 1992. The end result of this inaccuracy was that the initial resources allocated to implement these new benefits were insufficient and the mechanism for allocating additional resources to handle excess demand proved unsatisfactory. As one senior manager within the Agency reveals, 'Whilst there is an explicit approach to the handling of unforseen change reflected in the Agency's Framework Document, to either provide for additional resources in such circumstances, or, if not, to have the flexibility of adjusting existing targets or priorities, the reality is that this has not happened fully in practice'.

Management Accountabilities

The issue of accountability is at the centre of much debate surrounding agencies. A major reason for establishing agencies was to achieve more accountable management by placing responsibility and accountability for all operational matters under the control of a chief executive. This involves a change in accountability arrangements, where Permanent Secretaries, in their capacity as accounting officers, are no longer solely responsible to Parliament for all policy and operational matters relating to an agency. The extent to which accountability is 'shared' with an agency chief executive is both an important and sensitive issue. (See section A1.5 for details of financial flexibility.)

Many of the issues surrounding accountability appear, prima facie, to have been resolved with the establishment of chief executives as accounting officers who are now liable to answer to the Public Accounts Committee on the responsibilities allocated to them in the Framework Document. This, theoretically, leaves the Permanent Secretary, as Departmental Accounting Officer, liable to answer for matters in the Framework Document specially assigned to the Department, rather than the Agency.

The Efficiency Unit recently highlighted the need for on-going development of the accountability issue. It is recognized, for instance, that the current text of the Accounting Officer Memorandum needs to be reviewed. By reason of the implications that can be drawn from the current wording, wide responsibility is ascribed to the Permanent Secretary for ensuring good management and financial propriety throughout the Department, *including agencies*. According to the Efficiency Unit, interpretation of this wide responsibility can mean that 'Certain sponsor Departments feel that they have to carry out their control and monitoring role in a closer and more detailed manner than might otherwise be the case, so as to provide the Permanent Secretary with a reasonable level of assurance, not just on the adequacy of control systems, but also on the activities of the Agency.'

The scope of the Permanent Secretary's wide responsibility is reflected in the Social Security Agency Framework Document, paragraph 4.7: 'As Agency Accounting Officer, the Chief Executive can be summoned to appear before the Public Accounts Committee (PAC). Where the Committee is examining Agency matters, it may require both the Permanent Secretary and the Chief Executive to appear before it.' This relationship has been put to the test recently when the Chief Executive of the SSA was called before the Public Accounts Committee (PAC) on a wholly operational matter. The Chief Executive attended the PAC alone and the Department did not intervene. However, in the words of the Chief Executive: 'There still exists within the Accounting Officer relationship an indeterminate shade of grey where "the hands off – hands on" dilemma has yet to be determined.'

Devolving responsibility down the line, not only from departments to agencies, but also within agencies from senior levels of management to those at more junior levels, is a major issue. This mirrors the belief implicit in the *Next Steps Initiative* recommendation that real change is much more likely to happen if individuals are held personally responsible for action and results.

From its inception the SSA has recognized the importance of creating new forms of management accountability through its key principle of 'delegated personal responsibility'. Devolution of responsibility for budgets, estate management and personnel management functions have been instigated. Equally, the development of a new management style which encourages individuals at all levels to take responsibility for dealing with problems and making improvements is strongly supported by top management in the Agency. There are limits though to which this aspect of the Agency's vision might be pursued. As one senior manager puts it: The hard fact of life is that what is possible in terms of more enriched, responsible jobs for some of the lower levels of staff within the agency hits a bit of a brick wall when applied to the highly repetitive, specialised clerical work that people are engaged in. Of course, it is not impossible to change this, but it requires a root and branch revision of our business processes and also our culture.

Changing Personnel Practice

The Agency is committed to moving away from the traditional concept of management within the civil service as being about a process of management control and supervision. The Chief Executive of the SSA affirms the importance of the need for a more enlightened approach to management practice within the new agency framework:

> Our management and our staff resources are our greatest asset and it will be their commitment, their energy and their proficiency which will provide the spark of vitality needed for the Agency to succeed. Our objective is enlightened management policies, which take account of the expectations of our staff and the needs of a business and customer culture.

The way forward for the Agency is seen to require a major change in management style to bring about greater delegation, acceptance of responsibility and accountability, and greater scope for staff using initiative. The ideal state hoped for is that the Agency will move from 'management by command, driven by a system to be observed' to a new state of 'management by contract, driven by commitment to the job to be done'.

It is against this background that the SSA set about taking full advantage of its status to use whatever personnel flexibilities it could get towards achieving the desired cultural change. Section A1.6 outlines the flexibilities which the Agency enjoys in relation to the personnel regime, in relation to pay and grading, recruitment, performance appraisal and career development and training. It is in using the scope for personnel flexibilities that the SSA has sought to make progress in adopting a distinctive 'agency' approach to differentiate it from the personnel regime existing within the Northern Ireland Civil Service.

During its first operational year the Agency undertook a major review of its personnel strategies. The stated aim in its first business plan was 'to develop a personnel management strategy which is best suited to the needs of the Agency and makes best use of the personnel flexibilities delegated to the Agency in the Framework Document'. This strategy is focused on a move away from traditional personnel practice and aims to embrace the concept of human resource management. The key themes that underpin this strategy are:

1 Empowering line managers
   - devolution of personnel functions;
   - computer support;
   - discipline and inefficiency.
2 Performance appraisal
   - appraisal;
   - performance-related pay;
   - grading.
3 Proficient and valued staff
   - training and management development;
   - staff welfare;
   - induction;
   - staff benefits and incentives;
   - working patterns.
4 Right people in the right place at the right time
   - recruitment;
   - postings;
   - succession planning;
   - promotion;
   - manpower planning.

By setting a number of corporate objectives around the Agency's key principles of Proficient and Valued Staff and Delegated Personal Responsibility (see section A1.7), additional commitment is provided for a new HRM regime.

Immediate attention was given by the SSA to the deficiencies that existed in the NICS appraisal scheme inherited by the new Agency. The existing appraisal system was found to have a number of serious deficiencies:

- Over 70 per cent of staff are assessed as very good or better, which creates difficulties in setting higher standards and results in the silting up of the performance pay arrangements.
- There is insufficient rigour in the assessment of performance so that assessments have become inconsistent, bland and meaningless.
- Many of the aspects of performance which are assessed are unsuitable or irrelevant to the new values and culture of the Agency.
- Many forward job plans are poor and staff do not receive sufficient feedback on performance on a regular basis.
- Unnecessary time, effort and expectation is involved in annual promotion assessments.

A Human Resource Strategy for the Social Security Agency (NI), 1992 (internal document)

By 1993 the SSA was successful in introducing a new appraisal system which had a number of attractive features for staff. In particular, it provides open and optional promotion assessments, joint appraisal and regular reviews of performance and makes use of a competence framework to identify development needs. Introducing assessment based on outputs rather than inputs proved more problematical, however, as there was an inability to set consistent and meaningful standards at the individual level and to measure these objectively, especially for the qualitative aspects of performance. In the words of one senior manager:

> The new system failed in this respect not because of the concept of measurable output objectives but because of the overlapping roles/tasks between grades, especially at middle management level, which make performance standards difficult to determine and promotability difficult to assess, and because of the attitudes and culture within the Agency which give appraisal and other associated managerial skills a low profile.

A review of the SSA's personnel strategy also reveals that there was a strong feeling among staff that the current system of performance-related pay is not achieving its objectives, with only 20 per cent of staff feeling that the system has a positive effect. While acknowledging the need to conduct an overall strategic review of the SSA's grading structure which focuses on the Agency's business needs and the need to be more efficient, the Agency Management Board recognizes that there is a need to proceed cautiously in this area. This is because:

> The outcome of central pay negotiations is uncertain and the future direction volatile which does not allow for a sound planning foundation at present; there is a lack of empirical evidence on which to base decisions and a major pay and/or grading review could be potentially very disruptive at a time when substantial change is already underway.

From 1 April 1994, in line with government policy for Next Steps agencies, the SSA assumes responsibility for its own pay arrangements. In order to take full advantage of delegated pay arrangements it is envisaged that a full review of the existing pay and grading arrangements will be undertaken. Equal pay legislation is seen as a major limiting factor in devising new arrangements, as is the status of agency staff as employees of the DHSS. The net result, in the short term, of gaining delegated pay bargaining is described by one senior manager:

> Whilst delegated pay bargaining provides a platform to carry out a review of grading arrangements, there are limitations to the extent to which we can vary from the central settlement under the present grading arrangements. The other real issue to be addressed is the 'rules of engagement' for establishing future negotiations with Agency Trade Union Side – the latter will want a commitment to parity with the rest of the NICS, whilst the SSA will want flexibility to establish grading which best suits their needs and which they can afford.

Empowering Line Managers

Establishing clearer and more accountable management responsibility means that the SSA is committed, under its key principle of Delegated Personal Responsibility, to devolve responsibility and authority for the provision of services to the lowest appropriate level. In its Annual Reports the Agency has shown successful examples of delegating responsibility downward in the organization. For instance, managers locally are now responsible for a range of issues, from training through to manpower budgets, discipline, absentee management and inefficiency. However, not everyone in the Agency agrees that the existing process of devolution has led to radical results. One view is that the Agency is only tinkering with systems. In the words of one line manager:

> Local managers need the power to pull the levers that count in delivering a front line service. Operating under the existing terms and conditions of the NICS limits the flexibility of local managers as they have to work within the existing transfer and mobility restrictions. This can result in them having to manage with a surplus in one grade and an under supply in another. In particular, they need to have the right to 'hire and fire' if they are to create a more overtly based performance culture.

The most notable commitment from the SSA Management Board in carrying forward changes needed to improve performance and efficiency lies in the area of management training and development. A new training and development strategy has been developed which, in the view of the Personnel Director:

> . . . focuses on matching the business needs and new cultural change needed in the Agency through the introduction of competency based training. This approach requires renewed emphasis on roles and responsibilities to ensure

that everyone in the Agency knows what is expected of them and has the opportunity to acquire the skills and knowledge needed to perform their jobs and to fulfil their full potential.

The Agency believes that to match training against 'what staff need to be good at doing in order to meet business needs more effectively' requires a competence approach within training and management development. A bespoke competence framework has been developed by the SSA which clearly sets out the skills, knowledge and experience required for effective performance in any given grade. This competence framework is also being used in the further evolution of the staff appraisal system.

Management training in the Agency is ring-fenced since Agency Board members believe that commitment to training gives tangible expression to the Agency's key principle of 'proficient and valued staff'. The Chief Executive regularly affirms the Agency's commitment to training and management development:

> We will only be able to meet the challenges facing the Agency through a well trained and motivated workforce. We recognise that managers of to-morrow will no longer be people who have mastered one discipline as the passport to a lifetime's career. More than ever, we require our managers to be learning continually, updating old skills and acquiring new ones. They need to be flexible and innovative, to be visionaries and leaders and to be coaches and developers of staff much more than the controllers of the past. We are therefore committed to training and development and to providing managers with the necessary skills to meet the challenges and opportunities facing them.

■■■■ Staff Attitudes ■■■■

Through the mechanism of a staff attitude survey, the Agency Board attempts to gauge staff response to the ongoing process of change within the Agency. The following are the key findings of a staff attitude survey conducted during 1992:

- 89 per cent of staff are committed to improving the quality of service they deliver
- 44 per cent of staff say the quality and efficiency of the service has improved since the Agency was established
- 21 per cent of staff feel that most customers have a high opinion of the service delivered by the Agency
- 75 per cent of staff say they have a good understanding of their Branch's aims and objectives
- 49 per cent of staff are satisfied with their present job
- 13 per cent of staff feel that the Agency cares strongly for its staff
- 58 per cent indicated that they would leave the Agency if offered a comparable job in the wider Civil Service

- 89 per cent are clear about the standard of performance expected of them in their current job
- 58 per cent of staff do not regard the promotion process as fair to all staff
- 50 per cent of staff said that initiative and innovation were rarely praised
- 33 per cent of staff believe that the findings of the survey will be put to good use

(*Source*: Staff Attitude Survey, Social Security Agency (NI), 1992 (internal document))

The Future

In April 1994 the Department of Finance and Personnel announced that there were to be job losses within the NICS involving some 2300 staff. The pressure for cost efficiency continues to be a major fact of life facing all government departments in Northern Ireland.

Writing in the preface to the Agency's 1993–97 strategic plan, the Chief Executive highlighted the difficulties that lie ahead in turning the Agency's vision into reality:

> The incoming year is likely to be the most difficult we have had so far. It will require all of us to give our best and to tackle the tasks we face with determination and vigour. Although perhaps slower than we would wish, I am confident that we can still make further good progress in turning the Agency's vision into reality.

In August 1994 the Agency announced the details of a scheme for voluntary redundancies among staff.

Discussion Questions

1 How can agencies resolve the paradox inherent in the relationship between the agency and its parent department?
2 Are the performance measures adopted by the agency appropriate for measuring the agency's efficiency and effectiveness?
3 How compatible are the core values of 'delegated personal responsibility' and 'proficient and valued staff' with the realities of Social Security Agency life?
4 Does the agency meet the needs and demands of all its stakeholders?

APPENDIX

A1.1: The Vision for Agencies

Traditionally, the way the Civil Service is organized makes it difficult to achieve a proper balance between policy and delivery. This, argued the authors of the *Next Steps Initiative* report, has led to managerial weaknesses in government, with an emphasis, for instance, on the role of civil servants servicing ministers rather than managing their departments. The complexity and diversity of work in many departments, plus an imposed bureaucratic method of working, serves to constrain the freedom of civil servants to adopt a much-needed new approach towards the delivery of public services. Next Steps agencies, according to advocates of reform, create a more liberating approach to the business of government where civil servants have greater freedom to 'manage' rather than simply to 'administrate'.

The *Next Steps Initiative* recommended that agencies should be established to carry out the executive functions of government, as distinct from policy advice, and be headed by a chief executive. Agencies operate within a Framework Document which should clearly set out objectives and targets. Agencies should also enjoy a set of new financial and personnel freedoms if they are to achieve the required (better) performance.

It is recognized in the *Next Steps Initiative* report that structure alone cannot achieve the benefits to be gained from an increased business focus in the delivery of government services. To maximize results, and release the necessary managerial energy for the task, central constraints on managers ought to be loosened and a more overtly performance-based culture created.

Achieving the vision of agencies requires profound organizational change and this is neatly summarized in the *Next Steps Initiative* report as:

- greater clarification of roles and responsibilities to develop a clear sense of identity, purpose and direction and to establish clearer and more accountable management responsibility;
- contracts, clarifying the expected outputs and aggregate inputs and focusing greater attention on their achievement through greater precision about the results expected of people;
- greater incentives to good performance;
- greater management flexibility, putting the stress on results rather than processes; and
- strengthened commitment from the top, to carry forward the changes needed to improve performance and efficiency.

It is against this background that over 96 Executive Agencies have been established. There are various species of agency which differ in the range of activities they are concerned with and which have varied forms of financial regime. Some agencies are more clearly differentiated in their 'executive' role while others remain less clearly separated from their involvement in policy making.

Figure A1.1 Agency Management Board

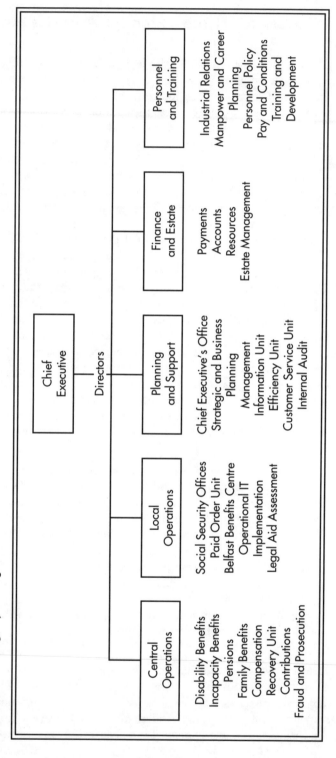

A1.2: Agency Management Board

Chief Executive

Directors

Central Operations

Disability Benefits
Incapacity Benefits
Pensions
Family Benefits
Compensation
Recovery Unit
Contributions
Fraud and Prosecution

Local Operations

Social Security Offices
Paid Order Unit
Belfast Benefits Centre
Operational IT
Implementation
Legal Aid Assessment

Planning and Support

Chief Executive's Office
Strategic and Business
Planning
Management
Information Unit
Efficiency Unit
Customer Service Unit
Internal Audit

Finance and Estate

Payments
Accounts
Resources
Estate Management

Personnel and Training

Industrial Relations
Manpower and Career
Planning
Personnel Policy
Pay and Conditions
Training and
Development

▬▬▬ A1.3: Roles and Responsibilities ▬▬▬

1 The Minister defines the scope of the Agency's activities; agrees its Strategic and annual Business Plans and sets its annual performance targets and resources.

2 The Permanent Secretary, as Permanent Head of the Department and principal adviser to the Minister, is responsible for those matters affecting the management of the department as a whole and for ensuring that adequate systems are in place across the department to support this role. The Permanent Secretary is also responsible for advising the Minister about the policy, resources plans, objectives, targets and performance of the Agency and for monitoring, on the Minister's behalf, the performance of the Agency and the Chief Executive.

3 The Chief Executive is responsible for the effective operation of the Agency in accordance with this document, his letters of appointment, and the Agency's agreed Strategic and annual Business Plans, and for meeting its objectives and targets within the resources allocated. In addition, it is his responsibility to:

- obtain the Minister's approval to changes in the Strategic and Business Plans which the Chief Executive considers necessary;
- alert the Minister and the Department to any aspect of the Department's activity which affects significantly the Agency's ability to perform effectively;
- provide the Permanent Secretary with the information required for monitoring, on behalf of the Minister, the Agency's performance against its specified targets and for policy development and related purposes, including the forecasting of benefit expenditure; and
- ensure that responsibility and management authority within the Agency is extensively devolved and keep all aspects of the management and organization of the Agency under review to ensure they best suit its business needs.

Table A1.1   Service targets and performance

Area of work	Targets 1992–93	Achieved 1992–93	Targets 1993–94
Social Fund			
Crisis loans	application cleared day need arises	same day	same day
Community Care grants	7 days	6.23 days	65% in 7 days 95% in 20 days
Income Support			
Claims	4 days	3.35 days	71% in 5 days 90% in 13 days
Accuracy	99%	99%	92%
Sickness – Invalidity Benefit			
Claims	65% in 12 days 95% in 30 days	68.84% in 12 days 89.08% in 30 days	65% in 10 days 95% in 30 days
Accuracy	98%	98%	97%
Child Benefit			
Claims	65% in 10 days 95% in 30 days	73.19% in 10 days 93.33% in 30 days	73% in 10 days 95% in 30 days
Family Credit			
Claims	60% in 13 days 95% in 45 days	61.15% in 13 days 98.03% in 45 days	60% in 13 days 95% in 42 days
Accuracy	96%	98.49%	92%
Disability Living Allowance			
Claims	60% in 30 days 95% in 55 days	35.45% in 30 days 52.29% in 55 days	65% in 30 days 85% in 55 days
Accuracy	96%	98.03%	96%
Disability Working Allowance			
Claims	95% in 5 days	68.49% in 5 days	
Accuracy	95%	98.45%	
Pensions			
Claims	65% in 20 days 95% in 60 days	74.23% in 20 days 94.37% in 60 days	65% in 20 days 95% in 60 days
Accuracy	99%	99.71%	99%
Unemployment Benefit			
Claims	8 days	7.62 days	7.5 days
Customer satisfaction			
% satisfied customers	90%	86%	90%

Source: *Social Security Agency (NI), Annual Report and Accounts 1992–1993,* HMSO, London.

Table A1.2 Efficiency and performance

Area of work	Target 1992–93	Achieved 1992–93
Social Fund		
Social Fund loan recovery	£13.62m of loan expenditure to be covered by loan recoveries	£15.07m of loan expenditure covered by loan recoveries
Live within gross allocation for loans and grants	£26.33m	£26.30m
Income Support		
Recovery of Income Support overpayments	£1.0m	£0.93m
Fraud		
Gross annual benefit saving	£10.40m	£10.56m
Contributions		
Increase the number of surveys to	5,000	7,987

Source: Social Security Agency Annual Report and Accounts 1992–1993, London: HMSO.

▬▬ A1.5: Financial Flexibilities ▬▬

Subject to normal supply procedures, and the Permanent Secretary's approval of the Agency's financial management systems, the Chief Executive has authority to:

1. authorize capital projects within such limits as will be specified from time to time by the Permanent Secretary;
2. deploy the Agency's overall running costs allocation flexibly, except that services undertaken for the Benefits Agency for the Department of Social Security are covered by a separate running costs budget;
3. carry forward underspends of running costs and capital within limits specified by the Permanent Secretary and with the agreement of the Permanent Secretary;
4. vire from running costs into capital or other non running-cost subheads within the same section up to a maximum of 5 per cent of the donor subhead and 10 per cent of the recipient subhead (whichever is the lesser) in any financial year subject to the approval of the Permanent Secretary. The ceiling will apply to the total involvement from or to any subhead over the financial year;
5. change provision within subheads where the change is below 10 per cent of the relevant entry provisions in any financial year, provided that the amount does not exceed 10 per cent of the recipient line entry;

6 reinvest each year in its business a proportion of efficiency savings, the proportion to be agreed with the Minister and, where appropriate, the Department of Finance and Personnel.

▬▬ A1.6: Personnel Flexibilities ▬▬

Pay and grading

1 The Agency's pay and grading structure is consistent with Northern Ireland Civil Service standards.
2 The Agency will, in consultation with the Department and the Department of Finance and Personnel, review its pay and grading structure to ensure that it meets its business needs.
3 Subject to the agreement of the Department and the Department of Finance and Personnel, the Agency may establish an efficiency-related bonus scheme for staff.

Recruitment

1 The Agency has authority to recruit permanent staff below Executive Officer Grade II directly through the Civil Service Commission.
2 Recruitment of permanent staff at Executive Officer Grade II and above is in agreement with the Permanent Secretary and through the Northern Ireland Civil Service Commission.
3 The Agency may bring forward proposals, for approval, by the Department and the Department of Finance and Personnel, for alternative methods of recruitment.
4 The Agency has authority to recruit directly staff, up to and including Grade 6, on short-service contract, or casual or limited appointment. All recruitment is by fair and open competition and on merit.

Staff appraisal

1 The Agency operates the performance appraisal system in use in the rest of the Northern Ireland Service.
2 It may adapt the system to meet its own requirements following consultation with the Department and the Department of Finance and Personnel.

Career development and training

1 The Agency is responsible for promoting the training and development of all its staff.
2 In pursuit of this, it will develop a training and development strategy which meets the needs of the Agency and takes account as necessary of the broader needs of the Department.

A1.7: Extracts from the Social Security Agency's Strategic and Business Plans

Good quality services

1 improve the Agency's understanding of and responsiveness to customer requirements by introducing regular independent sampling of customer opinion on the quality of service;
2 invest in customer care training for agency staff and recognize the importance of quality through the introduction of Quality of Service Officers in all Management Units;
3 make the service more accessible by trialing new Customer Service Access Points to provide the full range of services in some areas at present not well served by current outlets.

Efficient services

1 implement Operational Strategy Computer Systems to improve the services to the unemployed and the disabled;
2 set up service development teams to produce more efficient methods of working, taking account of the opportunities provided by Operational Strategy Computer Systems;
3 develop and improve the systems for financial and management accountability and control.

Proficient and valued staff

1 develop and implement a training and development strategy which is more appropriate to the changing needs of the Agency, with renewed emphasis on customer service training;
2 develop a personnel management strategy which is best suited to the needs of the Agency and which makes best use of the personnel flexibilities delegated to the Agency in the Framework Document;
3 develop and introduce revised and streamlined industrial relations arrangements which are focused more sharply on the business needs of the Agency and which encourage resolution of issues expeditiously and at the lowest level possible;
4 introduce regular sampling of staff opinion and satisfaction.

Delegated personal responsibility

1 devolve responsibility for personnel management to local management unit level;
2 devolve certain centrally held budgets to Management Units;
3 review roles and responsibilities of all grades within each Management Unit to ensure responsibility is delegated to the appropriate level;

4   encourage local and other initiatives by introducing a scheme to foster innovation.

References

CM 1760, *Improving Management in Government – the Next Steps Agencies Review 1991*, HMSO, London, November 1991.

CM 2101, *The Citizens Charter First Report: 1992*, HMSO, November 1992.

Social Security Agency (NI), 'A Human Resource Strategy for the Social Security Agency', 1992 (internal document).

Social Security Agency (NI), *Annual Report and Accounts, 1991–1992*, London: HMSO.

Social Security Agency (NI), *Report of Findings of Customer Survey*, 1992, HMSO, London.

Social Security Agency (NI), Staff Attitude Survey, 1992, (internal document).

Social Security Agency (NI), *The Business Plan*, 1991–92, London: HMSO.

Treasury and Civil Service Committee 7th Report, The Next Steps Initiative, (HC 496), London: HMSO, July 1991.

2

Capital Accounting Case Study – UK Local Government

Geoff Jones

This case is designed to illustrate a number of themes surrounding the introduction of a major change in UK local government accounting practice. Most elements of the change were first implemented in most local authorities for published accounts for the financial year 1994/5. This qualification of the extent of implementation highlights the major theme of the case: that significant changes of accounting practice are not simply a question of expert professionals devising a single, 'best' practice and accountants and managers applying them unproblematically. Although standardization of accounting practices has long been pursued as an aim of the accounting profession, encouraged or perhaps driven by certain interested users of financial information such as governments and providers of capital, diversity remains a key feature of all types of accounting activity.

Accounting professionals tend nowadays not to see accounting numbers as representing *the* truth about an organization's financial state of affairs but rather a particular version of the truth which coincides with the accounting conventions which governed the preparation of the accounts. Audit certificates under UK Companies Acts require the auditor to confirm their opinion that the accounts under audit represent a true and fair view of the financial affairs of the company. Thus there are two important qualifications to the truth of the accounts: the auditor's *opinion* that they are true (auditors can be wrong), and that truth is in some way inextricably linked with *fairness*, which in this context implies some kind of comprehensive, non-selective representation of accounting facts. In the UK public sector, the wording 'presents fairly' is used. So it is recognized that the same accounting 'facts' can result in significantly different sets of accounts.

The duty of the accountant, generally speaking, is to prepare accounts in accordance with the accepted conventions *and* to disclose in what ways and to what extent these conventions have not been complied with. This implies that there may either be difficulties in drawing up the accounts of an organization in compliance with the accounting conventions (for example, arising from the specified information being unavailable or too expensive to collect), or that producers of accounts may prefer one particular method of presentation to another (especially regarding the organization's assets and liabilities). Although accounting conventions (largely but not entirely codified as national and international accounting standards and 'Generally Accepted Accounting Principles' (GAAP)) attempt in principle to minimize scope for diversity, there are so many variables affecting an organization's financial standing (e.g. the industry and country in which its major activities take place, its recent and prospective profitability, its strategic intentions regarding major investments, merger or acquisition activity, the nature of its audit profession) that there remain many ways of representing its 'real' position. Consequently interpretation of accounting information has become a highly skilled activity practised by analysts of various kinds, usually with an eye to the interests of their corporate customers, e.g. the financial institutions.

Two interesting issues which have preoccupied the accounting community (i.e. including both producers and users of accounts) in recent years have been how to account for the value of so-called intellectual property (patents, software, performance rights, etc.) and for the value of company brand names. These are obviously not the only or even the most important emerging issues to have been tackled, but they have some similarities as accounting problems with the governmental accounting issue discussed in this case, namely that of accounting for the substantial capital assets owned and operated by UK local governments.

These similarities revolve around perceptions and definitions of the issue (i.e. how an issue becomes an issue), how the regulatory bodies search for and decide on a 'solution', and how (whether) the 'solution' is actually implemented as intended. Although these processes are played out differently, with different actors and concerns, nevertheless these three stages can be discerned in the case which follows, even though stages 1 and 2 occurred several times but stage 3 only once in the 125 years covered by the case.

The main point to bear in mind here is that commercial accounting has problematic issues of its own which it finds difficult to address despite the proliferation of apparently self-regulating yet prescriptive accounting bodies and institutions throughout the world. Accounting is not simply a question of applying agreed and autonomous rules to any given situation. Most importantly for this case, it is not just a question of applying 'good commercial accounting practice' to governmental institutions, even though there may seem to be good prima facie reasons for trying to do so.

Even 'fundamental' accounting concepts were introduced into different industries and organizations at different times and in different degrees, and although there may have been something of a convergence in the last 50 years or so (perhaps due to the concentration of ownership of capital in particular countries such as the US and the subsequent export of that capital into

US-controlled businesses throughout the world), new issues and problems continue to preoccupy accounting regulators and practitioners. Accountants tend to regard changes in accounting practice as developmental, i.e. progressive in the sense that accounting today is better than accounting in the past. Many researchers, however, look on accounting in much the same way as they do any other social practice, i.e. that these practices somehow are more reflective of the society which produced them and are therefore the result of a 'negotiated order' rather than the outcome of an objective search for new techniques and methods which better represent some underlying reality. Both parties acknowledge that there is no one set of permanent, objective, context-free 'laws' of accounting which apply to all conceivable circumstances. But they sometimes differ in their evaluation of the practices in use.

This case tells us a lot not only about UK local government but also about other parts of the UK public sector and possibly about the ways professionals of all kinds seek to retain their autonomy by owning and solving problems relevant to their practice area. Part of the impetus for the changes that were considered and adopted for local government arose out of successful application of new capital accounting regimes, first in the water industry and more recently in the National Health Service in the UK. Central government departments are preparing to introduce a similar regime for all UK state expenditure which will be completed early in the next century. So the example of local government may be seen as representing a much wider set of changes.

▬▬ Objectives of the Case ▬▬

This case has the following objectives:

- to illustrate the processes by which an important change in local government accounting in the UK came about;
- to highlight the roles played by different interests and stakeholder groups in these processes;
- to explore the different meanings that are given to accounting conventions.

▬▬ Capital Accounting – the Arguments ▬▬

Conventional accounting seeks to show the value of assets, usually based on their historic cost, with some recognition that most assets wear out, become obsolescent, etc. Depreciation is the accounting means of measuring and recording this depletion of value, and there are various ways of estimating the reduction in value which can be said to arise in a particular accounting period. For example, it is possible to depreciate an asset over its useful life so that at the end of the period it has no value and is written out of the balance sheet, or to provide depreciation so that at the end of its life enough depreciation has been provided so as to replace the asset at its then market price. The varying pace at which an asset's value declines can be accommodated, e.g. we are familiar with the idea that a new car loses a large percentage of its value as soon as it leaves the showroom yet declines in value more slowly thereafter. Some assets can appreciate in value: land, for instance, and in these cases capital reserves are created. Still others, for example railway tracks, will maintain their value so long as adequate repair and maintenance is carried out. Hence it may not then be appropriate to depreciate them. Despite sometimes heated debate, the historical cost convention is still the most widely used in all kinds of accounting: current or replacement cost bases, though used, are not so widespread.

From the mid nineteenth century to the introduction of the new capital accounting regime in 1994/5 local authority assets were shown in accounts in a way which emphasized the remaining amount owed on them rather than what they cost, let alone what their value was estimated to be. This was because other sources of finance, for example contributions from local income (such as markets and tolls), local authority trading undertakings (e.g. gasworks), or from rates, were extensively (and legally) used. Although there was usually great enthusiasm from reforming councillors to provide the new amenities the public were said to need, in the interests of prudence authorities frequently repaid debt early. After repaying the loan, no further charge for using the asset appeared in the revenue accounts. For those authorities which exceeded their minimum disclosure requirements set down by the Local Government Board and which did show the historic cost of their assets (mainly county boroughs, metropolitan boroughs and joint trading boards, i.e. the main urban areas of the country) the un-depreciated historic cost of the asset remained in the balance sheet and could remain there forever. For other authorities, only the loans outstanding were shown. It was the variety of practices in use, the emphasis on loans rather than economic cost and the pressure from the mainstream commercial accounting bodies which led to capital accounting becoming a big issue in the 1980s.

▬▬ The Issues ▬▬

Local Authority balance sheets portray councils as debt-ridden. They do not get anywhere near showing their true worth. Revenue accounts are downright whimsical in their portrayal of the cost of assets used up in providing services. The remarkable thing is that after a century of local government, that state of affairs should still exist. (*John Scotford, County Treasurer Hampshire County Council and Chairman of the CIPFA Capital Accounting Working Group,* **Public Finance and Accountancy,** *19 February 1993, p. 12*)

For any professional body to be worth the name, it has to be concerned with raising standards, including advocating new standards when old ones have served their time. What is acceptable in one circumstance may become quite unacceptable in another. *(Noel Hepworth, Director of CIPFA, **Public Finance and Accountancy**, 19 February 1993, p. 2)*

In a Utopian world the concept of asset rental would underpin all accounts in both the public and private sector . . . [W]e do not live in such a paradise, but rather in a mean spirited, anti-public sector environment. Acceptance of theoretical virtue of the nebulous aspiration does not provide a basis for extrapolating that into a mandate to impose an expensively irrelevant system of accounting on local authorities. *(Jeff Pipe, Assistant City Treasurer, Birmingham City Council, **Public Finance and Accountancy**, 19 February 1993, p. 20)*

These quotations identify two important aspects of the 'problem' of capital accounting in local authorities in the UK in the late 1980s. These issues relate primarily to local authorities in mainland Britain. Some local authority accounting terms, conventions and regulatory arrangements are different in Scotland from those in use in England and Wales. These differences do not affect the substance of this case. One aspect is historical: reforms, by definition, must have something to reform: no reformer starts with a blank sheet of paper and hopes to implement changes unhindered by the past (see section A2.1 for details). The second is the concept of interests in accounting: professional practitioners, for instance, have interests, probably in raising standards but also perhaps in retaining or enhancing their social position, which raising standards helps them to do. The implications of both these aspects as espoused by the practitioners themselves in these quotations are that accounting is not one fixed body of knowledge applicable for all time, and that changes to it may not necessarily be brought about simply because some experts see deficiencies which *could* be remedied.

▬▬ The Decisive Period 1980–1990 ▬▬

The oil crisis of 1973 is claimed as the turning point, but it seems likely that sooner or later some fundamental shock to the UK economy was bound to occur. The first budgets of the Labour Government elected in 1974 saw the official demise of Keynesian demand management and the beginnings of the turn to monetarism under the inflation/stagnation combination that affected many Western governments, but the balance of payments crisis of 1976/7 and the IMF loan terms to restrain public expenditure set in train the first round of local government budget pressures which have continued ever since.

Perhaps as the result of some combination of professional ambition and fiscal crisis, this period was also the beginning of the revival of interest in local authority capital accounting. In 1975 CIPFA's Accounting Panel published a pamphlet on Local Authority Accounting which proposed, *inter alia*, that capital assets should be depreciated if revenue costs were to be correctly stated.

As part of its attempts to accede to the mainstream of UK accountancy, CIPFA was also reviewing the applicability to local authorities of a wide range of accounting standards and proposed standards, and another working party recommended (in 1977) a system of notional loan charges (to be called capital charges) to attempt to reflect the true economic costs of using assets in the revenue accounts of local authorities.

Following the logic of the practice of emphasizing the amount owed on assets in the balance sheet, the 1972 Local Government Act had laid down specific requirements for pooling and charging the debt repayments to revenue accounts, and the changes proposed would have necessitated some revision or accommodation of this which would have been difficult and/or expensive to implement. But the main obstacle was the uncertainty about the way the accounting profession in general would deal with the problem of asset values following the period of high inflation in the UK economy. So–called Current Cost Accounting (CCA), which attempts to recognize the effects of inflation on company assets and performance, proved a minefield for all parts of the profession and, despite years of controversy, proposals and counter-proposals, no effective standardized accounting regime emerged, although some UK companies did, and continue to, produce current cost accounts.

The height of this uncertainty occurred in the late 1970s and early 1980s, and the proposals for reforming capital accounting were delayed pending some resolution. CIPFA felt obliged to show its commitment to CCA by recommending the adopting of current cost accounts for local authority trading activities. Enthusiasm for 'proper accounting' was again a strong force in the new Thatcher Government in the personality of Michael Heseltine in charge of the Department of the Environment and a strong prevailing feeling throughout the government that local authorities were overlarge and inefficient, and were contributing to the unnecessarily high interest rates the new monetarist outlook emphasized. The Department of Trade and Industry under Lord Young and others continued to signal the desirability of a unified UK accountancy profession.

One of the Thatcher Government's earliest pieces of local government legislation, the Local Government Planning and Land Act 1980, introduced the obligation for local authority Direct Labour Organizations (DLOs) – the parts of local authorities which existed to carry out approved local authority work such as refuse collection and highways maintenance – to expose themselves to competition with the private sector through the competitive tendering process. And here the issue of the value of local authority assets compared to their accounting treatment comes into focus, for the Act required DLOs to prepare their accounts (and hence their bids for contracts) on a current cost basis and to achieve a required rate of return on their assets valued at current cost (current cost here meaning current replacement cost – the highest basis for valuation and one which was not widely used by the private sector competitors for contracts). The general effect of this in accounting terms is to increase the prices which must be charged in order to maintain the current cost of assets while at the same time apparently depressing profitability because income is lower in relation to the highly valued asset base. This effect was one of the reasons it proved widely unpopular with companies at large.

But local authorities were encouraged to continue to find ways of extending the applicability of commercial accounting practices. However, many argued that the concept of depreciation, for example, entailed a conception of capital maintenance which was inappropriate for many local authority assets and, more importantly, could not form the basis of a charge to ratepayers.

Instead, a system of asset rents was proposed which could form the basis of a charge to operating departments for the use of assets but which would not be related to rates. In other words, the discipline of charging for use of assets would not affect the level of rates being charged – an important clarification of principle which had always been one of the key problems of reforming the accounting system, the separation of external reporting arrangements which would always need to show debt outstanding (yet was otherwise more or less incomprehensible to the non-accountant) from the fiscal pressure to make services like education do more with less.

▬▬ The Audit Commission ▬▬

The establishment of the Local Government Audit Commission for England and Wales in 1984 provided a further impetus to the reform of local authority accounting practices, bringing as it did a much wider involvement of private sector audit firms into local authority audit than existed under the previous 'approved auditor' system. Additionally, the Commission took seriously its role in promoting 'best accounting practice' in local authorities and one of its major initiatives was the development of a Code of Practice for Local Authority Accounts (1987) which took the accounting profession's Statements of Standard Accounting Practice and reconsidered the extent of their applicability to local governments. This code effectively became binding on local authorities since it redefined the meaning of the 'proper accounting practices' they were obliged to pursue.

One important part of accounting practice was left out of the Accounting Code: capital asset accounting was left on one side as 'too difficult' and would have significantly held up the introduction of the rest of it. But the Minister's (by then Nicholas Ridley) quoted response ('This is all very well but what about capital?') drove home the significance the Government attached to the issue. As before, the local authority accounting profession were left under the threat that if it failed to find an acceptable solution to the need to update its 'antiquated' conventions, the Department would impose its own solution. Whether it could ever have done this remains open to question; suffice it to say that not only was it a challenge to CIPFA's claim to be a self-regulating professional body, but many of its members believed that anything it could devise would be better than a scheme dreamt up and imposed by the civil servants. This possibility was repeatedly used later by the Institute's leadership as a means to deter sceptical opinion.

The Role of the Capital Accounting Steering Group

Whether real or imaginary, this threat, and the general embarrassment that the years of discussion had produced no workable proposals, led to a determined effort to resolve the issue once and for all. A high-profile Capital Accounting Steering Group (CASG) was set up on 1 January 1988 under the chairmanship of John Parkes, then Director of Finance of Humberside County Council and a CIPFA council member. The local authority associations (i.e. non-accountants) were represented as it was essential that non-finance Chief Officers and Councillors would not be automatically alienated from the Group's findings. The DoE, the Audit Commission, Scottish local authorities and academia also supplied members. Secretarial support (and guidance) was provided by CIPFA and Price Waterhouse provided technical support, e.g. in advising on commercial practice and in testing out some of the possibilities for change.

The CASG spent a year deliberating and finally came forward with a set of proposals for consultation in February 1989. These embodied many of the features previously favoured. A charge for assets in use was to be made in the service revenue accounts based on their current value (defined as net current replacement cost, i.e. current replacement cost after accumulated depreciation) plus a charge to reflect the cost of capital (i.e. the opportunity cost of tying up capital in its current use). The balance sheet would show assets at depreciated current replacement cost or market value. Assets would be grouped into four main types:

1 council dwellings;
2 other land and buildings;
3 infrastructure;
4 vehicles, plant, furniture and equipment.

The benefits of this arrangement were that it brought the economic cost of holding assets to bear on the service manager using them and at the same time allowed balance sheets to show 'proper' valuations without requiring additional funds from ratepayers (soon to be Community Charge payers).

The consultation period ended on 15 January 1990 – a lengthy gap, but in the meantime several authorities were to act as pilot sites for testing the practicability of the proposals, the biggest immediate problem being the drawing up of full asset registers. At the publication of the proposals (February 1989) the new system was envisaged as being implemented in the financial year 1991/2, i.e. beginning just after the close of the consultations.

The Response of the Professionals

The results of the consultations graphically illustrated the underlying tensions among the CIPFA membership and elsewhere. The perception of the leadership that the Institute needed to maintain its claim to be a 'proper' accounting body and retain its power of self-regulation in the face of governmental threats cut little ice with many of the membership who would have to implement the new proposals. The consultation document came at a difficult time (although it was argued that there had never been an easy time to make such changes). Following many years of legislative and structural changes in local government, and continued fiscal pressures, the government's sweeping reform of local taxation – the community charge or poll tax – was about to be introduced, the main feature of which was the transfer of the basis of assessment and charging of local tax from property (as it had been since time immemorial) to individuals on the grounds that it was they who actually consumed so many of the modern services which local government provided. Apart from the political controversy which surrounded its introduction, the logistical and practical difficulties of identifying, assessing and billing a new and wider range of local taxpayers in the time scale prescribed by Government fell heavily on CIPFA members. The problems inherent in adopting the proposed new system of capital accounting were widely seen as unnecessary in themselves and impractical to implement.

This type of response drew attention to one of the ambiguities in the situation. The stated intent of the CASG was to produce proposals which separated the capital cost of services from their financing, showed the full current costs of services and recorded the current value of fixed assets. This rather glossed over the important distinction between the external reporting requirements of local authorities (which the Code of Practice on Local Authority Accounting was concerned with and which, as we have seen, had excluded capital accounting) and the different issue of how efficiently authorities used the assets under their control. The DoE and the rest of the accounting profession, although interested in both, were primarily concerned with external reporting, mainly on the grounds that, in the DoE's case, it was still the formal accounts that provided the main basis for financial control of local authority expenditure and debt and, in the case of the accounting profession, from its assumption that internal efficiency depended on 'proper' accounting, meaning to them accountability to shareholders and stock markets.

CIPFA members, however, showed great scepticism about many of these assumptions. Something like 80 per cent of responses (including corporate bodies and non-accountant organizations) contained criticisms of the proposals. In general, they were unimpressed by suggestions that meeting DoE requirements was the same thing as improved accountability to rate and charge payers. Many felt the public were already well served by the financial information available to them. An alternative heresy put forward was that nobody bothered to look at local authority accounts anyway and that balance sheets, for example, simply did not have the same significance in the public as in the private sector since it was not part of the role of local authorities and other public bodies to aim primarily at increasing their net worth. Thus the internal disciplines were actually more important and many of the presumed benefits of this could be achieved by exhortation and comparative studies (as performed, for example, by the Audit Commission) rather than by a full-blown accounting system which might come to be regarded as just another accountants' wheeze unrelated to the 'real' concerns of managers. A surprisingly large volume of opinion seemed to regard many aspects of accounting as less important than delivering services. And some members implied that CIPFA should be finding better things to do than impose extra burdens on its members at the behest of the Government and the other accounting bodies.

The Role of CIPFA

This kind of response threatened the credibility of the leadership and the full weight of its disciplinary power was brought into play. The 'Why change?' kind of criticism was met with emphatic statements about how the imperfections of the current system had long been recognized and no longer proved adequate in the new competitive and constrained environment local authorities were now in. The 'Why now' kind of response was met with emphasizing the threat to self-regulation, supported by the evidence that during the consultation period the government had apparently considered the CASG report and imposed a similar system of capital charges in the NHS from the financial year 1990/1. It was easier to do this in the NHS since most of its accounting still used the cash basis and there were no loan accounts, but the implementation problems were simply brushed aside and a charge to services was introduced based on depreciation on all assets valued over £1000 (an absurdly low figure – later raised to £5000 – which spoke volumes for the outlook of the civil servants who devised it) and a charge to equate to a cost of capital. After years of deliberation by CIPFA, this single step by the Department of Health greatly added to the urgency of finding an acceptable solution for local government, and incidentally undermined many of the objections that the valuation task in local government would take an impossibly long time to get right.

Also at this time relations with the rest of the accounting bodies were further sensitized by the failure of a major merger attempt in 1990. This time, with the shrinkage of its public sector base and a worsening of its financial situation (though with a small but definite growth in active members) the long-term future of the Institute became less secure and prompted a rash of strategic and marketing initiatives designed to support an indefinite independent existence but still within the main professional regulatory bodies.

So the suggestion that the published accounts of local authorities were comparatively unimportant brought the most scathing response, expressed more moderately much later when the final revised proposals were adopted:

> The Institute as a professional accountancy body is committed to upholding professional accounting standards. The Institute cannot be seen to endorse a system which results in a completely meaningless financial statement, when

that statement, the balance sheet, ought to be of major significance – as it is elsewhere in the economy.

So there is no justification for the argument that no change should be made. *(Hepworth,* **Public Finance and Accountancy,** *19 February 1993, p. 2)*

But other objections proved more difficult to brush off. In particular, the costs of implementing the new system and the proposed time scale were seen as at best unnecessarily high and short. Complaints about the asset registers prompted the response that authorities would need to know what they owned anyway, either for competitive tendering purposes or simply for good housekeeping. As such, the costs could not be regarded as wholly additional. The Royal Institution of Chartered Surveyors which had been involved in the proposals offered advice on how to simplify and accelerate the valuation process, including the use of information then available as a result of the revaluing of businesses that took place at the time of the community charge introduction.

▬▬ Implementation ▬▬

Another line of criticism was that market valuations rather than current replacement cost could be the only basis for a 'real' economic cost, but the non-marketability of many local authority assets (e.g. roads and schools) made this difficult, although research was done at some of the pilot authorities to see how far this idea could be taken. The pilot studies, however, also threw up problems of their own. The involvement of other professional groups in endorsing and implementing the proposals was more difficult at grass-roots level than the attitude of the national bodies seemed to imply. Cost in particular was an issue, and later in the implementation phase some councils let it be known that their finance department would be expected to shoulder the additional financial burden. But problems associated with the assets themselves were unearthed. For instance, valuing roads proved even more difficult than had been envisaged since it turned out that for the purposes of depreciation a road had many different components which wore out at different rates, for example the wearing surface had a short life compared to the substructure. Was each of these components to be valued and depreciated separately?

All these reactions caused severe difficulties to the CASG and the Institute. Reaction was so unfavourable that despite producing a 'final report' in September 1990, the CASG recognized the difficulties and deferred the implementation of its proposals while yet more studies were carried out under yet another working group, whose remit was to find ways in which the new system could be implemented relatively simply and at minimum cost to local authorities. This time the pilot authorities were Solihull Metropolitan District Council, St Edmundsbury District Council and the London Borough of Croydon and this time the DoE was persuaded to finance the studies. Another 'interim' report was produced (on 8 May 1992) with the significant amendment to the earlier proposals that, subject to certain caveats relating to an authority's policy to maintain the economic life of the building by making adequate provision for repairs and maintenance and to depreciate if this were not the case, operational buildings and other properties should not be depreciated but included at current value (as previously defined).

This change was proposed 'primarily as a pragmatic response to the practical concerns expressed by commentators on the [CASG's] Final Report' (*Public Finance and Accountancy*, 8 May 1992, p. 10). The other main problem, council houses, were also to be valued on this basis, rather than on their value to their tenants under the 'right to buy' legislation (which was substantially lower). Finally, valuations were to be simplified by using a 'beacon' system where only one of a type in a neighbourhood would be valued. Infrastructure and so-called 'community assets' (parks, historic buildings, etc.) valuations would be based on historical cost and so would not need current valuations. The RICS was an important source of legitimation for these steps. The interim report of 8 May 1992 also reported that a survey had been carried out to see whether the new system was thought to be workable and in particular that it would be consistent with or unaffected by proposed changes by the DoE to the system of capital expenditure controls.

The interim report for the first time proposed implementation of the revised proposals for 1994/5 accounts, i.e. four years after the initial expectation of the CASG in 1988. Even then, the required approval by CIPFA Council was not entirely smooth with one council member voting against. A strong statement stressing 'professionalism' and 'proper standards' was made by the CIPFA Director (second quote under 'The Issues') to the membership following the adoption of the proposals on 29 January 1993 and an Institute Statement was issued. This stressed the 'limited room for manoeuvre', the 'full exploration of the options', the necessity of 'a degree of compromise and pragmatism', the need to recognize developments in other parts of the public sector, and finally that 'the proposals represent the best balance between action, pragmatism and principles'.

Further consultations were carried out, but the battle was essentially won (or lost, depending on your viewpoint). The revised proposals were incorporated into a revised Accounting Code of Practice for local authorities and became the Statement of Recommended Practice in 1993. One Treasurer wrote in PFA: 'the mood of practitioners I meet is one of mild acceptance, certainly not wild enthusiasm . . . there is general acquiescence.' (*Public Finance and Accountancy*, PFA 9 July 1993 p. 13). Many authorities were slow to get their asset registers set up and help was at hand from a wide array of valuers, software suppliers, private accounting firms and management consultants who were all able to benefit.

It remains to be seen whether the benefits in terms of accountability and better use of assets are actually realized (and how this is assessed), but it is clear that the main objective of being able to deliver a 'proper' accounting system for local authorities had at long last been achieved.

▬▬▬ Discussion Questions ▬▬▬

1 Who were the key stakeholders, and what were their interests, detailed in the case?
2 How appropriate are commercial accounting practices for the public sector?
3 What is the value of public assets and who should decide this?
4 What does the case pinpoint as the key issues facing public sector professionals?

▬▬▬ A2.1: The History of Local Government Capital Accounting ▬▬▬

There is no doubt that perception of capital accounting in local authorities as a 'problem' dates back in several important respects at least to the adoption of the system of accounting which prevailed for well over a century: the emphasis in local authority accounts from the mid nineteenth century onwards not on the value (current or historical) of the assets owned by local governments but on the amount borrowed to produce them.

The conventions which were imposed by central government on local authority accounting in the nineteenth century through the Local Government Board (created in 1871 through a merger of the Poor Law Board and the medical department of the Privy Council), together with the involvement of the Board of Trade and the Treasury (a triumvirate of departmental interests which was to remain crucial to local government down the years) could be said to embody the dominant values of the time within a workable regime. A feature of this regime was the pre-eminence of governmental administrative perceptions and requirements (represented by the Treasury and the Local Government Board) rather than accounting interests as represented through the Board of Trade and by the embryonic accounting profession. This perception emphasized the separate legal status of local authorities and their liability in respect of loans taken out by them, but also an apprehension over the size of the rising national debt and the need to ensure that local authorities behaved responsibly with the rapidly rising funds provided directly by ratepayers and indirectly by taxpayers through government grant-in-aid. Thus the departments sought to control the variables important to them through the legal and administrative methods they were familiar with rather than through the accounting regimes which shareholders and accountants had instilled into commercial concerns.

One consequence of this was an emphasis on cash accounting which has persisted up to the present day. For a long time, under an Act of 1882, authorities were required to keep accounts on a 'receipts and expenditure' basis – a misunderstanding by Parliament which was the subject of some derision from both local authority and 'commercial' accountants as it demonstrates clearly the lack of appreciation of accounting niceties of which the profession complained. It was generally accepted that what was meant was 'receipts and payments', i.e. the cash accounting convention rather than the 'income and expenditure' basis favoured by the accounting profession. The latter involves a recognition that events with financial consequences could have occurred but not yet affected the organization's cash flow – for example, goods having been received but not paid for by the end of the accounting period.

These 'accruals' remain one of the basic accounting conventions, even in public services (but not yet in all central government departments). A further aspect of the accruals convention is another non-cash charge on the accounts which is vitally implicated in the debate about capital assets: depreciation. A full accruals basis implies that the cost of asset depreciation is also recorded in the accounts even though no cash is involved. This was one of the main problems with introducing full accruals into local authority accounts which defeated a number of initiatives over the years.

The effect of all this was that, even on an historic cost basis, accounts did not clearly show the value and cost in use of the assets owned and operated by local authorities and, for instance, made it impossible to show the growing lobby of ratepayers concerned about the massive increase in rates which occurred during the nineteenth and early twentieth century that their money was being wisely spent on lasting assets rather than, as many suspected, being used to support municipal profligacy and to encourage idleness among the recipients of services.

Detailed accounting requirements were an intrinsic but only one part of the whole regulatory regime imposed by the Local Government Board and its successors. For large capital projects this included the granting of a private Act of Parliament to proceed, a loan sanction to borrow the monies required and a stipulation of the maximum period of the loan. This maximum period was intended to ensure that authorities did not owe money on assets which had decayed. Consequently they were set for periods not expected to exceed the useful life of the asset. Although originally the maximum period for the repayment of loans used for acquiring land was set at 120 years, this was quickly brought more into line with the life of the assets built on it, and a maximum of 60 years came into effect. It was later argued that the loan repayment was essentially the same as depreciation, since it corresponded to the depletion in value of the asset as the loan was redeemed. However, a range of issues including fluctuating interest rates, technological changes (e.g. the widespread use of gas and electricity), and variations in the use of loan finance meant that this correspondence was only approximate, although it almost certainly distorted values less than the historic cost convention itself.

By the end of the nineteenth century most municipal corporations had extended their activities into a wide range of undertakings including water supply, gasworks, electricity supply, tramways and canals. Some of these enterprises were new but some were acquired from private sector owners. The issue of appropriate compensation sparked a long-running debate about the accounting conventions of local authorities compared with those of their private sector equivalents. As with other developments, municipal corporations obtained the power to acquire or establish these trading undertakings by local Act of Parliament and with it the sanction to borrow the necessary funds. As with other assets, the balance sheets of the local authorities gave few clues to their current market value. However, since at this time the justification for these undertakings was the provision of public services, the question of their book value which would be needed for subsequent sale simply did not arise. It was thought (by the Local Government Board and the Treasury) to be far more relevant to concentrate on the extent of government indebtedness, hence capital accounts typically began with the entry 'loans outstanding – Town Hall'.

Other interests had rather different concerns. Private owners of utilities which were municipalized were interested in obtaining the maximum price they could, although here as elsewhere their accounts were unlikely to provide a basis for a transfer value, since valuation and depreciation practices varied widely and owners were anxious to stress the potential as well as the historic value of their assets. Privately, some owners were only too glad to get rid of decaying assets, such as obsolete water mains or old tram tracks, at a large profit, and the political tide to put these 'essential services' under public control meant that even otherwise shrewd councillor–businessmen were happy to go along with recommendations from their officers to acquire the patchwork of privately provided services to knit into the municipal fabric.

There were also, however, discordant voices. Political opposition to municipalization objected not only to the process itself (and the powers the corporations had secured for themselves) but also to the financial regime to which the municipal enterprises were subject. The latter not only involved increasing the national debt but also the presumed inefficient financial administration which would arise under municipal ownership and give rise to additional local taxation. These views became part of a strong lobby to bring 'proper accounting practices' to bear on local authorities and for them to be audited by trained, qualified accountants rather than the long-established system of audit which consisted of lay members of the community elected annually to inspect the accounts. These auditors tended to be either lawyers or worthy laymen; it was argued by the accounting lobby and its allies that they were hopelessly ill-equipped to pass judgement on the probity of complex corporation accounts which, moreover, included activities which had often been taken over from the private sector where they had been subject to private sector accounting disciplines.

This campaign was only partially successful and in a way which also demonstrates the relative power of government departments rather than the accounting profession: despite hostility from the municipal corporations, the audit eventually came under the control the Local Government Board itself and became the District Audit, but it developed its own specialized workforce which did not employ trained accountants in a big way until the 1960s. At the turn of the century the district auditors' insistence on cash accounts, reflecting the government's interests, was one of the sources of local treasures' antipathy towards them.

A potent force in the lobby for more 'professional accounting' was the ICAEW, who in a long series of articles in the *Accountant* in the 1890s and elsewhere drew repeated attention to the deficiencies as they saw them of municipal accounts. This culminated in a series of articles entitled 'The form of municipal accounts' in 1897. Praising Sheffield Corporation for showing its assets at historic cost less depreciation where appropriate, i.e. in accordance with commercial conventions (this was additional to the requirements of the Local Government Board), it took the opportunity to attack Bolton Corporation whose Treasurer was at the time president of the Institute of Corporate Treasures and Accountants (formed in 1885 and later becoming the Institute of Treasurers and Accountants and, eventually (IPFA)). But his balance sheets clearly demonstrated the local accountants' rationale for the predominant form of local authority accounts. He had three headings for his capital assets:

1   'Remunerative and Realizable Works', which included gasworks, electric supply, waterworks, markets and tramways, i.e. municipal trading undertakings;
2   'Unremunerative but Realizable Works', which included the town hall, parks, recreation grounds, museums, cemeteries ('less grave spaces sold'), depots, etc;
3   'Unremunerative and Unrealizable Works', including street improvements, sewage works, roads and a bridge.

The valuation basis of each of these classes of asset is revealing: the first two classes are stated at cost less sinking fund provision (a method comparable to depreciation whereby amounts are set aside as investments which eventually provide funds for the replacement of assets). The final class, however, is treated as being worth only 'the amount from time to time due upon them', i.e. the balance of loans outstanding. The logic for this, in the perspective of the time, is understandable, although criticized by the *Accountant*: since there was no thought or intention to sell things like roads and sewers and no alternative to local government being responsible for them, it follows that their most definite determinable value is the amount of any liability owing on them. This logic underlies the whole debate about asset valuation of governmental assets and is only really challenged when the idea of transferring assets from public to private control (or vice versa) is raised. It is not quite as straightforward as this, however: proposals for nationalization or privatization also revive or reflect interest either in the alleged inefficiencies and poor financial control of public bodies (as a critique of nationalization) or their alleged inadequate accounting procedures (as an obstacle to privatization). In both cases, 'proper accounting' is one of the remedies offered.

What perhaps is most remarkable is the durability of the administrative regime imposed by the Local Government Board throughout a period where its validity was frequently challenged by a range of different and often powerful interests. This in turn raises the question of what was different about the forces and arguments deployed in the late 1980s and early 1990s which eventually succeeded in changing it.

The post-war period

This issue again became prominent in the immediate post Second World War period when a wide variety of industries were nationalized. The new nationalized industries frequently consisted of both private companies and former municipal undertakings and again the question of compensation assumed prominence and again the differences in accounting practice were crucial. In the electricity industry, for example, compensation to private companies was contested and said by their owners to be unfairly low, but the terms on which municipal electricity undertakings were to be taken under central government control provoked an outcry from local authorities and their ratepayers. Compensation was offered on the basis of 'net debt', i.e. the amount outstanding on the loan used to provide the asset. The paradox was that not only did the net debt basis not reflect the current and future value of these usually profit-making entities, but the more prudent a council had been in building up that enterprise through being more reluctant to borrow and perhaps relying on higher contributions from the rates, etc., the lower their compensation was to be. Some 370 municipal electricity undertakings on which an aggregate of £400 million of capital monies had been spent were to be nationalized for a capital sum of about £200 million, while the capital sum payable to about 190 company undertakings with assets at cost of some £300 million were to be nationalized at something more than that. In the gas industry it was estimated that the market value of the assets was £91 million yet the outstanding debt on which compensation was to be paid was only £22 million. Needless to say, the net debt basis for the transfer of municipal assets prevailed.

The role of the accounting profession

It is often argued that the post-war nationalizations represented some kind of high-water mark for collective aspirations and consensus in the UK whatever assessment is made of the subsequent performance of these industries and whether or not they achieved the hopes of the originators. This consensus more or less prevailed for over 30 years. Although there were always comments about the control of local spending and the extent of central government support of the rates, on the whole public expectations of public services continued to rise and Labour and Conservative governments vied with each other to build more roads or houses. Meanwhile, the accountancy profession was busy extending its membership and influence. Municipal accountants were no different, and throughout the 1940s and 1950s tried repeatedly to obtain a Royal Charter for their Institute. This was finally granted in 1959 with the appearance of a deal whereby district auditors, by then employees of the Ministry of Housing and Local Government, were able to become members, i.e. recognized as qualified accountants, a status which had previously been denied them. Later, auditors from the Government's Exchequer and Audit department were also allowed to join.

The structural reforms of local government put in place by the Heath administration (1970–74) spread municipal accountants widely beyond local government with the establishment of new separate entities for health, water, gas, electricity, transport and urban development. Seeing this as an opportunity to break out of the municipal corral, and following a failure to merge with the ICAEW in 1970, the IMTA obtained a supplementary Royal Charter, becoming the Chartered Institute of Public Finance and Accountancy in 1973, and began to seek a stronger voice on the governing committees of the accounting profession. Influenced by its new proximity to the mainstream of accounting views, a continuing perception that a unified profession could achieve more than its component bodies alone and by pressure from the new Department of the Environment, the CIPFA leadership began to encourage discussions about 'improvements' to accounting and reporting practice based on the application of commercial accounting conventions, such as Accounting Standards, into public authorities.

Municipal accounting practice during the 1960s and 1970s had concentrated on the new possibilities opened up by statistical techniques, for instance in resource allocation decisions, and the computers to run them. Inter-authority comparisons became easier to perform and highlighted the huge range of accounting and reporting practices in use. Internally, great emphasis was placed on integrated structures and new management techniques, largely imported from America, such as PPBS and MBO. The new county councils and metropolitan authorities were heralded as being the evangelists for a new scientism and rationality in local government affairs. Local government professionals like lawyers and valuers began to be ousted by a new profession in local government – managers. And treasurers and accountants were their natural allies.

Glossary

ADC   The Association of District Councils
ACC   The Association of County Councils
AMA   The Association of Metropolitan Authorities
ASC   Accounting Standards Committee (now Accounting Standards Board – ASB)
CIPFA   The Chartered Institute of Public Finance and Accountancy
DoE   Department of the Environment
DTI   Department of Trade and Industry
ICAEW   Institute of Chartered Accountants of England and Wales
MBO   Managing by Objectives
PPBS   Planning, Programming and Budgeting System

References

Public Finance and Accountancy, 8 May 1992, p. 10.
Public Finance and Accountancy, 19 February 1993, pp. 2, 12, 20.
Public Finance and Accountancy, 19 July 1993, p. 13.

CASE STUDY

3

Implementing Community Care*

Alan Lawton

Formulating policies is a key element in the strategic process. However, attending to the implementation of those policies is also crucial. Implementation is a crucial part of strategy. This case is concerned with issues of implementation. As such it is concerned with a number of key themes:

- the suitability and feasibility of policy proposals from the perspective of financial and human resources;
- the acceptability of policy proposals to the affected stakeholders including politicians, managers and service users;
- the challenges of implementing policies that require the co-ordination of different professionals and organizations;
- solving the operational problems;
- the relationship between strategy formulation and implementation.

The case focuses upon the implementation of care in the community in a fictional local authority. The Background Note (pp. 228–233) gives information concerning care in the community and illustrates some of the issues that it has generated.

  Stourvale and Community Care

Stourvale was a traditional multi-functional local authority characterized by a hierarchical departmental structure where interdepartmental disputes were common. Stourvale has a history of non-party rule and at present no political party

* The case study represents a fictional authority. However, the author would like to thank Madeleine Knight and her colleagues in S. Tyneside Social Services Department for the invaluable advice and insights that they offered.

has overall control. Its political make-up comprises Conservatives, Liberal Democrats and Independents; the Conservatives are in the majority but a number of committee chairs are held by the Liberal Democrats, including the Chair of Social Services.

Traditionally, the members have allowed the officers to be proactive in formulating policy, leaving the members to represent the interests of their particular wards. Members have long believed that their most important role is representing their constituents. Pressures on local government throughout the 1980s have forced the members to take a much more active interest in authority-wide issues and face up to the reality of reduced resources and the contract culture.

It will not be easy for them to come to a common view in determining the role of the local authority in community care. Some members interpret the 'enabling authority' as one where all contracts are given out to the private sector. Other members wish the authority to be involved in provision, while several of the Independents have strong links with the voluntary sector. The private sector has won a number of contracts including cleaning and catering in residential homes and day-care centres.

At the same time other services, such as education, will have a claim on any new resources. Traditionally Social Services, Housing and Education have not worked in a co-operative fashion.

The authority is coming under closer public scrutiny with Citizens Charter marks. There is an election due in May for one-third of the seats. Local government reorganization is very much on politicians' minds.

The local authority is committed to the provision of high-quality social services. The authority's mission statement recognizes that:

- services provided or purchased must respond to the assessed needs of the individuals who use them;
- such services need to be of the highest quality;
- services should be easily accessible to all irrespective of age, disability, race, religion or gender;
- services should be monitored to ensure quality and appropriateness.

The Social Services Department is increasingly a purchaser rather than a provider of services. In the past the Social Services Department has been a traditional bureaucratic local authority department characterized by empire building and interdepartmental rivalries. It has little experience of getting 'close to the customer', of contracting out services, or of management development. Market philosophy has not had an impact upon the department.

The senior management team responsible for drawing up the community care proposals has thus to ensure that it has in place the appropriate organizational structures, processes and personnel as well as the appropriate mechanisms for collaboration, consultation and co-ordination with other stakeholders. Traditionally, managers tend to have professional qualifications such as the Certificate of Qualification in Social Work (CQSW) rather than Master of

Business Administration (MBA). Front-line managers are rarely consulted about changes and feel that their views are often ignored.

Stourvale Social Services Department has a budget of £30 million which is approximately 15 per cent of Stourvale's total budget. Of that £30 million approximately £15 million is used for other Social Service Department activities, particularly those concerned with the care of children. The current budget of Stourvale, 1994–5, for spending on community care, is therefore £15 million. Section A3.2, Tables A3.1–A3.5 show how the money is spent.

The Council is reluctant to impose a high council tax but will consider charging for the services it provides.

Stourvale Social Services Department is divided into three districts:

1 *Western District* Geographically the largest, but with the smallest population. It is predominantly rural and includes a coastal region. It is popular with the elderly and is considered a retirement area. Transport facilities are poor and there is only one day centre for the elderly.
2 *Central District* This district has a higher population and is considered a desirable place to live. It is mostly suburban with good facilities and it is inhabited mainly by young families.
3 *Eastern District* The smallest in size but the most densely populated in three large towns. The towns are a mixture of Victorian terraced housing, with certain areas run down, modern flats for the single employed and council estates. The population is a mixture of age groups and ethnic minority groups. There is a substantial elderly Asian population who traditionally have not used social services facilities.

Section A3.3 provides background information on Stourvale's demographic features.

Relations with stakeholders

The relations between the Social Services Department and other organizations and agencies in the area has been mixed.

1 With the *voluntary sector*, relations have been distant. Some money is given to voluntary groups, particularly those who organize Meals-on-Wheels. The local authority has never monitored this expenditure.

   Locally, the voluntary sector has been concerned with advocacy and has been dominated by members of the middle class. It has traditionally provided transport, luncheon clubs, sitting services and help in day centres. There has been a lack of organization and no one body to represent the interests of the voluntary sector as a whole. Because of this lack of organization the voluntary sector has had little access to the decision-making forums of the statutory agencies other than support from individual members of the Council. Traditionally, the voluntary sector's strengths are seen as altruism, the absence of professional values, the absence of overt political viewpoints, accessibility to citizens, informality and cheapness. There is little information available of the contractual specifications that the local authority might adopt in terms of quality, evaluation or different types of contract. It is likely that different stakeholders will have different definitions of quality.

A group has now been formed to bring together voluntary groups in the area and this group believes that the community care proposals give the voluntary sector an opportunity to be more proactive, to widen the scope of its activities and to achieve a higher profile in the local community. In addition local branches of national organizations such as MIND and MENCAP are looking to make more of an impact at local level.

2   With the *private sector* the local authority has not had good relations in this field. One large company provides a majority of the residential care for the elderly and is considered to provide a reasonable service. However, in the past three to four years a large number of small independent residential homes have sprung up and some provide a questionable service. The local authority has failed to keep up with this growth and many of these small operators have not been inspected or monitored.

Private sector involvement in the provision of local authority services in Stourvale has been fairly limited. However, one large company primarily involved in residential care for the elderly has a large share of the market. This company is dubious about the profitability of other areas of community care and it envisages barriers to entry. Similarly, other private sector organizations are unlikely, without inducements, to bid for contracts for other than residential care for the elderly. One other company is, however, looking to form strategic alliances to enter other markets. This company has already won contracts from the local authority to provide cleaning and catering services in local authority residential homes and day centres.

There are likely to be opportunities for private sector organizations to exploit. It is anticipated that growth areas will be day-care provision and respite care. Changes in legislation means that even in residential care the business will not be as profitable in the future. In the past social security payments, which were more generous than local authority rates, made residential homes a profitable business. Under the new arrangements the local authority purchases the service from the providers.

The nature of future arrangements with the local authority are unclear and there is little available information on contractual specifications in terms of quality, unit size, evaluation and the different forms of contract. In addition different definitions of quality are likely to exist.

3   With the *local health authority* relations have been distant. In theory, joint funding is available but neither Stourvale nor the health authority have had much interest in developing joint initiatives.

In 1991 the Government introduced a programme of reform within the National Health Service and NHS trusts were created along with GP fundholders. The purchaser–provider split was introduced and GP fundholders can purchase services from several providers including NHS trusts. In Stourvale there are four GP fundholders serving 30 per cent of the population. There is one trust – Stourvale Health Care Trust set up in 1993. In Stourvale the District Health Authorities and the Family Health Service Authorities have established the Stourvale Health Commission which acts as the purchases of community-based health care. It can purchase services from neighbouring areas. The Health Commission has a budget of £1 million for the purchase of care in the community. At present there are no plans to increase this figure.

Traditionally, the medical profession is extremely powerful and is committed to high-profile medical care. Most resources go into acute care with community care a real Cinderella service.

There has been little commitment to management training and most clinicians are sceptical of management skills. Because of resource constraints one hospital is due to close with long-stay patients having to move to residential or nursing homes in the community.

4   Traditionally *users and carers* have had little impact on the services that have been delivered to them. This group of people have traditionally little power and no access to decision-making processes. They have little confidence in their ability to get their views known and have been ignored by the statutory agencies. Their knowledge of what is available is usually limited.

A group of families has got together to try and influence the decision-making process but has little experience of advocacy or of articulating its views. Informal carers traditionally are isolated, need respite on a regular basis and are usually women. There is an absence of help outside normal office hours. The group is concerned that resources will be allocated according to what the Social Services Department thinks it has available rather than on the basis of need. It also wants consultation and not merely information.

5   The *Housing Department* has to prepare its strategy for 1994/5 and thereafter. It is required to show specifically how the demand for housing from people with special needs will be met. The Standard Spending Assessment for 1994/5 is down 3.5 per cent over 1993/4. Capital grants are at a post-war low in real terms. The Housing Management Function must be exposed to competitive tender by October 1997.

Right-to-buy has been popular and almost 35 per cent of the stock has been sold. Houses with gardens have been the most popular with buyers. All sheltered accommodation has been handed over to a local housing association. There is no foreseeable prospect of all single parent families currently on the waiting list being housed in the next ten years. Election manifestos of all parties contain pledges to remedy this. The local branch of Shelter is campaigning on this issue.

Homelessness has been increasing. The department has a policy of not using bed and breakfast accommodation except as a last resort. This puts considerable pressure on such temporary accommodation as is available, e.g. voids, and the situation could get worse. New building starts are the lowest since 1963. Several staff are members of the Institute of Housing. The Director is a member of the Chief Officers Management Team.

Morale within the department is fragile, especially in the 'front-line' services. Citizens Charter targets are not being met fully.

All the bodies involved in community care planning are committed to joint working and planning. A Joint Consultative Committee formed from members of the local authority and the Health Commission meet regularly. Consideration is being given to set up joint planning teams to look after specific client groups. There are obstacles, however, arising from historical and traditional differences in training and approach.

One of the tasks of the Joint Consultative Committee was to seek to improve the information to users and carers. The committee has published 15 leaflets in five different languages indicating what services are available.

Further information is also available through GPs surgeries and through the Health Care Trust. The Social Services Department is seeking other ways to make sure that people are better informed about community care.

Implementing Community Care

Implementing community care requires managers to develop new skills: managing contracts, assessing need, working with other agencies, handling budgets and so on.

I believe a good manager is a good manager, whatever discipline they come from. But there is an important element in managing social services that involves caring, and I would always want to see that mixture is there. I would prefer to have a social work practitioner, and provide the financial tools to play the part. (Local Authority deputy director)

An enabling role to my mind requires in some ways a higher degree of management skill than a providing role because it calls for a real concentration on the precise content of contracts or arrangements with third parties. It requires clarification of the outputs expected from the contract in the sense of clarity as to the quality to be achieved, standards to be attained, as well as the financial aspects. It calls for real management understanding as to how to devolve responsibility effectively and to set local budgets. It calls for advocacy in the broadest sense of community needs through the planning process and more narrowly of individual needs in the assessment process. *(Sir Roy Griffiths)*

Stourvale is now implementing its community care strategy and after a difficult first year appears to be coping as well as could be expected given its problems in producing its strategy.

The views of different stakeholders are reproduced below.

Politicians

We were far too slow in preparing for community care. We assumed that the Conservatives would lose the 1992 election and that a Labour government would rethink the whole idea. Our politicians are also interested in the nuts-and-bolts and not in the airy-fairy of trying to formulate a strategy.

It is yet another attempt to reduce the power of local authorities. How can you have market principles determining care. The market might be OK for street cleaning or leisure but surely not for caring for the needy?

Unfortunately there is an increasing concentration of people who are dependent upon state and council benefits and services, especially the very elderly who require intensive care and support.

Money is always tight but I believe that if we introduced a system of charging for, say, use of day centres, or do more in the way of means testing then the problem of lack of resources will lessen.

Citizens charters and patient charters raise expectations about the services but, as usual, central government does not give us the money to deliver high quality services.

Senior Manager

I don't think money is the problem. In fact the government has just announced an extra £20 million. The problem we have is that we can't spend all our allocation. We now have to spend 85 per cent in the Independent Sector and quite frankly the supply is just not there.

To be honest it is the information systems, or lack of them, that causes the problems. The financial systems that we had in place were antiquated and nothing was ever costed properly. More importantly though we had no idea of what was being provided and by whom. We have had to get information from the health authorities, voluntary sector and private sector as well as individual users and carers. To co-ordinate all this has proven a nightmare. It is also difficult getting the right information to the right level.

Social Services Director

Quite frankly we were not ready for community care. Nevertheless we have made great strides in the past year. The problem is we are still practising crisis management. It only takes one Ben Silcock and the publicity is unremitting. Whoever said that managing public services is all about managing in a goldfish bowl was absolutely right.

The government can speak the language of quality, developing a market for community care, the enabling authority, etc. but it is fairly meaningless when it comes to implementing changes. What we need is time and resources. Time to train people, to understand the legislation, to change the whole culture of this organization. As usual government with its eyes on the next election wants everything to happen overnight.

Social Services Contracts Manager

Its been a nightmare – half my staff have not received any training. The guide-lines were quickly drawn up and we are all terrified of conflicts of interests and stepping over the boundaries of probity. Some of our colleagues in the health service see nothing wrong with accepting gifts from providers – they have been doing it for years with the drug companies. For us accusations of corruption have to be taken seriously.

Care Manager 1

I am between a rock and a hard place. On the one hand I am trying to put together a menu of care but I don't have any authority over budgets or contracts. If I want to purchase a particular care package I have to refer upwards to the contracts manager. It's very frustrating.

Care Manager 2

I have social work qualifications and I did not come into this job to act as a resource rationer. There is no way that we have a needs-led service. As usual it depends upon the resources available.

Care Manager 3

It's all very well for the Department and the local health authority to preach about the virtues of joint planning but when it comes to the crunch it's the GPs who I have to deal with and they have the money and the power.

Area Team Leader 1

I am spending more and more time running a budget than managing the job. As it is my team is struggling to keep up with the case load. Devolving budgets is all very well but we don't have the time or the expertise to do financial assessments and work out the individual user needs. I am lucky in having a dedicated team – we get by on good will.

Area Team Leader 2

I quite like having control over my own budget. It allows me to make decisions and gives me some flexibility. There is a perception that social workers can't and shouldn't control budgets and I suppose that my management diploma has taught me not to be afraid of figures.

Area Team Leader 3

My team might just be able to keep on top of assessments. But there is a real problem of monitoring the quality of provision and I don't know what the solution is. We just don't have the time to assess the quality of every residential or day centre place and there are no national guidelines to help us. How do you define quality of life?

Mentally ill patient

When the hospital closed down what was I supposed to do? Sleep on the streets? OK the hostel is a pig-sty, the owner is a crook and there is overcrowding. But Social Services can't get its act together: it takes too long to do the assessment, it's too bureaucratic and there ain't enough accommodation anyway.

Local authority training manager

We try and bring together managers from different backgrounds with different expertise in, for example, physical disability or people with learning difficulties. For example we ran a two-day course on assessment and care planning for a mix of field social workers, hospital social workers, occupational therapists and home care organizer.

Local authority training manager 2

It's all very well working up these elaborate plans and strategies: they require a fundamental change in the culture of the organization. You need training and development to achieve this. Yet training is always the first budget to be hit.

Carer 1

It's impossible to work out who is responsible for what. It seems to me that the only difference between a health care bath and a social care bath is that you put Dettol in one and bubble bath in the other. Trying to get information on what is available and from whom is very difficult.

Carer 2

It's so confusing. There have been so many changes it's impossible to keep up. All you hear is 'we are a purchaser not a provider' and 'we are not contracted to do this'. In the old days you knew who was providing help and you built up a relationship of trust with them.

Carer 3

Despite the rhetoric of putting our needs and those in our care first, I found some of the staff still patronizing – it's the 'we know best' attitude and they make assumptions without really listening.

Carer 4

We have a reputation for looking after our own. The family is very important to us. But we can't always cope. The younger ones no longer are prepared to look after their grandparents or even parents like we did before. OK so the information is printed in Urdu but they do not really understand the needs of our community. I do know that the post of Ethnic Rights Officer has been vacant for some time.

Health Authority Manager

On the whole we now have good relations with our counterparts in social services. Yet they are still too bureaucratic: we are keen to increase the through-put and improve our efficiency. Quite frankly social services just takes too long in assessment and beds are being blocked. Not only that but the committee cycle in local government does not lend itself to quick decision making.

District nurse

We are getting there. At first I used to resent all the bureaucracy, like filling in forms for someone to get a disabled car drivers badge. But I recognize that home care staff are just as anxious that the patient or the client is at the centre of what we do and it doesn't matter who delivers the service. I am working closer with the social workers and on the ground we get things done. The problem is higher up where there is a lot of political in-fighting between the

GPs and the hospitals, between senior managers in the local authority and the Health Commission.

Housing managers (local authority)

Nobody ever really thought about our contribution to community care. We have been marginalized. Social Services don't appear to be aware of our problems. We can't build new houses, we are under pressure form CCT and yet they want us to spend our budget on aids, adaptations, home support and so on without ever thinking to consult with us.

Voluntary sector volunteer

I started volunteer work because I wanted to make a contribution to the community around me. I know it sounds do-gooding but I wanted to help people. Now we are run like a business – it's all about value-for-money, fulfilling contracts, controlling budgets. Some of my colleagues welcome this. They think that it gives us greater status and we are no longer totally reliant on grants. But we still need donations, and 'give us a fiver: a director of finance and a personnel director to support' does not have quite the same ring to it.

User 1

I think that community care is a great idea. For the first time, I feel that Social Services are beginning to take me seriously. In the past the attitude has been 'aren't these people lucky to receive our services'!

User 2

It's not much to ask for – somebody to collect my pension and do the cleaning and ironing. All I want is a guaranteed service, having a choice of who does it is irrelevant to me.

User 3

I get sick of the 'office hours' mentality'. I want a service that is convenient for me, not for the local authority. They don't really understand what it is like to be disabled.

Private Sector 1

It's all very well pushing for spot contracts. I agree that this is the most flexible for the user. But what guarantees do we have? For small operators it creates uncertainty. We would much rather have block contracts where places are bought in advance. It gives us some stability and helps us in our planning and secures our immediate future while we come to terms with this new climate.

Private Sector 2

Our residential care business is doing well; local authorities no longer resent us and where we have poor relations it is often because some politicians are reluctant to give up the provider role and they mistrust our profit motive. On the other hand, domiciliary care is, quite frankly, not worth our while even though local authorities are keen to develop this aspect of community care. Different authorities use different accounting procedures; and there are too many restrictions on our staffing policy imposed by local authority contracts.

Private Sector 3

Quite frankly I think that there is over-provision in residential care. With stricter monitoring of homes and with the reduction in income following on from the money being switched from Social Security to the local authority, there will be a shakeout and some homes will go under.

▰▰▰ Discussion Questions ▰▰▰

1 What appear to be the major problems in implementing community care?
2 How can Stourvale ensure that its implementation strategy is consistent with its vision for community care?
3 How can the demands of different stakeholders be reconciled?

▰▰▰ Background Note ▰▰▰

The concept of Care in the Community has been with us for some time. For the past three decades politicians, academics and practitioners have felt that certain types of care are best carried out in the community rather than in institutions. Thus, care of the elderly, mentally ill, mentally handicapped and the physically disabled have all been subject to scrutiny for Care in the Community. A good example of this approach has been the All Wales Strategy, initiated in 1983, which was committed to giving people with mental handicaps a normal pattern of life within the community.

The most recent expression of Care in the Community is the National Health Service and Community Care Act 1990 which gives legislative effect to the proposals first put forward in Sir Roy Griffiths, *Community Care: Agenda for Action*, following on from an Audit Commission report of *Making a Reality of Community Care*. The main recommendations of the Griffiths report included.

- primary responsibility for community care should lie with local authorities;
- collaboration between local authorities and the health service should precede the presentation of plans to the Minister for Community Care;
- local authority social service departments should be re-oriented towards the design and co-ordination of packages of care largely provided by others.

The report suggested that a mixed bag of provision should be encouraged where agencies from the private and voluntary sectors actually provided the service. Thus the concept of welfare pluralism was used to indicate how different bodies should be involved in the provision of community care. The responsibility of the local authority was to set local priorities, design individual packages of care, arrange delivery and make maximum use of the private and voluntary sectors. The local authority was to act as an enabling authority. The principles of the Griffiths Report were endorsed by the Government insofar as it believed that such an approach would encourage consumer choice and flexibility, stimulate competition and improve efficiency and effectiveness in service delivery. The Government's views on community care were, then, no different to its views on the rest of local authority activities.

The Act itself recommended:

1 that local authorities be given major responsibility for providing and/ or organizing social care for the elderly, for the mentally ill and for those who have physical or learning disabilities;
2 that responsibility for the funding of residential care for elderly people and others be transferred to local government from the Department of Social Security;
3 that a case management and assessment system be introduced to which all of those likely to need community care will be entitled and through which they must pass to be eligible for certain publicly funded services;
4 that a comprehensive planning system for community care be developed in consultation with other authorities such as health, housing and voluntary organizations;
5 that an arms-length inspectorate be introduced to monitor standards in local authority residential care as well as the independent residential sector;
6 that a statutory complaints procedure be instituted;
7 that a specific grant to accelerate development of the mental illness services be introduced;
8 that the emphasis for local authorities be on purchasing rather than directly providing services.

The Act did not endorse the view put forward in the Griffiths Report that monies for community care should be ring-fenced. However, this has since changed.

The Government proposed that money would be transferred from the social security budget to local authorities. Previously Social Security paid for residential care for those in private sector residential homes. Local authorities resented this as social security payment was invariably higher than local authority payment and many felt that the private sector made a 'killing'.

Originally, £539 million, all ring-fenced, was to be provided for community care of which £399 million would be transferred from Social Security and £140 million will be new money for one year only. Local authorities argued that this was insufficient and would lead to a shortfall of some £200 million and that 12,000 elderly and disabled people would be at risk of not getting the care services they require. This funding has since been increased.

The Government also announced that 75 per cent of this money would have to be spent on care in the independent sector.

The original proposals were to be introduced in April 1991. However, the Government later decided on a phased implementation in three stages over two years:

1   By April 1991:

- the establishment of inspection units for residential care homes which is independent of day-to-day management;
- the introduction of specific grants for people with mental health problems and for people who have drug or alcohol abuse problems;
- the introduction of comprehensive complaints procedures.

2   By April 1992:

- the publication of community care plans which take the form of joint planning agreements with other organizations including health authorities, service users and carers, the voluntary and private sectors;
- preparatory work to introduce a unified assessment procedure for people in need of community care support;
- preparatory work to introduce a case management scheme for people whose service needs are complex.

3   By April 1993:

- a unified assessment procedure in place;
- a care management scheme fully introduced which includes care planning and the regular review of people's needs.

At the heart of the proposals is a move away from a service-centred to a needs-led approach to community care. Historically, the service provided has depended on the funds available, determined partly by political choice, and by the *perceived* needs of the population. The Audit Commission Bulletin 'Taking Stock: Progress with Community Care', argues that a needs-led approach requires authorities to be more 'sensitive, flexible and responsive'. Being more sensitive requires a clearer understanding of the numbers requiring help and the type of help they require. Greater flexibility requires operational arrangements that allow local managers to respond to individual needs quickly. Being more responsive recognizes the diversity of need and that new patterns of care may be appropriate.

The achievement of a more sensitive, flexible and responsive approach will partly depend on funding arrangements, and Section A3.1 provides information on these.

Commentators on the changes to the provision of community care raise a number of issues.

The issues

What is community care? What do we mean by community care and is there general agreement on what it should encompass? Different groups may have different perceptions so that we might find a definition of health care in competition with social care. Where are the boundaries between them? A further definitional problem is that the concept of community care assumes that there is something called 'the community' out there. It may well be that some areas/neighbourhoods are more sympathetic to the disabled than others. This is an important consideration if the aim of community care is to integrate individuals back into a community.

Who is to provide it? Not all local authorities go along with the concept of the enabling authority that is in use, i.e. acting as a purchaser rather than a provider. For political/ideological reasons some authorities do not see their roles in the same way. Similarly, what happens if there does not exist the private sector or voluntary sector to undertake the work? The assumption is that there are a host of other agencies that are able and willing to provide the service. The voluntary sector may have a tradition of advocacy and may be unwilling to get involved in large-scale direct provision. Similarly, the private sector might find providing residential care for the elderly to be attractive but may be less interested in providing services for highly dependent people.

What will be its impact on existing provision? The proposals also require a profound shift from a services-led delivery to a needs-led delivery, needs which are notoriously difficult to define. In the All Wales Strategy for the Mentally Handicapped mentioned earlier it was often the case that rather than individual care packages being drawn up, the individual received what was available.

It will require a change in the role of local authorities which now have to:

- stimulate a mixed delivery;
- introduce competitive tendering and contracting out;
- introduced cost-centre management and devolved budgeting;
- introduce resource management systems;
- separate out the purchase and supply of services;
- establish key indicators and performance measurement.

It will also have an impact on the roles of professionals in so far as new skills of management will need to be developed by the medical profession, new skills of contract management by local authority officers and new skills of collaboration by all concerned. At the same time service users and informal carers will need to be articulate in their demands to ensure full use is made of consultation.

How will it be done? Joint planning and action is crucial. Does it exist already, is there a tradition of working together? At what stage should the voluntary sector be involved? The All Wales Strategy found problems here with the voluntary sector resenting their treatment as inferior partners by the statutory agencies involved.

At the very least we would expect there to be agreement on common goals, on defining needs, on priorities and on the implementation of a common strategy. The success depends on the interorganizational production of community care plans and the inter-professional production of individual care packages. We can legitimately ask: how do local authorities and health authorities collect, share and agree on basic information such as demography, dependency characteristics and the scale and scope of needs within geographical areas, particularly if there is no tradition of inter-agency collaboration?

The vehicle that drives the partnership approach must include trust, commitment and common goals.

Possible problems

1   What happens with market failure? Is the local authority in a position to provide the services itself?
2   In the event of the local authority giving up any commitment to service provision how does it deal with monopoly provision?
3   The private sector may be interested in providing a standard service for a mass market rather than individual care.
4   We must also consider the problems of yet more changes for the NHS to deal with. How much time and effort can the NHS devote to community care given all the other recent changes of internal markets, trust status etc.?
5   Will there be a tendency to discharge people early into the community to free beds or meet targets based on throughputs. This will place an increasing stress on community care.

6   How compatible are the organizational structures of the NHS and the local authority? Are they based on area, function or client group?
7   Will the voluntary sector be prepared to enter into contract agreements?

Despite the fact that community care has been in operation for two years many of the above issues and problems remain unresolved. Indeed new problems have arisen.

A3.1: Special Transitional Grant

Flexibility requires the ability of care managers to purchase services when and where necessary so it is important that money is available to 'spot' purchase. 1993–4 saw the introduction of the Special Transitional Grant (STG) which provided funds not assigned for specific services but available for flexible purchasing. The main purpose of the grant was to transfer responsibility for the funding of care from the social security system to local authority services. The Audit Commission (1994) has calculated that the STG now forms 21 per cent of the total social services budget; in 1993–4 that figure was 14 per cent.

The STG in brief:

1   STG in 1993–4 = £565 million; 1994–5 = £736 million.
2   Funds transferred from Social Security make up the largest element: 1993–4 = £339 million; 1994–5 = £652 million. Of this 85 per cent has to be spent on non-local authority services.
3   The allocation of STG to individual local authorities depends on the formula for distributing the overall block grant from central government and the number of people who were already being supported by social security benefits in independent homes.
4   This formula was changed in 1994–5 and is now wholly allocated according to the overall block grant. Some authorities gained and some lost.

A3.2: Stourvale Social Services Department

Table A3.1   Expenditure by client group 1994–1995

	£ million
Elderly	8
Mental health	0.7
Physical disability	2.5
Learning disability	3.8
	15

Table A3.2 Expenditure on elderly 1994–1995

	£ thousands
Residential care	3,500
Domiciliary care	2,000
Day centres	500
Day centres (voluntary sector)	500
Meals-on-wheels (private and voluntary)	500
Grants to voluntary sector	200
Management and support services	800
	8,000

Table A3.3 Expenditure on people with physical disabilities 1994–1995

	£ thousands
Residential care	450
Domiciliary care	500
Day centres	500
Occupational therapy	500
Grants to voluntary sector	300
Management and support services	250
	2,500

Table A3.4 Expenditure on mental health and illness 1994–1995

	£ thousands
Residential care	100
Domiciliary care	200
Specific grant for mental illness	250
Grants to voluntary sector	50
Management and support services	100
	700

Table A3.5 Expenditure on people with learning disabilities 1994–1995

	£ thousands
Residential care	1,000
Day centres	1,700
Domiciliary care	500
Grants to voluntary sector	250
Management and support services	350
	3,800

Table A3.6 Stourvale social services departments

Type of establishment	Number of establishments	Number of places
Homes for the elderly	10	420
Day centres for the elderly	5	200
Homes for adults with a learning disability	10	250
Day centres for adults with a learning disability	10	200
Homes for adults with a physical disability	2	70
Day centres for adults with a physical disability	5	160
Homes for people with a mental illness	1	20

Table A3.7 Private sector and voluntary establishments

Type of establishment	Number of establishments	Number of places
Homes for the elderly	22	540

Table A3.8 Location of social services departments' establishments

District	Type of establishment	Number of establishments	Number of places
Western	Homes for elderly	5	250
	Day centres for elderly	1	30
	Homes for adults with a learning disability	5	150
	Day centres for adults with a learning disability	3	70
	Home for adults with a physical disability	0	
	Day centres for adults with a physical disability	1	
	Homes for people with a mental illness	0	
Central	Homes for elderly	2	70
	Day centres for elderly	1	45
	Homes for adults with a learning disability	2	40
	Day centres for adults with a learning disability	3	55

Table A3.8 (cont'd)

District	Type of establishment	Number of establishments	Number of places
Central	Home for adults with a physical disability	0	
	Day centres for adults with a physical disability	1	
	Homes for people with a mental illness	0	
Eastern	Homes for elderly	3	100
	Day centres for elderly	3	125
	Homes for adults with a learning disability	3	60
	Day centres for adults with a learning disability	4	
	Home for adults with a physical disability	2	
	Day centres for adults with a physical disability	3	
	Homes for people with a mental illness	1	

Table A3.9 People aged 65 years and above by district

District	% of people aged 65 and over
Western	25
Central	12
Eastern	20

A3.3: Demographic Features of Stourvale

Stourvale consists of three distinct areas, comprising a rural, coastal region Western District; a suburban Central District; and an inner-city Eastern District. It has a population of 4,000,000.

There are several distinct population trends:

- a reduction in the number of children and adults of working age;
- an increase in the number of elderly people as a proportion of the overall population;
- an increase in unemployment in Eastern District.

Currently:

- 35 per cent of the population of Stourvale is wholly or mainly dependent on welfare benefits:
- 18 per cent of all households are dependent on income support;
- 35 per cent of all households contain at least one pensioner;
- 20 per cent of all households contain one or more persons with a long-term illness;
- 7 per cent of the population are registered with the Social Services Department as disabled;
- non-whites account for 7 per cent of the population in the Eastern District.

Glossary

Assessment	The process of defining need and determining eligibility for assistance against stated policy criteria. There are different levels of assessment depending on the complexity of need. It is a participative process involving the applicant, their carers and other relevant agencies.
Contracts	Agreements purchasing a range of services and facilities from a provider which are enforceable in law.
Care manager	Any practitioner who undertakes all, or most, of the core tasks of co-ordinating the assessment of a person's needs, who may carry budgetary responsibility but is not involved in any direct service provision.
Care package	A combination of service designed to meet the assessed needs of a person requiring care in the community.
Carers	Relatives and friends who provide support.
Day care	Communal care normally provided in a setting away from the user's place of residence, with paid or voluntary carers present. Day care can cover a wide range of services.
Discharge plan	Plans drawn up before a patient's discharge from hospital making appropriate arrangements for any necessary continuing care or treatment. The plans should include a checklist of action to be taken by all those concerned with the patient.
Enabling authority	An authority whose main function is to secure and fund services to reflect the assessed needs of its local population; selecting the most cost effective from among its own provision and that of other agencies.
Independent sector	Individuals, bodies or organizations not wholly controlled or maintained by a government department or any other authority or body instituted by Special Act of Parliament or incorporated by Royal Charter. The term may be taken to refer to the voluntary sector and the private sector.

Purchaser/ provider split	Local authorities, for example, are encouraged not to directly provide services but to purchase services from a wider choice of providers including the voluntary sector and private sector. It is believed that this makes for greater choice and competition than if the local authority itself provided the services.

References

Audit Commission, *Making a Reality of Community Care*, London: HMSO, 1988.
Audit Commission, 'Taking Stock: Progress with Community Care', London: HMSO, 1994.
Griffiths, R., Community Care: Agenda for Action, London: HMSO, 1988.

4

The Metropolitan Police Plus Programme*

Garry Elliott

As Sir Peter Imbert, the Commissioner of the Metropolitan Police (the Met), prepared to hand over to his successor in 1993, problems surrounding the policing of London appeared to be as great as ever. Calls for greater accountability and value for money were strong. The view of many of those involved in police funding or competing with the police for a share of the public sector funds could be summed up in the tone of an earlier editorial in *The Times*: 'For the Police Federation yesterday to accuse the Government of undervaluing its work is little short of cheek. No group in the public sector has been more succoured by Home Secretaries since Mrs Thatcher came to power in 1979. Certainly no group has been treated so well with so little obvious return' (*The Times*, 23 May 1990).

Early rumours about the findings of an enquiry into police pay and conditions chaired by the industrialist Sir Patrick Sheehy were affecting morale, and amalgamations of forces and changes in methods of funding and control were expected in a Government White Paper soon to be published. On top of this some *cause célèbres* and highly publicized allegations of police malpractice were still fresh in people's minds and affecting public confidence in the police service generally. The next five years looked as full of interest, change and problems as the previous five.

As Sir Peter prepared for his retirement he was asked which of his achievements as Commissioner he would put first. He replied, 'Well, I haven't really achieved it yet. I intended the Plus Programme to change the Met from a force to a service, not only in the eyes of the serving officers, but more importantly in the minds of the public' (*The Job*, January 1993).

---

* The case was made possible by the generous assistance of the Metropolitan Police Service.

The PLUS Programme, a project to change the culture of the Met, had been ambitious. It had started in 1987 when, as one of his first actions at being appointed, Sir Peter commissioned a team of consultants to look at the corporate identity of the Met in response to a perception of falling public confidence and a belief that internal problems and divisions were hampering the effectiveness of the force (see Background Note 'The Metropolitan Police' pp. 248–251).

This case examines how a public service seeks to change its culture in the light of competing objectives and perceptions of its function.

■■■■ The Environment ■■■■

The Metropolitan Police was unique among British police forces in that the Home Secretary acted as the police authority charged with ensuring that the force was properly resourced and efficiently managed, a function that for forces outside London was performed by a committee of elected councillors and magistrates. It was a matter of dispute by some groups whether the needs of Londoners would be better served by their own elected police authority. One of these groups which was quite vociferous was the Police Monitoring and Research Group of the London Strategy Policy Unit which had been set up by nine London boroughs to carry through the policy initiatives of the disbanded Greater London Council. In the conclusion to the report on the Metropolitan Police financial estimates for 1987–8 they wrote:

> Public dissatisfaction with the organisation and management of the Met's finances is growing. Primarily this is caused by a lack of commitment within the force to provide value for money services. This year's estimates contain ample proof of the waste in resources caused by a poor structure of exercising management controls. This has been picked up by the House of Commons Public Accounts Select Committee which, although not in a position to propose that control of the police service should transfer from the Home Secretary, was evidently very unhappy about the way financial matters and policy co-ordination has failed (Police Committee Support Unit, London: Greater London Council, February 1986).

The financial environment for the Met was changing. In common with all public sector organizations it had been cash limited for the past three years and although it had enjoyed increases in its funding it was having to come to terms with a tightening on budgetary control. The funds came from two main sources: about half the net expenditure of the force was met from local authority rates and the remainder by way of government grants. See section A4.3 for a summary of the functional cost information.

The world for the police was also changing in other ways. Responsibility for the prosecution of offenders had been taken away from the police in the previous year with the creation of the Crown Prosecution Service and officers were still coming to terms with their altered role.

Figure A4.1 Offences and clear-ups in the Metropolitan Police Division – 1939–1989

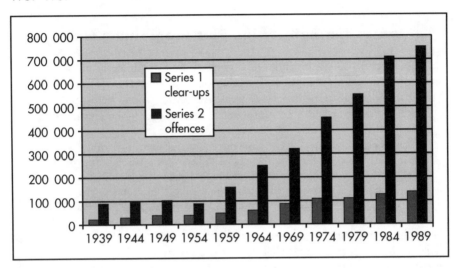

Source: Annual Report of the Commissioner of the Metropolitan Police, London, 1988.

Cause célèbres of police wrongdoing surrounding some high-profile court cases had been guaranteed to reach the front pages of national newspapers and had appeared to dent the support and confidence of the vast majority of the public which the Met had enjoyed. A survey in 1988 found that 69 per cent of Londoners polled thought that the police were doing a very or fairly good job (section A4.4). Whether this was itself a good or bad message for the organization was less important than the fact that the figure was showing a distinct downward trend and this was a cause for concern especially as the survey went on to suggest that people in non-White ethnic groups were less likely to have a high opinion of the work done by the police.

Coupled with this the British Crime Survey suggested that nationally crime had increased by 30 per cent in the past six years and that only 37 per cent of crime was reported to police. Reported crime was increasing sharply in London and the proportion of crimes cleared-up by police was not keeping pace (figure A4.1).

The surveys commissioned annually by the Met were part of a broad process of consultation whereby the force determined the views of the people in London. Despite minor variations, the results of these had shown a consistency over several years (section A4.5).

At a local level consultative committees had been set up on all London boroughs as a result of the 1986 Police and Criminal Evidence Act. These were innovations which followed the recommendations of Lord Scarman in his report following the riots in Brixton several years previously. Consultative groups were committees of councillors and other local people and it gave them the opportunity to meet and question the chief superintendent in charge of policing their area. As a group they had no executive power but were a vehicle for consultation and communication.

The Birth of the Plus Programme

In September 1988 the consultants commissioned by Sir Peter published their report, 'A Force for Change' and, while pointing to great strengths within the Met, it made suggestions in several areas, the principal one being their perception that the Met lacked a common sense of purpose. They commented:

> There is no consistency of views on the overall mission of the Met, nor how each individual contributes to the whole. Police work is based on the principle that individual police officers are given a high degree of independence of action and discretion. This means that each police officer interprets policing in the way he thinks best (Metropolitan Police Service, 'A Force for Change', 1989).

They also highlighted other matters which exacerbated this, such as internal divisions between police and civil staff or even between officers performing different roles. They felt that presentation and channels of communication should be improved and the role and structure of management should be reviewed in the light of the changing environment in which the Met was working. The report also pointed to the strengths of the Met, the renowned centres of excellence and the willingness to face change, but it gave Sir Peter significant cause for thought and concern.

The Commissioner tasked DAC Charles Pollard to take the report and turn the recommendations into an action plan. At the same time he considered further the idea of a mission statement which would be relevant to all the Met's personnel and act as a focus and vehicle for the change he knew was necessary.

The Metropolitan Police had always had a statement of its primary objects which was credited to Richard Mayne and was still learned word perfect by every constable when they did their initial training:

> The primary object of an efficient police is the prevention of crime. The next that of detection and punishment of offenders if crime is committed. To these ends all the efforts of police must be directed. The absence of crime, and the maintenance of public tranquillity will alone prove whether these efforts have been successful.

How relevant was this to the late twentieth century? Traditionally, police mission statements were concerned with:

- upholding the law and guarding the peace;
- preventing crime;
- detecting criminals and bringing them to justice;
- helping the public.

Much of police work has a social services/education flavour to it such as assisting people who are locked out of their homes or working with school children. Previous research into modern police work had shown that the majority of calls from the public were not crime related and incidents such as domestic occurrences, road accidents, lost and found property, missing person cases, errands, health- and animal-related matters accounted to 59 per cent of all incidents.

Sir Peter had already started the debate on this subject around the service and he used a conference in October 1988 to discuss and develop these ideas with his senior staff. A need to keep any statement short and simple was recognized and there was a general dislike for the term 'mission statement', the preference being for a 'statement of purpose'. A draft was produced – 'The purpose of the Metropolitan Police is "To serve and Protect"'. The draft went on to list ten values of every member of the organization including adopting 'the highest standards', upholding 'individual rights', being neither 'racist nor sexist' and being 'cost effective'. This was circulated in the organization, inviting comment.

◾◾ 'Making it Happen' ◾◾

In April 1989, DAC Pollard's report 'Making it Happen' was published which recommended work under nine components and launched the Statement of Common Purpose and Values of the Metropolitan Police Service.

Statement of our Common Purpose and Values

The purpose of the Metropolitan Police Service is to uphold the law fairly and firmly; to prevent crime; to pursue and bring to justice those who break the law; to keep the Queen's Peace; to protect, help and reassure people in London; and to be seen to do all this with integrity, common sense and sound judgement.

We must be compassionate, courteous and patient, acting without fear or favour or prejudice to the rights of others. We will need to be professional, calm and restrained in the face of violence and apply only that force which is necessary to accomplish our lawful duty.

We must strive to reduce the fears of the public and so far as we can, to reflect their priorities in the action we take. We must respond to well founded criticism with a willingness to change.

The project taking forward this report was called 'Plus' and a team was set up with separate groups looking at each of the nine components. When launching the project, Sir Peter said that it was 'one of the most important steps we as an organization are to take over the next few years' (*The Job*, 14 April 1989). He added that he was determined that the bulk of the programme of change would be carried out during his term of office. The Plus programme is best described as an attempt to change philosophy and culture rather than a specific set of tangible reforms.

The components of the programme were:

1 adopting the Statement of our Common Purpose and Values;
2 policy making and command systems;
3 composition of front-line teams;
4 deployment of front-line teams;
5 rewards and sanctions;
6 communication;
7 paperwork and bureaucracy;
8 appearance of the force;
9 performance indicators.

Sir Peter realized that action in all these areas was necessary if his ideas for the service were going to come to fruition. Teams were set up under the control of a specially selected commander to pursue each component individually. John Smith, the Assistant Commissioner in charge of Management Support, was appointed as project manager and at the launch he gave his view of a rationale behind the ideas: 'We are putting the emphasis on service to the public, forging relationships with the community. This is not a softly, softly approach. Every good detective knows for example that he can obtain more information if people are treated well. Our contract with the public will mean that we learn more about crime' (*The Job*, 14 April 1989).

Despite the breadth of the Plus programme, two items lay at its heart: the adoption of the Statement of Common Purpose and Values and the senior policy-making structure. It was important that action on these had top priority.

The Implementation of Common Purpose and Values

Sir Peter was always aware that the statement would need action to support it if it was to be accepted and be of value. He knew that it would need to overcome some resistance if it was to become part of the core values of the service. The issue of the Metropolitan Police Service (MPS) internal newspaper, *The Job*, following the launch carried a letter to the editor which stated, 'The expression of our Purpose and Values for the 1990s seems little different to those pertaining in the 1890s or the 1830s. It is perfectly acceptable as a statement of intent although I thought that it was already part and parcel of everyday police work' (*The Job*, 28 April 1989).

Although wide consultation had been carried out prior to the statement being decided, it was new to most of the service and it was important that it was discussed and reinforced. Framed copies were distributed and very soon were displayed in all MPS buildings and most offices. The Component 1 Team then set to work on how ownership could be achieved since values statements are never absorbed by being pinned to a wall.

In the winter and spring of 1990 four seminars for 600 of the most senior police and civil staff in the organization were arranged at the training school at Hendon. These were designed to introduce the most senior management to the plans and processes being prepared and to set the scene for day-long seminars which were being arranged for all staff which were planned to start in June.

During the summer the Commissioner addressed large groups of his middle management at specially prepared presentations at the Westminster Theatre. The sessions were designed to ensure that the managers on the divisions and in the branches at headquarters understood the change that was taking place and played their part in selling it throughout the organization. Sir Peter summed it up:

> PLUS will make us a more effective organisation. How will it do that? By giving us a sense of unity, a common purpose. By improving leadership across the organisation. By giving us a positive attitude to the concept of service both between ourselves and in our dealings with the public. By making us less defensive and isolated. By improving the way we communicate both within the organisation and outside. All this amounts to profound cultural change . . .

The magnitude of this task of putting all 44,000 members of staff through the seminars was not underestimated and careful plans were prepared to ensure that the days involved a mixture of ranks, roles and lengths of service. A video explaining the issues and featuring the Commissioner was produced which would be used to start and end each day. Glossy briefing packs were prepared for each attendee and a process to ensure that they were briefed before and debriefed after the day by their line managers was arranged.

The seminars started on 3 September 1990 under the title 'Working together for a better service', and a year later 99 per cent of the workforce had been through the process. Not all the reaction was positive. The facilitators had to deal with a full range of views and feeling about the programme. Some officers who felt that they were already giving a good service felt hurt. In the feedback from one of the sessions a detective constable said: 'Some senior officers fail to understand the problems affecting constables and sergeants and the officers react somewhat unfavourably towards the statement [of purpose] when rammed down their throats by such officers.'

It is a difficult task to restore a sense of corporate identity when relationships between senior and junior officers are strained. Authoritarian management breeds cycicism and mistrust. Others saw the programme as being too much like a business, taking away from the principle of public service. A uniform constable commented: 'In general the Plus programme is ideal – however the seminar on the day reminded me of working in industry again. I can't see how we can compare the service to outside industry.'

▬▬ The Operational Policing Review ▬▬

At the same time as the Plus team were struggling with the difficult issues and the seminars were being held, a major review sponsored jointly by the ACPO, the Superintendents Association and the Police Federation was published. It was a lengthy document covering all aspects of the service and among its headlines it pointed to an erosion in the level of 'traditional' policing and felt that the drive towards efficiency had reduced the sense of service.

Surveys had been carried out to gain the views of members of the public, members of consultative groups and police officers. While there was broad agreement in some areas, e.g. the priority of the police in dealing with emergencies, it was evident that there was a mismatch between the attitude of the public and the police and not a clear agreement between the public and members of consultative groups.

There was a strong consensus among members of the public that more police should be patrolling on foot and more than 80 per cent said that, of the police officers they saw, too many were in vehicles. The great majority saw preventing crime as a particularly important police activity and many more people said that they preferred the caring, community style of police officer to the firm, law enforcement style (section A4.6).

Although public opinion strongly favours uniformed patrol, there appears to be little evidence that, as a deterrent to crime, it is that effective. The PC on the beat passes within 100 yards of a burglary in progress once every eight years. However, the physical presence of the police is seen as reassuring.

In comparison, police officers responding conversely placed relatively low importance on the community constable type role and did not see an increase in foot patrols as desirable.

The Home Secretary may take a different view of the role of the police. The government identified a number of priorities for 1994 in order to reduce violent crime and increase the number of detected burglaries. These priorities were crime fighting, upholding the law, bringing criminals to justice and providing value for money. ACPO has sought to identify other priorities. They involve community relations, public reassurance and the maintenance of order. ACPO recognize that much of police work is not directly involved with catching criminals and that the development of good police–community relations is of paramount importance to them.

The Policy-making and Command Structure

Soon after the launch of the Plus programme a consultant was commissioned to work with a small team of a chief superintendent and a senior civil staff member to pursue component 2 and look at the senior policy-making structure of the Met. Six years previously an annual planning cycle based loosely on management by objectives had been introduced where divisions set their own objectives in the light of published force goals. These were monitored and co-ordinated by units on each area and by the Force Planning Unit at New Scotland Yard who was responsible to the Commissioner for preparing strategic reports to the Home Secretary.

Separate to this, resources were bid for through a process governed by the Government Public Expenditure Survey (PES) cycle. Bids were aggregated and prioritized by areas. The Receiver was then responsible for preparing the submission to the Home Office for resources that would be needed in the financial year two years following the bid.

The team reported in 1990, highlighting a need for:

- the Metropolitan Police to take a longer forward view and consider a five-year strategy;
- the Policy Committee to delegate as much as feasible and concentrate on the most important decisions affecting the service including the strategic review;
- operational and resource planning to be aligned.

They suggested a structure where operational policy could be delegated to ACTO and ACSO, and support issues to the Receiver, and at the same time ensuring users and providers of resources were both involved in decision making. Three new committees ('Executives') were recommended:

1 the Territorial Operations Executive (TOE), chaired by ACTO and involving not only all DACs but the directors of the departments under the control of the Receiver;
2 the Specialist Operations Executive (SOE), chaired by ACSO and with a similar membership to the TOE but considering operational issues falling to SO Department;
3 the Support Executive, chaired by the Receiver and involving the directors of his departments and also the assistant commissioners 'MS' and 'PT' and the DACs 'TO' and 'SO'.

The new structure was set up at the end of 1991 and in November the first five-year plan was presented to the Home Office as the Police Authority, setting out the 'Strategic Intention' and containing manpower and budget proposals for the years 1993–7. The Strategic Intention had seven principal strands:

1 To remain a visible, predominantly unarmed, approachable police service in order to provide a reassuring presence across London. This, our overriding policing style, has its roots deep in the community.
2 To increase consultation with the public and their representatives; to inform and to respond to their views, and their particular and changing needs, as far as we can; and to improve our internal communications. We intend to maintain our place as leaders in policing philosophy and practice.
3 To establish a clear view of the relative importance of policing tasks, and improve our performance in those areas of police activity which are identified for priority attention. It may be necessary deliberately

to divert manpower away from some areas of work to address these priorities.

4 To maintain a range of specialist services which, in support of our general policing style, reflect the changing and dynamic needs of those living and working in London. Such specialisms must also encompass those national responsibilities we presently bear.

5 To achieve a sufficiency and disposition of personnel – both police and civilian support staff – to make us more effective in the delivery of our service and to realize the full potential of all individuals within the service promoting professionalism together with high standards of personal conduct. All personnel must be well trained, led and managed.

6 To ensure technical and other appropriate support for our workforce. Investment here must be sustained and have as its twin goals the greater effectiveness of staff and the provision of better working conditions for them;

7 Finally, to give a high quality service to all our customers, particularly the public, delivered in a way that represents good value for money. This requires exacting self-scrutiny of our performance, against agreed standards, through inspection and review procedures. We will continue to promote good practice and correct errors; if we are wrong and grievances are justified, we will accept our mistakes.

▬▬ Discussion Questions ▬▬

1 How well has the Met responded to the interests of its key stakeholders?
2 Has the Met been successful in moving from a police force to a police service?
3 What lessons can be learned concerning changes in public services culture?

▬▬ Background Note: the Metropolitan Police ▬▬

The force which Sir Peter had taken over was very similar to that which he had joined as a constable 34 years previously and in some ways it had not changed in over 100 years. Primacy was still given to the idea of the unarmed uniformed constable patrolling on foot supervised by a structure similar to the army one on which it was based. Written reports were often passed through several layers of hierarchy before achieving their object. CID officers (or detectives) working in plain clothes investigated crimes which had been reported.

The Met had about 28,000 police officers supported by 16,000 civil staff. Apart from patrolling in uniform and investigating crime the police officers' roles varied between traffic policing, dealing with accidents, illnesses and deaths, and managing demonstrations. In a *Guide to the Met* published in 1986 the Greater London Council had attempted to list the range of police duties and had suggested that some of them were controversial and could be done by local authorities. The list was:

- crime prevention;
- crime detection;
- assisting people (e.g. providing information, lost property);
- social services (e.g. children in care, missing persons);
- traffic control;
- public order, e.g.
  - day to day control of streets,
  - control of large crowds (e.g. football crowds, demonstrations),
  - dealing with public disorder,
  - policing industrial disputes;
- national functions (e.g. royalty and diplomatic protection);
- political and industrial surveillance (work of special branch);
- public and community relations.

The hierarchy of ranks of police officers is shown at section A4.1. Legislation prevented officers from being part of a trade union, but three staff associations existed to represent members at a local and national level. The Association of Chief Police Officers (ACPO) represented the most senior, and through a series of committees acted as a means of making and co-ordinated national policy. The superintendents' association similarly represented superintendents and chief superintendents and the Police Federation acted for constables to chief inspectors.

Civil staff roles included traffic wardens, scenes of crime examiners and photographers, engineers, surveyors, drivers and administration work. The grade structure broadly followed civil service lines. Programmes to civilianize jobs which were felt not to require the skills, training, experience or powers of a police officer had been an important part of efficiency measures for a number of years. Civil staff were represented through several trade unions which recognized the range of civil staff roles covering both industrial and non-industrial work.

Police and civil staff had separate career structures and usually separate lines of reporting. All promotion for police was from within the service. All senior officers for a number of years had once walked the streets as constables.

The structure of the organization had been radically changed three years previously (figure A4.2) and the force was now split into eight geographical areas, one covering the central area and the rest dividing London like slices of cake. Each area was under the control of a deputy assistant commissioner (DAC). Each DAC was responsible for the work of about nine police divisions together with units attached to the area headquarters such as traffic enforcement and a mobile reserve. A policing division was an area usually covered from a single station but containing more than one station in the larger divisions towards the edge of London. A division was headed by a chief superintendent.

Figure A4.2 Metropolitan Police area structure

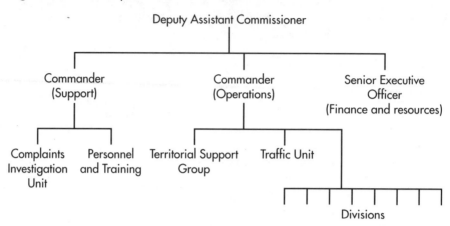

The force headquarters centred around a tower block in Central London where Sir Peter had his office on the eighth floor. Known throughout the world as New Scotland Yard it carried on the name of the site of the first Metropolitan Police headquarters over 150 years previously. Management of the Metropolitan Police was actually shared between Sir Peter, who as Commissioner was the operational head, and the Receiver, a senior civil servant responsible for finance and resources. This division of responsibility had been the case since 1829 when the Metropolitan Police had been set up with joint Commissioners Charles Rowan and Richard Mayne and a Receiver 'to administer all monies applicable to the [Police] Act'.

The headquarters was divided into 11 departments, four under the control of assistant commissioners and seven under the Receiver. Section A4.2 shows the structure of headquarters and the responsibilities of the departments. The police departments were:

1   *Territorial Operations* – responsible for all police functions on divisions and areas and central functions such as public order and obscene publications.
2   *Specialist Operations* – responsible for all crime not capable of being dealt with on a local basis including terrorism, fraud, robbery and international crime. Also provides national functions such as protection of the Royal Family and diplomats.
3   *Management Support* – responsible for enhancing management practice, planning and policy.
4   *Personnel and Training* – responsible for recruiting, career development and training of police officers.

The senior decision-making group was called the Policy Committee and met fortnightly, chaired by the Commissioner. It comprised the Deputy Commissioner, the four Assistant Commissioners, the Receiver and the Deputy

Receiver. Meetings were often preceded by a co-ordinating committee attended only by the police officer members where operational matters were discussed.

The police force that Sir Peter inherited when he joined the Met was not dissimilar in culture and structure to police forces elsewhere. Police forces were traditionally hierarchical, centralized and authoritarian and with strict adherence to a rigid set of rules. As police forces increasingly split into specialized divisions the development of a coherent and integrated service delivery could be hindered by the divisions between central headquarters and operational elements.

In common with many other parts of the public services, the police force was slow to recognize the importance of meeting public expectations and tended to be producer-driven.

A4.1: Ranks of Police Officers in the Metropolitan Police

Commissioner
Assistant Commissioner
Deputy Assistant Commissioner
Commander
Chief Superintendent
Superintendent
Chief Inspector
Inspector
Sergeant
Constable

The ranks constable to chief superintendent have equivalent 'detective' ranks for officers working in the CID.

A4.2: Senior Management Structure of the Metropolitan Police in 1989

Figure A4.3 Senior management structure of the Metropolitan Police in 1989

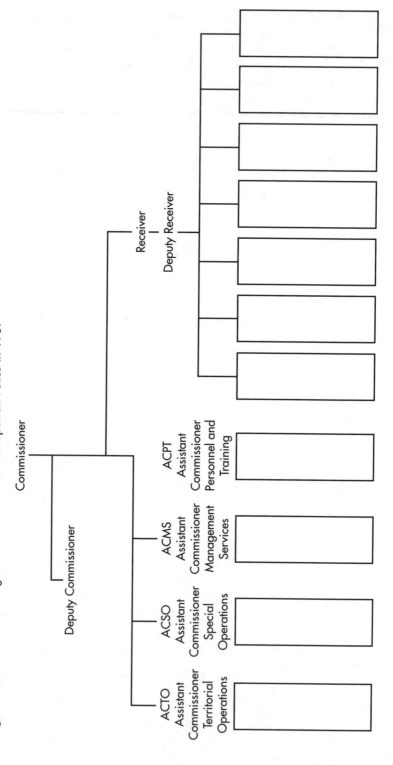

A4.3: Metropolitan Police

Table A4.1 Summary of functional cost information

	Annual cost £K of function	% of gross force budget
Patrol	341,805	28
CID	155,271	13
Uniform officers in crime squads	50,945	4
Traffic	74,968	6
Community relations	16,532	1
Public order	25,507	2
Training	53,357	4
Complaints and discipline	9,743	1
Protection duty	41,357	3
Police: Other HQ functions	29,557	3
Other Area and divisional duties	236,054	20
Civil staff: Other HQ functions	110,569	9
Other Area and divisional duties	22,024	2
Civil staff overtime	19,064	2
	1,186,753	98

The remaining 2 per cent reflects expenditure which cannot be usefully apportioned to individual functions.
Adapted from the *Annual Report of the Commissioner for the Metropolis*, 1988.

A4.4: Perception of Police Performance 1983–1989

Table A4.2 'Taking everything into account, would you say that the police in this area do a good job or a poor job?'

	1983 %	1984 %	1985 %	1986 %	1987 %	1988 %	1989 %
Very good	25	25	22	18	18	18	16
Fairly good	47	48	47	48	49	51	48
Combined positive image	72	73	69	66	67	69	64
Neither	10	9	10	11	12	11	14
Fairly poor	6	6	7	8	7	7	8
Very poor	2	3	3	4	4	4	4
Combined -ve image	8	9	10	12	11	11	12
Uncertain	10	9	10	12	10	10	11

From annual public attitude surveys commissioned by the Metropolitan Police Service.

A4.5: Personal Safety and Policing
━━━ Priorities 1983–1989; Safeguarding ━━━
Property 1986–1989

Table A4.3 'How safe do you feel walking alone in this area after dark?'

	1983 %	1984 %	1985 %	1986 %	1987 %	1988 %	1989 %
Very unsafe/unsafe	48	51	56	48	48	50	47
Women only	65	72	74	70	66	70	67
Reasons							
Fear of mugging	62	43	52	43	30	32	28
General fear	12	31	31	29	26	29	29

From annual public attitude surveys commissioned by the Metropolitan Police Service.

Table A4.4 'What do you feel are the most important problems in this area that the police should concentrate their efforts on?'

Rank order Offence	1983 %	1984 %	1985 %	1986 %	1987 %	1988 %	1989 %
1 Burglary	38	39	35	39	38	31	34
2 Mugging	27	22	24	19	26	24	20
3 Vandalism	15	15	13	14	14	13	14
4 Traffic	10	6	6	7	8	8	11
5 Loitering	8	6	8	9	9	9	9

Subjects were asked to place 18 categories in order of priority. The chart shows the top five categories and the percentage of people giving that category the highest priority. From annual public attitude surveys commissioned by the Metropolitan Police Service.

Table A4.5 'In what ways, if any, do you think that the police could help the public safeguard their own property from theft?'

	1986 %	1987 %	1988 %	1989 %
More police on foot	38	50	50	51
Encourage Neighbourhood Watch Schemes	22	24	27	28
More police patrols	12	20	20	23
Information/leaflets	19	13	12	15
Visits from Crime Prevention Officers	15	13	10	13
Property marking	3	4	5	6
Advertising	7	3	3	3

From annual public attitude surveys commissioned by the Metropolitan Police Service.

▬▬ A4.6 Policing Priorities ▬▬

There is a high level of agreement about the order of policing priorities.

Table A4.6 Policing priorities – Tasks

	Rankings	
	Public	Police
Respond immediately to emergencies	1	1
Detect and arrest offenders	2	2
Investigate crime	3	3
Patrol the area on foot	4	5
Set up squads for serious crime	5	7
Provide help and support to victims of crime	6	9
Get to know local people	7	4
Give advice to the public on how to prevent crime	8	8
Patrol the area in cars	9	6
Work closely with local schools	10	10
Work with local council departments, such as housing, to plan crime prevention	11	12
Control and supervise road traffic	12	11

Source: Operational Policing Review, Joint Consultative Committee, 1990, quoted in Audit Commission, undated.

The consensus begins to break down over the offences which the police should devote most time to fighting.

Table A4.7 Policing Priorities – offences

	Rankings	
	Public	Police
Sexual assaults on women	1	3
Burglary of people's houses	2	1
Drunken driving	3	8
Vandalism and deliberate damage to property	4	9
Robberies in the street involving violence	5	2
Crimes in which firearms are used	6	4
Use of heroin and other hard drugs	7	5
Theft of and from motor cars	8	7
Fighting and rowdyism in the streets	9	6
Litter and rubbish lying around	10	14
Use of cannabis/pot/marijuana	11	13
Parking and general traffic offences	12	12
Bag-snatching and pick-pocketing	13	10
Racial attacks	14	11
Noisy parties and domestic disturbances	15	15

Source: Operational Policing Review, Joint Consultative Committee, 1990.

References

Annual Report of the Commissioner of the Metropolitan Police, 1988.
The Job, 14 April 1989.
The Job, 28 April 1989.
The Job, January 1993.
Metropolitan Police Service, 'A Force for Change', 1989.
Police Committee Support Unit, *Guide to the Met*, London: Greater London Council, February 1986.
The Times, 23 May 1990.

CASE STUDY

5

Wellcare Hospital Trust

Alan Lawton and David McKevitt

John Prideauz looked out of his office window to the beautifully manicured lawns below and to the executive car park beyond. He saw his own company Saab gleaming in the sunlight. All appeared to be well with the world. And yet John was a worried man. He had been in post as chief executive of the hospital for only a few months and the job was very different from what he had expected. He had been recruited from the private sector after a successful career in manufacturing. He had qualified as an engineer and later gained his MBA through part-time study. John formerly believed that running a hospital could not be that different from running a ball-bearing factory and had relished the challenge of improving the hospital's productivity, reducing its costs and making it more efficient. John had taken the job with firm views on how he could turn the organization around. After all, he had done it successfully on two occasions in the private sector. However, the financial figures for the previous six months made depressing reading and the lead story in his daily newspaper was about how many Trust hospitals had got into financial difficulties. Perhaps he had been over-confident, perhaps he had not realized the complexities of managing in the public sector. After idly wasting the first half-hour of his day with these thoughts he realized that he had better start being more constructive. He decided to review the progress he had made in the past few months and decide on his strategy for the future. Immediately, he realized that much of this time had been spent with day-to-day crises and with trying to defuse long-standing tensions between the different groups that made up the hospital's workforce. He decided to go back to basics and start from scratch. John pulled out the briefing papers he had been given prior to his appointment. They contained information about the hospital, and about the NHS (see section A5.1). At the time it had seemed fairly straightforward but he realized that the complexities of organizational life in the NHS were far greater than he had imagined.

John thought that the key to improved performance lay in setting out clear targets and measuring their achievement. He decided to have a more thorough examination of the existing system for measuring performance and turned to a series of papers that had been produced by one of his middle managers. He recalled that the middle manager had carried out only the first part of an investigation into performance measurement. She had left the hospital shortly before John's arrival, under something of a cloud. Apparently she had kicked up a fuss about lack of co-operation and had committed the cardinal sin of criticizing the medical staff for not taking performance measurement seriously. She was seen as something of a troublemaker but John did know that she was now working for another Trust hospital and was seen as a rising star. Section A5.2 contains a summary of her report on the performance measurement systems currently used by Wellcare Hospital. John did remember asking whether the investigation was continuing and was given an evasive reply by one of his senior managers.

John had always believed in MBWA (Management By Walking About) and felt that he needed to have a higher profile among all staff in the hospital. He realized that he still did not have a real feel for how the hospital worked and felt that informal chats with staff would give a sense of how people felt about the performance of the hospital. Reproduced below are some of the comments he received.

Perspectives on Performance Measurement

Consultants

All this paperwork erodes clinical time!

The current system needs to be bespoke rather than externally imposed.

We will need a strong executive lead on this.

There is pressure on managers to reduce costs without regard to effectiveness.

Performance measures are a paper exercise and just used to increase the political profile of the Trust: internally they are frequently used as a tool in the allocation of resources by powerful interests.

The only performance measurement that is worth anything is peer review. I don't want some jumped-up MBA telling me that my performance could be improved. Only my colleagues have the knowledge to comment on that.

Nurses

It is difficult measuring individual performance since it is so difficult working out who actually owns it. Patients' well-being is dependent upon so many different people from the medical staff, to the porters, the ambulance crews or the social workers who look after them when they leave here.

There are league tables for hospital performance (waiting lists, times etc) but the system still isn't truly responsive to the patient's needs.

Attitudes must change, such that doctors do not see themselves as all-important and managers see that they have greater control. Many of the barriers to entry of the profession remain. Such change is definitely seen as unacceptable from the doctor's perspective.

Target setting is currently only for arrival contacts with patients or for waiting times at appointment.

Most staff are indifferent to the current performance measures. They bear little resemblance to the service delivered, they are time consuming and provide minimal feedback to the staff.

Whatever system we use it must reflect the care and attention that we give to individual patients. It must also reflect the complexity of individual patient needs.

Middle managers

Technical barriers can be overcome but the behavioural barriers are still present.

Most stakeholders view the Government, closely followed by consultants, as the most powerful and patients and their representatives as least powerful.

I want to know how well neighbouring OPDs perform in terms of overall budget, activity and quality because this will help me develop a marketing strategy to influence purchasers.

I want to influence directly those groups of patients most likely to seek a choice of hospital such as pregnant mothers or those seeking non-emergency treatment.

If quality is defined as the ability to satisfy need, it begs the question of whether this is felt (expressed) need or expertly defined (normative) need. Measures of expressed need can be tapped in a variety of ways – not simply the patients complaints and satisfaction surveys, but also user forums or panels lead by 'neutral' facilitators. The former methods are easily quantified, but can fail to tap much opinion that the patient may not express to staff in fear of adverse influence on their care and general loyalty to the NHS, or low expectations.

The acceptability of patient satisfaction feedback data collected by patients organizations is more threatening to hospital staff than in-house data collection, precisely because it can be less easily biased in favour of the hospital.

There is a weakness in the current arrangements in deciding *who* should be monitoring performance – the providers or the purchasers.

Networking, collaboration, co-operation and communication have to be improved among all stakeholders if performance assessment in the public domain is to be improved.

The current systems are the result of demands from central government departments or oganizational management needs. Even with the Patients Charter monitoring standards are selected centrally rather than based on users local interest.

The trust will need to provide a proven value for money, quality service that is responsive to the GPs needs. Failure to do so will inevitably lead to a loss of business. The role of PIs to prove effectiveness should not be underestimated in this process.

Greater emphasis must now be placed on making both financial and information systems more accurate because in future the commissioners will be basing contracts on such information and this will affect the ultimate *survival* of the Trust. Professionals must recognize this and managers must be flexible to allow more time to be spent on information collection. This could lead to a small increase in admin and clerical staff who are normally used to collate and record such information.

Accurate information is required by both sides: the purchaser needs a clear idea of what services it requires: the provider needs to know how much and when it is required to provide.

Performance indicators usually mean reducing costs at any price without any thought given to effectiveness.

Unlike in business, I do not know who my customers are. Is it those who use us, is it the medical staff, is it the community generally? It is not just the patient.

Stakeholders

John realized that the views expressed were fairly selective and represented only the internal stakeholders of the hospital. He quickly drew up a list of all the possible stakeholders and tried to think through what their interests might be:

Stakeholders	*Possible interests*
Nurses	Patient care, interesting job, career progression
Patients	Better health!
Doctors	Quality of care, career progression, research

GPs	Quality and cost of care
Managers	Costs, efficiency, patient satisfaction, level of competition, business growth
Government	Costs, avoid possible scandals, leagues tables of performance
Health authority	Costs, equitable treatment, league tables and comparisons, access
Local politicians	Avoid scandals, no hospital closures
Professional bodies	Quality of health; protection of members and maintenance of standards.
Trust board	Survival, achieve a surplus, levels of remuneration.

John recognized that not all of these interests could be reconciled and that performance measurement might mean different things to different people. He also recognized that the brief summary of the current system of performance indicators (section A5.2) left much room for improvement. He dug out his notes from a conference he had recently attended on performance measurement in the public services (section A5.3).

John was left reflecting that in the 'new' NHS, the internal market would judge performance. Hospitals which provided an effective and efficient service which gave the customer what he or she wanted would survive and prosper. Those that did not would go under. Whether or not this would be politically acceptable, John had his doubts but managers had to recognize that they were running a business. In this new world, the purchaser was of crucial importance as GPs, for example, sought to get the best value for money from the providers for their patients. Fundholders were key players in the market and they were becoming adept at exploiting their new strengths.

Managing in the NHS was all about being responsive to the customer and managers had to be flexible in response to consumer demands. However, John was beginning to appreciate that the manager's hands were often tied in crucial areas of performance. The power of the professional bodies had made it difficult to move to a more flexible pay system which allowed him to pay for good performance and to penalize poor performance. Certainly the Government was reluctant to be seen to be battering the nurses.

▬▬ Discussion Questions ▬▬

1 What would you recommend as a new performance measurement system for Wellcare?
2 How would you recommend that John Prideaux satisfy the needs of the different stakeholders?
3 How can quality of health service be defined?

▬ A5.1: The Changing National ▬
Health Service

Wellcare Trust Hospital is an acute general hospital with 300 beds. It has 20,000 outpatients per year. It is structured into clinical directorates comprising obstetrics/gynaecology, general surgery, orthopaedics and trauma, paediatrics and general medicines.

The percentage spent on administrative costs is slightly higher than the national average. The physical quality of the buildings is poor and will need extensive refurbishment.

There is one other Trust hospital 20 miles away and four district general hospitals in the next district.

The Trust is run by a board of directors, the chairperson being appointed by the Government and with a number of local businessmen on the board. The board can run the Trust as an independent business and has the powers to determine staff levels and mix and can negotiate outputs with a variety of purchasers with whom it enters into contracts.

The Trust's Mission Statement is: 'To provide high quality healthcare across the full spectrum of general hospital services to its local population. That care must be patient-centred.'

The NHS has undergone profound changes in its structure, financing and operating environment in recent years. The major piece of legislation introducing these changes was the National Health Service and Community Care Act 1990. The Act was intended to bring about the introduction of market-like mechanisms into the NHS through the separation of the providers of health care from the purchasers. The relationship between the purchasers and providers was to be regulated through the use of contracts. The reform would, it was argued, allow purchasers to shop around to get the best deal from providers, increasing choice and ensuring that competition improved efficiency.

The purchasers of health care would be the District Health Authorities and General Practitioner (GP) fundholders. GP practices of a certain size were allowed to control their own budgets and purchase health care for their patients. Other possible purchasers include insurance companies and employers.

The providers of health care were classified as those hospitals directly managed by the health authority and a new breed of hospital Trusts. Trusts are independent self-managed units run by a board staffed by government appointees and representatives of the medical profession. A Trust can retain its financial surpluses and invest in the business. It has flexibility over levels of remuneration and the numbers and mix of staff.

Other providers may include ambulance or community services. Purchasers can buy health care from neighbouring districts if they so desire. Funding for purchasers is determined, partly, on a capitation basis depending on the number of patients on a GPs list or the size of the resident population.

The intention is to place patient interests above those of the providers and alongside the Patients Charter which defines the service that patients can expect to make a public service more responsive to the needs of its 'customers'.

A5.2: Wellcare's Performance Indicators

Performance indicators in the NHS were introduced in the 1980s and concentrated on activity levels. Performance indicators were concerned with increasing the number of, for example, open heart operations or hip replacement operations; other indicators measured cost per case treated, staffing levels related to patient numbers, waiting lists and so on. Early performance indicators were criticized for using already generated statistics and 'rebadging' them, for concentrating on throughput rather than outcome and for not measuring quality.

Critics have argued that performance indicators were issued as a control mechanism by central government to ensure the economic use of taxpayers' money.

Wellcare's current system of performance indicators focuses on:

- cost of staff;
- cancelled appointments;
- waiting times;
- attendances;
- non-attendances;
- number of clinics per 1000 population;
- budget statements;
- complaints;
- workload.

A major problem that Wellcare faces is lack of information. We tend to 'rebadge' statistics collected for different purposes and call them performance indicators. Managers lack basic financial data to make decisions. If we are serious about pushing responsibility downwards then we have to allow managers the 'freedom to manage'. Part of this involves making financial decisions: they cannot do this if they do not have the basic information concerning the costs of operations, X-rays, equipment, etc.

Nurses are frustrated because they cannot get quick access to patients records. We installed the new computer system but did not spend enough time training nurses on how to use it.

Consultants resent what they see as yet another encroachment on their territory by managers who do not have medical expertise.

Increasingly the nature of our business will be governed by contracts with purchasers. We need to develop skills in contract management as performance targets will be an integral part of the 'contract culture'. At present most contracts are likely to be block contracts in which we receive an annual fee in return for a broad range of services and which are measured in terms of length of stay, waiting lists, and so on. Quality is not clearly specified. We can expect, however, pressure to move to cost-per-case contracts where quality and targets are much more clearly specified and costed.

A5.3: Performance Indicators in the Public Sector

Can be used to:

1 clarify objectives;
2 evaluate outcomes;
3 input into incentive schemes and staff appraisal;
4 enable consumers to make informed choices;
5 indicate standards and allow monitoring;
6 calculate the contribution of different activities to overall performance;
7 spotlight problem areas;
8 help in cost-benefit analysis;
9 indicate potential areas of cost reduction.

Six Dimensions of Quality in Health Care

1 Access to services
2 Relevance to need
3 Effectiveness
4 Equity
5 Social acceptability
6 Efficiency and economy

Criteria for Performance Indicators

1 Timeliness
2 Accuracy
3 Acceptability
4 Suitability
5 Feasibility
6 Usefulness
7 Consistency
8 Comparability
9 Clarity
10 Controllability
11 Availability

Dimensions of Performance Measurement

Structure	Process	Outcome
Inputs	Activity	Outputs
Economy	Efficiency	Effectiveness

QUALITY

APPENDIX

Questionnaire

QUESTIONNAIRE

■■■ **Accident and Emergency** ■■■
(Casualty Department) Patients

Q.1   How long ago did you last attend an A&E/casualty department?
       [TICK ONE BOX]

                                                            (9)
       In last month   1☐
       In last 2–3 months   2☐
       In last 4–6 months   3☐
       Longer ago   4☐

Q.2   At which hospital was this? [WRITE IN]

Q.3   Was this on behalf of yourself, or for someone else? [TICK ONE
       BOX]

                                                            (11)
       Self   1☐
       With a child aged 0–2 as the patient   2☐
       With a child aged 3–5 as the patient   3☐
       With a child aged 6–10 as the patient   4☐
       With a child aged 11+ as the patient   5☐
       With another adult as the patient   6☐

Q.4   How did you get to the Accident & Emergency department? [TICK
       ONE BOX]

                                                            (12)
       By private car   1☐
       By taxi   2☐
       By ambulance   3☐
       On foot   4☐
       Other [WRITE IN]   5☐

Q.5   What time of day did you arrive? [TICK ONE BOX]

                                                      (13)

9 am – 12 noon	1☐
12 noon – 5 pm	2☐
5 pm – 8 pm	3☐
8 pm – midnight	4☐
midnight – 9 am	5☐

Q.6   And what day of the week was this? [TICK ONE BOX]

    (14)

Sunday	1☐
Monday	2☐
Tuesday	3☐
Wednesday	4☐
Thursday	5☐
Friday	6☐
Saturday	7☐

Q.7   How did you regard the injury? [TICK ONE BOX]

    (15)

Very serious	1☐
Serious/potentially serious	2☐
Probably minor, but wanted reassurance	3☐
Other [WRITE IN]	4☐

Q.8   How did you think the injury should be treated? [TICK ONE BOX]

    (16)

Definitely needed to be dealt with in the hospital	1☐
Could probably have been dealt with by a GP	2☐
Not sure	3☐
Other [WRITE IN]	4☐

IF IT COULD HAVE BEEN DEALT WITH BY A GP PLEASE ANSWER Q.9, IF NOT GO TO Q.10.

Q.9   Why did you come to the hospital? [WRITE IN]

_____ (17)

_____ (18)

_____ (19)

Q.10   Was there any choice of which hospital to go to? [TICK ONE BOX]

    (20)

No, only one hospital round here/
only one that I can get to   1☐
Yes, there is a choice   2☐
IF 'YES' PLEASE ANSWER Q.11, IF NOT GO TO Q.12

Q.11   Why did you come to this hospital? [WRITE IN]

_____ (21)

_____ (22)

_____ (23)

Q.12   When you arrived at the Accident & Emergency department, were
there many other patients there already waiting? [TICK ONE BOX]

		(24)
None		1☐
1–5		2☐
6–10		3☐
11+		4☐

Q.13   How long did you have to wait before someone looked at you/the
patient to decide how serious the injury was? [TICK ONE BOX]

		(25)
0–5 minutes		1☐
6–10 minutes		2☐
11–15 minutes		3☐
16+ minutes		4☐

Q.14   Were you given any idea as to how long you might have to wait
before you could be treated? [TICK ONE BOX]

		(26)
Yes		1☐
No		2☐

Q.15   And how long were you in the department altogether before you/the
patient was treated? [TICK ONE BOX]

		(27)
Less than half an hour		1☐
Between half an hour and 1 hour		2☐
Between 1 hour and 2 hours		3☐
Between 2 hours and 3 hours		4☐
More than 3 hours		5☐

Q.16   Did you ask for, or were you offered, any painkillers during this time?
[TICK ONE BOX]

		(28)
I asked for them and was given some		1☐
I asked for some but none were provided		2☐
I was offered some without asking		3☐
I did not request any and none were offered		4☐
Other [WRITE IN]		

Q.17　And how long had you finally been in the department before you were sent home/sent elsewhere in the hospital? [TICK ONE BOX]

(29)

Up to one hour　1☐
Between one and two hours　2☐
Between two and three hours　3☐
More than three hours　4☐

Q.18　Overall, how did you feel about the time you had to wait before treatment? [TICK ONE BOX]

(30)

Much too long　1☐
Rather too long　2☐
It was acceptable　3☐
Pleased to be seen so quickly　4☐

Q.19　And, secondly, how would you describe the staff? [TICK ONE BOX]

(31)

Very caring　1☐
Fairly caring　2☐
Not particularly caring　3☐
Rather off-hand　4☐
Very off-hand　5☐

Q.20　How did the staff seem? [TICK ONE BOX]

(32)

Very efficient　1☐
Fairly efficient　2☐
Not particularly efficient　3☐
Not at all efficient　4☐

Q.21　What did you think about the number of staff in the department? [TICK ONE BOX]

(33)

More than needed, just at that point　1☐
Just the right number　2☐
Enough to just about cope　3☐
Definitely too few　4☐

Q.22　When you left the hospital/were referred to another department, how well informed did you feel about what you should do in the way of aftercare? [TICK ONE BOX]

(34)

I was told exactly what to do/what not to do　1☐
I felt I had been given a reasonable idea of what to do　2☐
I did not have any idea what I was supposed to do　3☐
Not relevant　4☐

Q.23   What did you think of the waiting room facilities for patients in the
Accident & Emergency department? [TICK ONE BOX]

(35)

Excellent   1☐
Good   2☐
Adequate   3☐
Poor   4☐
Very poor   5☐
IF 'POOR/VERY POOR' PLEASE ANSWER Q.24, IF NOT GO
TO Q.25.

Q.24   What needed to be improved? [WRITE IN]

_____ (36)

_____ (37)

_____ (38)

Q.25a   Overall, how satisfied were you with your visit to Accident & Emergency? [TICK ONE BOX]

(39)

Very satisfied   1☐
Quite satisfied   2☐
Not particularly satisfied   3☐
Not at all satisfied   4☐

Q.25b   Why, in your own words, did you feel this way? [WRITE IN]

_____ (40)

_____ (41)

_____ (42)

Q.26   How could the service offered by Accident & Emergency to people
like yourself by improved? [WRITE IN]

_____ (43)

_____ (44)

_____ (45)

Q.27   Have you heard of the 'Patient's Charter'? [TICK ONE BOX]

(46)

Yes – IF 'YES', PLEASE ANSWER Q.28   1☐
No – IF 'NO' GO TO Q.30   2☐

Q.28   Do you know what it says specifically about Accident & Emergency
departments? [TICK ONE BOX]

(47)

Yes – IF 'YES' PLEASE ANSWER Q.29   1☐
No – IF 'NO' GO TO Q.30   2☐

Q.29   What does it specify? [WRITE IN]

_____ (48)

_____ (49)

_____ (50)

Q.30   If you were unhappy with your experience at the Accident & Emergency department, did you complain? [WRITE IN]
If YES

To whom _____ (51)

What happened _____ (52)

_____ (53)

If NO

Why not _____ (54)

_____ (55)

_____

Q.31   Have you had to have any follow-up to your treatment since your visit to the Accident & Emergency department? [TICK ONE BOX]

                                                                                    (56)

Yes – IF 'YES' PLEASE ANSWER Q.32   1☐
No – IF 'NO' FINISH   2☐

Q.32   Was it suggested to you at the Accident & Emergency department/the hospital that you might need this? [TICK ONE BOX]

                                                                                  (57)
Yes   1☐
No   2☐

THANK YOU VERY MUCH FOR YOUR HELP.
Finally, we would very much appreciate your just giving us some details about yourself.
ALL QUESTIONS REFER TO THE PATIENT UNLESS A CHILD UNDER 16, WHEN THE ACCOMPANYING ADULT SHOULD ANSWER.

Q.33   What age are you? [WRITE IN]

_____ Years   (58)

Q.34   Are you? [TICK ONE BOX]

                                                                                   (59)
Male   1☐
Female   2☐

Q.35   What is the occupation of the head of the household? [WRITE IN]

_____ (60)

REFERENCES

Chapter 1

Arrow, K. (1975) *Economic Development, Present State of the Art*, Papers of the East–West Communications Institute, no. 14.

Baumol, W. (1952) *Welfare Economics and the Theory of the State*, London, Bell and Sons.

Coase, R. (1937) *Nature of the Firm: Economica*, London, London School of Economics.

Oakshott, M. (1991) *Rationalism in Politics and Other Essays*, Indianapolis, Liberty Press.

Stewart, J. (1989) 'In search of curriculum for management of the public sector', *Management Education and Development*, vol. 20, no. 3.

Wrigley, L. (1970) *Divisional Diversification and Autonomy*, unpublished DBA, Harvard.

Wrigley, L. (1989) 'Foreword' in McKevitt, D. *Irish Health Care Policy*, Cork, Hibernian University Press.

Chapter 2

Arrow, K. (1975) *Economic Development, Present State of the Art*, Papers of the East–West Communications Institute, no. 14.

Caves, R. and Porter, M. (1977) 'From entry barriers to mobility barriers', *Quarterly Journal of Economics*, vol. 91, pp. 230–49.

Department for Education and Employment (1996) *Higher Level Vocational Qualifications: a Government Position Paper*, London, Department for Education and Employment.

Halsey, A. H. (1987) *Change in British Society*, Milton Keynes, Open University Press.

Hood, C. (1995) 'Contemporary public management: a new global paradigm', *Public Policy and Administration*, vol. 10, no. 2, pp. 104–17.

Hudson, B. (1989) *Disability and Dependence*, (ed.) Barton, L., London, Falmer Press.

Lipsky, L. (1980) *Street Level Bureaucracy,* New York, Russell Sage Foundation.

McKevitt, D. (1989) *Irish Health Care Policy*, Cork, Hibernian University Press.

McKevitt, D. (1996) 'Strategic Management in the Irish Civil Service: Prometheus unbound or Phoenix redux?', *Administration*, vol. 43, no. 4, pp. 34–50.

Oakshott, M. (1991) *Rationalism in Politics and Other Essays*, Indianapolis, Liberty Press.

Scott, B. R. (1962) *An Open Systems Model*, unpublished DBA, Harvard.

Simon, H. (1947) Administrative Behaviour, New York, Free Press.

Simon, H. (1994) 'The criterion of efficiency', in McKevitt, D. and Lawton, A. (eds) *Public Sector Management, Theory, Critique and Practice*, London, Sage.

Smith, A. (1776) *An Enquiry into the Nature and Causes of the Wealth of Nations*, Chicago, University of Chicago Press.

Wrigley, L. (1970) *Divisional Diversification and Autonomy*, unpublished DBA, Harvard.

Wrigley, L. and McKevitt, D. (1995) 'Professional ethics, government agenda and differential information', Open Business School Research, *Working Paper 95/5*.

Chapter 3

Anell, A., Rosen, P. and Svarvar, P. (1996) 'Health care reforms in Sweden' Swedish Institute for Health Economics, *Working Paper 1996:8*, Lund.

Audit Commission (1993) 'Putting quality on the map', *Occasional Paper, No. 18*.

Bateson, J. (1995) *Managing Services Marketing*, Fort Worth, Dryden Press.

Child Support Agency (1994) Framework Document.

Citizen's Charter Complaints Task Force 1995, *The Citizen's Charter, Second Report 1994*, London, HMSO.

Foucault, M. (1994) 'Governmentality' in McKevitt, D. and Lawton, A. (eds) (1994) *Public Sector Management, Theory, Critique and Practice*, London, Sage.

Gyford, J. (1991) *Citizens, Consumers and Councils*, London, Macmillan.

Hakansson, S. and Nordling, S. (1997) 'The health system of Sweden', in Raffel, M. (ed.) *Health Care and Reform in Industrialized Countries*, Pennsylvania State University Press, pp. 191–215.

Hambleton, R. and Hoggett, P. (1990) 'Beyond excellence: quality local government in the 1990s', *Working Paper no. 85*, School for Advanced Urban Studies, University of Bristol.

Harrison, S. (1993) 'Resource management' in *Managing Public Services*, Open University MBA, Milton Keynes, The Open University.

Health Service Commissioner for England, Scotland, Wales (1995) *Annual Report 1993/94*, London, HMSO.

Hirschman, A. (1970) *Exit, Voice and Loyalty*, Cambridge (MA), Harvard University Press.

HMSO (1997) *Social Trends*, London, HMSO.

Hutt Valley High (1993) *School Charter*, New Zealand, Hutt Valley High.

Kanter, R. and Summers, D. (1987) 'Doing well while doing good', in McKevitt, D. and Lawton, A. (eds) (1994) *Public Sector Management, Theory, Critique and Practice*, London, Sage.

Kommunal (1993) *Facing the Future Now*, Stockholm.

March, J. and Simon, H. (1958) *Organisations*, New York, John Wiley.

McKevitt, D. and Lawton, A. (1996) 'The manager, the citizen, the politician and performance measures', *Public Money and Management*, vol. 16, no. 3, pp. 49–55.

National Advisory Committee (1993) *Core Health and Disability Services*, New Zealand.

National Economic and Social Forum (1995) Quality Delivery of Social Services, Report No. 6, Dublin.

Osborne, D. and Gabler, T. (1992) *Reinventing Government*, Reading (MA), Addison-Wesley Publishing.

Peters, T. and Waterman, R. (1982) *In Search of Excellence*, New York and London, Harper and Row.

Pfeffer, N. and Coote, A. (1991) 'Is quality good for you?', *Social Policy Paper No. 5*, London, Institute for Public Policy Research.

Pirie, M. (1991) *Empowerment*, London, Adam Smith Institute.

Potter, J. (1988) 'Consumerism and the public sector: how well does the coat fit?', *Public Administration*, vol. 66, Summer, pp. 149–64.

Waldegrave, W. (1993) *The Reality of Reform and Accountability in Today's Public Service*, London, Chartered Institute of Public Finance and Accountancy.

Walsh, K. (1994) 'Marketing and public sector marketing', *European Journal of Marketing*, vol. 28, no. 3, pp. 63–71.

Wellington Action Committee (1992) *Health Reforms: A Second Opinion*, Wellington.

Zeithmal, V., Berry, L. and Parasuraman, A. (1988) 'Communication and control processes in the delivery of service quality', *Journal of Marketing*, vol. 52, pp. 35–48.

Chapter 4

Arrow, K. (1985) *Collected Papers*, Boston, Harvard University Press.

Audit Commission (1993) *Compulsory Competitive Tendering*, Audit Commission.

Baier, V., March, J. and Saetern, H. (1986) 'Implementation and ambiguity', in McKevitt, D. and Lawton, A. (eds) (1994) *Public Sector Management, Theory, Critique and Practice*, London, Sage.

Bower, J. (1970) *Managing the Resource Allocation Process: A Study of Corporate Planning and Investment*, Boston, Harvard University Press.

Brunnson, N. (1989) *The Organisation of Hypocrisy*, Chichester, Wiley.

Cuyler, A. (1976) *Health Status Measures and Health Care Planning*, Toronto, Ontario Economic Council.

Financial Times (1994) *Resource Management in the Public Sector*, London, Financial Times.

Florio, M. (1990) 'Cost-benefit analysis and the control of public expenditure', *Journal of Public Policy*, vol. 10, no. 2, pp. 103–31.

Hayes, R. and Wheelwright, S. (1984) *Restoring Our Competitive Edge*, New York, John Wiley.

Hogwood, B. and Gunn, L. (1984) *A Policy Analysis for the Real World*, Oxford, Oxford University Press.

Hood, C. (1991) 'A public management for all seasons', *Public Administration*, 69, pp. 3–20.

House of Commons Health Committee (1994) *Better Off in the Community?* Vol. 1, London, House of Commons.

Jenkins, K., Caines, K. and Jackson, A. (1988) *Improving Management in Government: The Next Steps*, London, HMSO.

Kanter, R. and Summers, D. (1987) 'Doing well while doing good', in McKevitt, D. and Lawton, A. (eds) (1994) *Public Sector Management, Theory, Critique and Practice*, London, Sage.

Le Grand, J. (1982) *The Strategy of Equality*, London, Allen & Unwin.

March, J. (1976) 'The technology of foolishness' in March, J. and Olsen, J. (eds) *Ambiguity and Choice in Organisations*, Bergen, Universitete forlaget, pp. 69–81.

McKevitt, D. (1996) 'Strategic Management in the Irish Civil Service: Prometheus unbound or Phoenix redux?', *Administration*, vol. 43, no. 4, pp. 34–50.

Ministry of Health (1992) *Analysis of Submissions on 'Support for Independence'*, New Zealand.

Mintzberg, H. (1983) *Structures in Fives: Designing Effective Organisations*, Englewood Cliffs, London, Prentice Hall.

National Advisory Committee (1993) *Core Health and Disability Services*, 1994/95, New Zealand.

National Interim Provider Board (1992) *Providing Better Health Care for New Zealanders*, New Zealand.

Rowntree, B. (1901) *Poverty: A Study of Town Life*, London, Macmillan.

Schmenner, R. (1982) *Making Business Location Decisions*, New Jersey, Prentice Hall.

Simon, H. (1947) *Administrative Behaviour*, New York, Free Press.

Simon, H. (1994) 'The criterion of efficiency', in McKevitt, D. and Lawton, A. (eds) *Public Sector Management, Theory, Critique and Practice*, London, Sage.

Stewart, J. and Ranson, S. (1988) 'Management in the public domain', *Public Money and Management*, Spring/Summer, pp. 13–18.

Tyson, S. (1990) 'Turning civil servants into managers', *Public Money and Management*, Spring, pp. 27–30.

Chapter 5

Arnold, T. (1935) *The Symbols of Government*, New Haven, Yale University Press.

Audit Commission (1997) *What the Doctor Ordered: A Study of GP Fundholding in England and Wales*, London, Audit Commission.

Battistella, R. and Eastaugh, S. (1980) 'Hospital cost containment' in Levin, A. (ed.) *Regulating Health Care: The Struggle for Control*, Academy of Political Science.

Child, J. (1984) *Organisation: A Guide to Problems and Practice*, 2nd edn, London, Harper and Row.

Hakansson, S. and Nordling, S. (1997) *Health Care Reforms in Sweden*.

Huhn, D. (1994) 'Measuring performance in policy advice – a New Zealand perspective' in OECD, *Measurement in Government: Issues and Illustrations*, No. 15, Paris, pp. 25–34.

Macara, A. (1994) 'Reforming the reforms', *Junior Members Forum*, British Medical Association.

McKevitt, D. (1989) *Health Care Policy in Ireland*, Hibernian University Press.

McKevitt, D. (1993) 'Performance measurement in health care delivery', *Administration*, vol. 41, no. 3, Autumn, pp. 307–22.

McKevitt, D. (1996) 'Strategic Management in the Irish Civil Service: Prometheus unbound or Phoenix redux?', *Administration*, vol. 43, no. 4, pp. 34–50.

OECD (1993a) *Health Policy Studies*, vol. 11, no. 3, Paris.

OECD (1993b) *New Zealand Economic Survey Reports*, Paris.

Osborne, D. and Gaebler, T. (1992) *Reinventing Government: How the Entrepreneurial Spirit is Transforming the Public Sector*, Reading (MA), Addison-Wesley.

Raffel, M. (ed.) (1997) *Health Care Reform in Industrialised Countries*, Pennsylvania State University Press.

World Health Organization (1984) *Planning and Management for Health*, EURO Reports and Studies, no. 102.

Wrigley, L. (1989) 'Foreword' in McKevitt, D. (1989) *Health Care Policy in Ireland*, Hibernian University Press.

Chapter 6

Burns, T. and Stalker, G. (1994) *The Management of Innovation*, revised edition, Oxford, Oxford University Press.

Dearing, R. (1994) *The National Curriculum and its Assessment*, London, School Curriculum and Assessment Authority.

Douglas, R. (1993) *Unfinished Business*, New Zealand, Random House.

Harrison, R. (1993) 'The powers, duties and responsibilities of school boards of trustees' in *Education and the Law in New Zealand*, Auckland, Education Management Centre, pp. 62–93.

McKevitt, D. (1996) 'Strategic Management in the Irish Civil Service: Prometheus unbound or Phoenix redux?', *Administration*, vol. 43, no. 4, pp. 34–50.

Ministry of Education (1988) *Tomorrow's Schools. The Reform of Education Administration in New Zealand*, Wellington, New Zealand.

Ministry of Education (1993) *Three Years On: New Zealand Education Reform 1989–1992*, New Zealand.

Mintzberg, H. (1979) *The Structuring of Organisations*, London, Prentice Hall.

OECD (1993) *New Zealand, Economic Survey*, Paris, OECD.

Powell, W. and Di Maggio, P. (1991) 'The iron cage revisited: institutional isomorphism and collective rationality in organisation fields' in Powell, W. and Di Maggio, P. *The New Institutionalism in Organisational Analysis*, Chicago, University of Chicago Press, pp. 63–82.

Scott, R. (1991) 'Unpacking institutional arguments' in Powell, W. and Di Maggio, P. *The New Institutionalism in Organisational Analysis*, Chicago, University of Chicago Press, pp. 164–82.

Scott, W. and Meyer, J. (1991) 'The Organisation of Societal Sectors' in Powell, W. and Di Maggio, P. *The New Institutionalism in Organisational Analysis*, Chicago, University of Chicago Press, pp. 108–43.

University of Waikato (1993) *Hear Our Voices, Final Report of Monitoring Today's Schools*, Waikato.

Weber, M. (1947) *The Theory of Social and Economic Organisation*, trans. Henderson and Parsons, Oxford.

Chapter 7

Alcorn, N. (1992) *Walking the Tightrope: The Role of School Leadership in the New Climate of New Zealand Education*, Herbison Lecture, Deakin University.

Baier, V., March, J. and Saetern, H. (1994) 'Implementation and ambiguity', in McKevitt, D. and Lawton, A. (eds) *Public Sector Management*, London, Sage.

Brunnson, N. (1989) *The Organisation of Hypocrisy*, Chichester, Wiley.

Burris, B. (1991) 'Business, the state, and health-care politics', *American Journal of Sociology*, vol. 96, no. 4, pp. 1016–7.

Carter, N. (1991) 'Learning to measure performance: the use of indicators in organisations', *Public Administration*, 69, pp. 85–101.

Dearing, R. (1994) The National Curriculum and its Assessment, School Curriculum and Assessment Authority, London.

Education Review Office (1993) *Accountability in Action*, Wellington, New Zealand.

Guth, W. and Macmillan, I. (1989) 'Strategy implementation versus middle management self-interest' in Asch, D. and Bowman, C. (eds) *Readings in Strategic Management*, Basingstoke, Macmillan.

Kotter, J. and Schlesinger, L. (1989) 'Choosing stragegies for changes' in Asch, D. and Bowman, C. (eds) *Readings in Strategic Management*, Basingstoke, Macmillan.

March, J. and Olsen, J. (1989) *Rediscovering Institutions*, New York, Free Press.

McDonald, K. (1995) *The Sociology of the Professions*, London, Sage.

REFERENCES

McKevitt, D. and Lawton, A. (1994) 'The manager, the citizen, the politician and performance measures', in McKevitt, D. and Lawton, A. (eds) *Public Sector Management*, London, Sage.

McKevitt, D. and Lawton, A. (1996) 'The manager, the citizen, the politician and performance measures', *Public Money and Management*, vol. 16, no. 3, pp. 49–55.

Metcalfe, L. and Richards, S. (1990) *Improving Public Management*, London, Sage.

Meyer, J. and Rowan, B. (1992) 'Institutionalised organisations: formal structure as myth and ceremony' in Meyer, J. and Scott, W. (eds) *Organisational Environment*, London, Sage.

Mintzberg, H. (1979) *The Structuring of Organisations*, London, Prentice Hall.

Oakshott, M. (1994) 'Rationalism in politics' in McKevitt, D. and Lawton, A. (eds) *Public Sector Management*, London, Sage, pp. 4–10.

OECD (1981) *The Welfare State in Crisis*, Paris, OECD.

OECD (1992) *The OECD International Education Indicators*, Paris, OECD.

Ofsted (1993) *The New Teacher in School*, London, HMSO.

Rae, K. (1993) Te Hutinga O Te Harakeke – *The Plucking of the Flaxbrush*, paper to ACEA Conference, Adelaide, September.

Simon, H. (1994) 'The criterion of efficiency' in McKevitt, D. and Lawton, A. (eds) *Public Sector Management*, London, Sage, pp. 37–53.

Standaert, R. (1993) 'Technical rationality in education management: a survey covering England, France and Germany', *European Journal of Education*, vol. 28, no. 2, pp. 159–76.

State Services Commission (1992) *Principals Model Contract*, Wellington, New Zealand.

Terhart, E. (1994) 'The ethics of school teachers: between administrative control, professional autonomy, and public interest', Fourth International Conference on Ethics in Public Service, Stockholm.

Chapter 8

Johnson, J. and Scholes, K. (1997) *Exploring Corporate Strategy*, London, Prentice Hall.

INDEX